TAKEDOWN

THE ATTEMPTED POLITICAL ASSASSINATION OF

PATRICK BROWN

Published by Optimum Publishing International a division of JF Moore
Lithographers Inc. Toronto, ON

Canadian Cataloguing in Publication Data
ISBN: 978-0-88890-291-7

Patrick Brown
TAKEDOWN, The Attempted Political Assassination of Patrick Brown

Cover and Jacket Design by Matthew Flute
Cover Photo, PB File
Back Cover photograph, Chris Young/ Canadian Press
Printed and bound in Canada by Webcom

All Photos used in this book were obtained from the author and publisher and
where required, permission was obtained or credited to the photographer.
Chapter 5 transcript of caucus call. Permission obtained from Macleans
Magazine, Toronto, ON.

For information, address:
Optimum Publishing International
144 Rochester Avenue
Toronto, Ontario M42 1P1
Dean Baxendale, President

For rights, submissions and media inquiries go to www.optibooks.com

Dedication

To my mentor William Grenville Davis who taught me that a proud Conservative can also care deeply about the environment, social justice issues and labour rights. He taught me the importance of a big tent and being open to good ideas from all sides. I thank him for showing me there is a better path than the deeply divided ideological battles we see dictating the politics of our day.

CONTENTS

NOTE FROM PUBLISHER

Mr. Brown filed an $8 million defamation suit against CTV in April of 2018. The matter is still before the courts. After consulting with legal counsel, we at Optimum Publishing International made the decision to respect the accusers' requests for anonymity even though their identities have been exposed on social media and through various news outlets. Please note the following:

Accuser 1 will be referred to as "Joanna Bloggs"

Accuser 2 will be referred to as "Jane Doe"

INTRODUCTION

It was January 24, 2018, a date I would love to forget, but never will. I was playing tennis at the Toronto Lawn Tennis Club, where I was a member. I knew something was up when my assistant, Shan Gill, walked onto the court halfway through the allocated time. Staff is not allowed on the court at a private club, and this was unusual. Shan looked as if he'd seen a ghost.

He told me not to shower. "The guys need you back at your apartment ASAP, so that no media comes."

What the hell was going on? I wondered. I insisted on showering, anyway.

My downtown Toronto apartment was located at Bay Street and St. Mary Street. Many MPPs have apartments close to the Ontario Legislature when they live outside Toronto, as I did. My home in Barrie, Ont., was a 90-minute drive north of Toronto.

I arrived at about 5:30 p.m. and waited for 20 minutes for my executive team to arrive: Dan Roberston, my chief strategist; Walied Soliman, my campaign chair; Andrew Boddington, my campaign manager; and Alykhan Velshi, my chief of staff.

We were now all in my small apartment bedroom. Gill and Rebecca "Becky" Thompson, my communications director, were asked to wait outside by my executive team.

As I waited, I thought about some calls I had received the night before. Two individuals phoned to give me a heads-up that CTV was asking questions in connection to some stories about me that it was pursuing. One caller was

Samantha Flynn, who had worked in my office while I was MP. The other was Tyler King, my buddy from the Red Bull company, the makers of my favourite energy drink.

The CTV reporter asked both Flynn and King if they recalled a fight that took place at the Barrie bar called The Bank after a Hockey Night in Barrie event that I had organized. King was also asked if he ever recalled being alone with me and Jane Doe in my bedroom following that event. Flynn was asked if she recalled me doing anything inappropriate. Both defended me to CTV and told the reporter that there was no story. Tyler ended the call by hanging up on the reporter, and Flynn told them that there was never any inappropriate behaviour by me whatsoever at any time. That's what I knew about CTV and the stories its reporters were pursuing. I found it disconcerting that CTV hadn't tried to reach me.

After I hung up, I reported these calls back to my senior campaign team. They assured me that they would seek a meeting with CTV and put them on notice that the events, as had been shared with me by Flynn and King, were fabrications. And they would remind CTV that it should not broadcast any story that had not undergone due diligence and which was a lie.

You could imagine my surprise and horror, then, when I was finally briefed on the allegations that had been made against me and were about to air on the *CTV National News* at 10 p.m. that night.

The way it was presented to me, an email had arrived at 4:24 p.m. It had been sent by Glen McGregor of CTV Bell Media to Sarah Letersky, my assistant. It was marked "URGENT" for Velshi and it read as follows:

> Hi Alykhan,
>
> This is a media inquiry to Patrick Brown. Because it is highly sensitive, I am sending it directly to you to give to him rather than to his public-facing email address. Please call me to discuss soonest.
>
> Thanks Glen

A letter written to me followed this email note, which contained all that CTV was prepared to share with me:

> I am a reporter with CTV National News in Ottawa. We are looking into allegations against you of sexual misconduct, made by two women. We would like to arrange an on-camera interview with you to address these allegations in more detail.

It named the first accuser as "Joanna". Her surname was withheld. She was identified as having been a high-school student at Innisdale Secondary School in Barrie at the time of the incident.

Few details were provided in the allegations other than she and a "mutual friend" — no name provided—met me in a Barrie bar, also no name provided. There was also no date, nor year provided in the letter.

It went on to say that I had allegedly invited the two to my home "even though Joanna was under the legal drinking age at the time." At this point, I allegedly asked Joanna to tour the house, while the mutual friend stayed downstairs.

When we were in the bedroom, according to the letter, I supposedly closed the door and exposed my penis to her. I asked for oral sex after, to which she left "very distressed" and went to a nearby friend's home.

The letter went on to inform me that there was another accuser. This time, the full name was provided. It was Jane Doe, a former employee. This allegation came with a few more details. Briefly, her allegation claimed that I sexually assaulted her on the morning of August 15, 2013, after a Hockey Night in Barrie charity event, which I organized to raise money for the local hospital.

She had come to my home with others, where she continued to drink, though I did not. Once again there was mention of another "mutual friend" who was with her, but no name was provided. Doe allegedly came to my bedroom upon my invitation to look at photos, and that when we were alone, according to the letter, I "forcibly" kissed her and "pushed her back on the bed."

The allegations went on to explain that she told me to stop kissing her because she had a boyfriend. Then, she asked me to drive her home to her parents' house. I agreed. The letter essentially accused me of taking advantage of her because she was drunk, my employee and because she hadn't given consent for me to be kissing her.

The letter also mentioned that Doe asked and obtained work during summer 2014 at my office in Barrie. (This, despite the alleged inappropriate behaviour, for which I was now being outed.)

I could barely get through the letter. It was sickening.

I was informed that at 4:58 p.m., Velshi advised McGregor that I had not been reached. Velshi asked to know when exactly CTV was planning to run the story.

A minute later, at 4:59 p.m., McGregor responded. "We are planning to run a story tonight, beginning with our 10 p.m. national news broadcast."

By 10 p.m.? Was this some sick joke? I was essentially being asked to respond on the spot to allegations that were no doubt compiled after months of deliberations. I was being asked to appear on television within hours to defend allegations by accusers, one of whom I had no idea who she was, as well as two unnamed mutual friends. Who they were was anyone's guess, and I had no real contextual information.

I was sick, nauseated and frantic. None of these allegations actually happened. I simply could not place any story similar to the ones being presented.

I called Genevieve Gualtieri, my girlfriend, who was nicknamed "GG." She was working at SickKids Foundation, and I told her that some awful stories about me were going to break and that there were going to be nasty things said and written about me as a result. I explained that I was with my team, and we were trying to figure out how I could deal with the allegations on such short notice. Finally, I asked her not to come to the apartment. GG was *persona non grata* to many on my team because of our age difference — I'm 16 years older than her. Our relationship was the "big scandal" that no one could know about. The irony wasn't lost on me that, in comparison to the allegations I was facing, our age difference seemed rather trite.

GG was in tears and sick with worry. My final words to her: "Don't believe anything you're about to hear. I love you and you need to give me time to sort this out." We hung up. I could only imagine the anxiety she must have been feeling, sitting there alone in her office.

It was then that I remembered that there was someone who was at my place the night of August 15, 2013, after Hockey Night in Barrie, the night of the alleged "Doe" incident. *That's it! I had a witness.* The witness was my then girlfriend, Mikaela Patterson. I called her and asked her to come to my apartment. Patterson did recall the evening of August 15, 2013, very differently from what had been provided to CTV.

Patterson jumped in the car and made her way south to Toronto from Collingwood, Ont. What I didn't realize was that she would never be allowed to talk and would be sent home by members of my team. And that will be discussed in an upcoming chapter.

Meanwhile, I had that awful, sinking feeling. My chest was pounding harder than having run a marathon, and I had that prickly, hot, flushed sensation that comes over you when you're neck deep in shock.

Why would these women do this to me? I knew Doe, and I also knew this was utter bullshit, because apart from the fact that the evening didn't unfold as she described, I knew that Doe was a huge supporter of mine.

In 2016, she had liked a post on Facebook that described me as a great boss, leader and friend, and that I would make a great premier. She had worked on my leadership bid in 2015. And in 2017, while working for The Hill Times, Doe reached out to me for help as she covered the 2017 federal Conservative leadership. *Good Lord, that wasn't even a year ago.* And then I remembered that at my Canadian Club speech in Ottawa, in 2016, Doe had asked to attend, and she was seated at a table reserved for my friends and supporters. She later lined up to speak to me. When she finally made it up to the front of the line, I didn't recognize her at all. Her long hair that had once been brown was now cut very short and jet black, sort of goth style. When I realized who she was, we spoke for a short time, and she thanked me for inviting her to the table. There was nothing to indicate to me that she had any issues with me at all. *So how is it that someone who sought me out and provided me with unsolicited kudos came up with this bullshit? Clearly, there was a mistake.*

Seated at the edge of my bed in the small room, I told the team that it was bullshit. Absolute bullshit. We simply couldn't allow these lies to stand. My team asked me if I wanted to fight. Of course I did! But CTV was offering no real time in which to do so. The advantage was theirs.

I considered my options: I could try my best to cobble together some response based on these allegations, but I would have been reaching to make sense of allegations I didn't understand with incomplete information. Or I could let CTV carry a story that would no doubt set a false narrative that could ultimately destroy my career and certainly damage my reputation. Some choice.

Velshi, Robertson, Boddington and Walied said they would devise a plan. Shan and Becky were now brought back in after the huddle. So was former Stephen Harper staffer Dimitri Soudas, who had been hired by Velshi to do "black ops" (finding damaging information about your opponents) and damage control.

I had faith in all of them. They would help me figure this out. After all, I wasn't thinking straight. *But that's why you have a team of professionals, right?* They are the ones who would think straight when my mind was jumping from allegation to allegation, trying to remember a "Joanna" and trying to reach back into the cobwebs of my memory to figure out what the hell Doe was referring to.

The team crafted a statement that they told me I would need to read at a press conference that night, before CTV aired the story. *A statement? What the hell would I say? What the hell could I say with so little information? Just another guy, denying some victims' claims?*

I wasn't sure this was the right thing to do. But they were the professionals and likely thinking more clearly than I was. They insisted that I needed to respond immediately and emphatically. Goldy Hyder, my debate coach, arrived at the apartment.

He was a good, decent man, and privately he told me he didn't think I could survive the allegations. But the core team insisted I could.

Obviously, what I wanted was to be able to prove that these allegations were false. But there were only a few hours before the national news. I had no time.

I was instructed to turn my phone off and wait in my bedroom. I was not to talk to anyone while they prepared the response. I desperately wanted to speak to my family. So I called my sisters, who at first didn't pick up, but then immediately called me back.

Once I got them on the phone, I could barely speak. I love my family, and this was very humiliating to describe to them what was being alleged and what was happening was sickening to me. They wanted to come over. But the team was adamant; no visitors right now. No distractions. I told my sisters this.

I then called my mom and dad to tell them what was happening. We had to respond to CTV by 10 p.m. They were asking for an on-camera interview, and regardless, the story was going to be the lead item on the news. I could barely breathe. I told them someone or some force was trying to get me.

I assumed that the Ontario Liberal Party was behind these allegations. I had heard rumours of provincial Liberal backroom operatives desperately pitching stories to the media to dig up dirt on me. What scum bags! *But what the hell was CTV doing running with this pack of lies?* They were supposed to be a legitimate news source. *Why were they not giving me a proper chance to respond before shooting me in the head? Surely, they should realize that their story would legitimize these accusations. Why were they acting so recklessly?*

My mom immediately said she felt things had been going too well for me. She feared that someone was going to take a run at me and try to tear me down. But no one predicted this.

In the meantime, my sisters didn't give a rat's ass about what my team wanted. They showed up at my apartment 30 minutes later. They were not going to leave their older brother alone. Stephanie and Fiona came into my room and warned me: "These political advisers are hired guns and won't be loyal to you."

Stephanie and Fiona had an immediate sense of certain players I had in my apartment. What they sensed was disloyalty.

I was grateful that they were there. And I was relieved when my long-time friend, Mike Richmond, joined us at the apartment. He came to help protect me. Richmond is a lawyer. He felt something was wrong with some of the people I had around me.

At 8:14 p.m., we advised McGregor by email that, among other things, I denied the false and defamatory allegations. And, we put McGregor on notice that the last-minute request for an on-camera interview, mere hours before broadcast, was an attempt at ambush.

CTV didn't seem to care if the story was real or false. They had something juicy, and they planned to make a splash.

Sometime before 10 p.m., *CTV National News* published a sensational "teaser" tweet.

"EXCLUSIVE: Two women come forward with graphic sexual misconduct allegations against Ontario Progressive Conservative Leader Patrick Brown...watch @glenmcgregor's report tonight."

Good God. They were promoting a story, and they hadn't even tried to contact me while they were researching it? Were the so-called "mutual friends" contacted? Was anyone who might have been a witness to my side ever contacted about these allegations? And if they were, what did they say?

At some point, Robertson asked if there would be other women coming forward. He just sort of put the question out there for anyone to answer. My answer was obvious: "Other women? There shouldn't even have been these allegations."

Richmond replied dryly that if they could make up two, they could make up 10. Robertson freaked out. "What? There might be 10? I'm outta here!" and he darted out of the room.

It wasn't exactly the response I was expecting from a professional in communications and strategy. There was a lot that night I didn't expect that was still to come.

The team went back and forth on the content of the speech that I was advised to read in a hastily called press conference to be held later that evening in the PC caucus room on the third floor of the Ontario Legislature. The speech was crafted by Robertson and Soudas. Becky, Hyder and Soudas prepped me. I was lightheaded. The team insisted this presser was a good idea and that it should happen before CTV aired the piece.

I was not so sure.

We were running out of time. We needed to be at Queen's Park for 9:45 p.m., for the press conference.

Soudas told my sisters they couldn't come with me to the legislature, and the team backed him. Fiona and Stephanie erupted; they wanted to be by my side.

Eventually, at my sisters' insistence, it was agreed that they would accompany me to Queen's Park. But Robertson, Velshi and Soudas were adamant that they needed to wait in the car. They could not go into building with me. "Patrick needs to do this on his own. No props, no supporters, no family."

My sisters continued to fight this. Finally, Robertson, Velshi and Boddington tried to reassure Fiona and Stephanie that I would not be alone. They would be with me at the press conference and would leave the caucus room with me after my statement was delivered. Robertson, Velshi and Boddington would escort me back to the car. The gentle coaxing quieted my sisters. We loaded ourselves into the car.

I arrived at Queen's Park with my sisters in the car driven by Shan. I entered alone from the west entrance and walked up the flights of stairs to the caucus room on the third floor. Becky was waiting for me in the anteroom, outside the caucus room.

I fought back tears.

When I entered the room, it was packed —a feeding frenzy. I was taken aback by the number of media there on such a short notice. I was in a daze of shock and anger. It was all a blur.

At about 9:45 p.m., I delivered the brief statement my team prepared, knowing as the world did that at that point, CTV was going to break the story at 10 p.m. I could barely hear myself speak. The clicking sound of cameras was distracting. The lights felt hot, and the words danced on the page. But I read them as I had practised. I read every single God damned word:

>Ladies and gentlemen:
>
>A couple of hours ago, I learned of troubling allegations about my conduct and character.
>
>I'm here tonight to address them.
>
>First, I want to say: these allegations are false. Every one of them.
>
>I will defend myself as hard as I can, with all the means at my disposal.
>
>I can't speculate on the motive of my accusers; I can only say that what they are saying is categorically untrue.
>
>It's never OK for anyone to feel they have been a victim of sexual harassment or feel threatened in any way.
>
>Let me make this clear.

A safe and respectful society is what we expect and deserve.

I looked up and unscripted I added: No one appreciates that more than I do. I've got two younger sisters who are my best friends. I've grown up in a family that has taught me good values. It's not how I was raised. It's not who I am.

I looked back down and continued from the text: My values and beliefs are those that we need to move forward to eradicate sexual violence and harassment across the province — across the country. Everywhere.

I know that the court of public opinion moves fast. I have instructed my attorneys to ensure that these allegations are addressed where they should be: in a court of law.

In short: I reject these accusations in the strongest possible terms.

Media was throwing me questions from all sides but I walked out taking none. All I remember saying was that I intended to be back to work the next day. *Where was Robertson? Where were Velshi and Boddington?*

I made my way down the staircase alone. There were no supporters, team, friends or family. I was alone, except for the shouting reporters and cameras. With each step, I thought of three words: "dead man walking."

I was in a trance. I made it to the side entrance, found the car and got in. The lights and cameras were unbearable. White lit faces peered into the windows. The black sedan rolled onto Queen's Park Crescent and back to my small apartment.

CHAPTER 1

THE YOUNG POLITICIAN

If Brian Mulroney was a catalyst for my self-identification as a PC supporter at the age of 10, Jean Charest solidified that certainty.

The year was 1978.

Andy Gibb's "Shadow Dancing" and the Bee Gees' "Stayin' Alive" topped the music charts.

In May of that year, Pete Rose got his 3,000th career hit, en route to becoming the all-time Major League Baseball hit king. Years later, Rose would be banned from baseball for betting on the game.

In another part of the world, the Red Brigades, an anti-establishment terrorist group, killed Italy's former Prime Minister, Aldo Moro. Moro was loved by the Italian people, yet there he was in May '78, dead in the trunk of a car.

Also in May 1978, Sarajevo, Yugoslavia, was selected to host the 1984 Olympic Winter Games. No one knew at the time that after having welcomed the world to its shores, Yugoslavia would disintegrate as a nation less than a decade later.

These were three big stories of May 1978, and all were connected by one common theme: a tragic end to a glorious beginning. It makes you think of that old Sinatra tune that says something about ridin' high in April, and then being shot down in May. Maybe it was not coincidental that in May 1978, I was born.

The name on my birth certificate reads *Patrick Walter Brown*, but everyone in my family just calls me "Paddy," with the Irish spelling.

I was born from a fiery combination that includes Irish/Scottish and Italian heritage. This is somewhat ironic since I don't drink alcohol, nor am I known to have a tempestuous personality.

My grandparents on both sides had a profound impact on me. On my dad's side were my grandparents, Teresa and Walter Brown. Teresa hailed from County Cork, Ireland. After her mom died when she was six, she was raised along with her four sisters in a convent. Teresa moved to England, where she worked as a nurse and later helped in a mobile health unit at the scene of the London bombing blitz. It was there that she met my grandfather, Walter. He's descended from Scottish and British stock.

Walter was also in London contributing to the war effort, working on radar systems. The two married in 1941. My dad, Ed, was a product of the marriage, the oldest of their three kids. While he was born in England, he also lived in Ireland and Scotland before moving to Canada, at the age of 11 years.

Eventually, Walter immigrated to Canada through a circuitous route and settled in North Bay, Ont., where Teresa and the kids joined him a year later. In North Bay, Walter sold X-ray equipment for General Electric throughout northern Ontario and Quebec. Eventually, the family moved to Oakville, Ont., when my granddad was promoted. Walter died in 1997.

Today, my grandma Teresa lives in a seniors' home in Toronto. I've always made it a point to visit her each week. I'd say she gets around pretty well with a walker, even though she is blind. She is still pretty sharp at 104 years of age.

Nanny Teresa is among my biggest supporters. I remember how she loved listening to the campaign videos we put out when I was leader of the Ontario Progressive Conservative (PC) Party. My mom would play them over and over for her, and she'd memorize every word. Her big desire was to stay alive long enough to see the election on June 7, 2018, after which she had plans to go visit Walter in the afterlife. She'd tell him all about what Paddy did; about the great videos that she could recite by heart; about the election; and about how Paddy had become premier of Ontario.

Of course (spoiler alert), that didn't happen. Nor did the visit with Walter.

Nanny took my takedown hard. Really hard. After the awful, career-ending CTV newscast of January 24· she stopped eating as much, and her health deteriorated. She called me every day to make sure I was OK. And, while those events upset her terribly, she was still a great source of strength for me at a time when strength was the one thing I needed most of all. I don't think she really recovered. I don't think any of us has.

Giuseppe (Joe) and Edna (Miller) Tascona were the parents of my mom, Judy. Joe and Edna married in 1940 and eventually settled in Barrie, Ont., where they raised their kids. My mother is the fourth born of their five kids.

Joe was born in St. Boniface, Man., and Edna was born in North Battleford, Sask. Edna was descended from a family of United Empire Loyalists whose family farm in Kingston, Ont., had been the site of a battle during the War of 1812. She was a pistol–brilliant, sharp-witted and devoted to family. Grandma Edna instilled in her kids the need for higher education and expected them to work hard. I now know where my mom got her insistence on education and good grades.

From Edna I learned about the importance of volunteerism and giving back to the community. Edna dedicated her life to volunteering for good causes and received special recognition for her 50 years of service. But the big thing we shared was her love of politics. Even while in her 70s, Edna would go door-knocking for me during my runs at public office.

Unfortunately, dementia robbed all of us of the person she was. She had to leave Joe and went to live in a home. I visited her twice a week to keep her company and helped feed her until she died.

My grandpa Joe was Italian through and through. His family had emigrated from Sicily, taking the long voyage through to Ellis Island. He learned to speak French fluently growing up in St. Boniface. His hero was Louis Riel, the young Manitoba Métis activist.

Joe also served in the army as a mechanic. His work was excellent, and during the war in 1943, Base Borden stopped sending vehicles to Toronto for servicing because Joe was able to repair the tanks and trucks at the base.

After the army, Joe set up a car lot in Barrie with a huge sign that read: *We speak French here — ici on parle français*. In an age when bilingualism wasn't an asset, he was proud to declare his bilingualism loudly.

His business took off. Soldiers from the base and people from all over northern Ontario came to buy cars from him and have their badly damaged vehicles repaired. Apart from customers, his car lot office was always filled with local dignitaries, including the likes of the mayor and the head of police, as well as friends and other car dealers. People just wanted to be around him and listen to his hilarious storytelling. Joe was a character.

He worked for 63 years and only stopped working shortly before he died, at 93. I believe I got my work ethic from him. I always say that if you want something done, ask a busy person. My grandpa was always that —busy. Joe spent the last years of his life living alone since Edna was in a nursing home, and I spent a lot of time with him, which I will always treasure. Every Sunday, I brought him dinner, and we sat and chatted for the evening. I really miss him.

My parents, Judy and Edmond, met, married and later settled in the Bathurst Street and St. Clair Avenue area of Toronto. My dad, Ed, commuted to his criminal law practice in Brampton, Ont., for years, and it's where I articled and also practiced law.

I was exposed to politics at an early age. When I was a year old, my father ran federally for the New Democratic Party (NDP) in Toronto's Davenport riding. Yes, that's right, my father was a candidate for the NDP. I obviously don't recall any of that, except that one of the earliest photos taken of me was featured in my dad's campaign literature. Perhaps it was a foreshadowing of things to come. Dad stayed connected to the NDP, and by the age of six I was helping him put up lawn signs.

My only real family connection to the PC Party was on my mother's side, when in 1995 my Uncle Joe Tascona Jr., mom's baby brother, became an MPP under then Premier Mike Harris. But that was much later on. My dad talked a lot about the "great and undefeatable" Bill Davis, who was premier of Ontario. Despite my dad's NDP roots, he clearly admired the man a great deal; an admiration that he passed on to me. As a young man, I met Davis while volunteering in Brampton for Jean Charest in 1997 and again at a federal PC fundraiser. These were encounters that I'm certain Davis will not remember, and ones that I will not forget.

I suppose my grandparents Edna and Joe were likely Liberals. They never would have dreamed of taking a PC lawn sign until Uncle Joe ran in '95. I think it's fair to say that I was exposed to a wide range of political perspectives. Ultimately, the choice to join the conservative movement was all my own.

Mom never got involved in politics, though she would be my greatest supporter behind the scenes. Mom was a school teacher all her working life and taught almost every grade, including classes for special needs children. She finished her teaching career as a principal and is now retired. Mom was big on good grades— something I didn't always completely appreciate.

I grew up with a debilitating stutter and suffered throughout much of my elementary school years. It wasn't until junior high that I overcame it, largely thanks to grandma Edna, who saw an ad for a free speech clinic in The Globe and Mail. She called my mom and said, "Take Paddy to this."

Each week, Mom would pick me up from school and take me to speech therapy. Decades later, after I became leader of the Ontario PC Party, I opened up about my challenging stutter in a Toronto Star article. That article prompted my former speech therapist, Melissa Potashner, who I hadn't heard from since I was a child, to contact her PC MPP, Gila Martow. She told Martow that she remembered all those speech therapy sessions vividly and was so happy to see that I had succeeded in my life. That was a pretty neat moment, along with my discovery at the 2015 leadership convention, where I was elected PC Party leader, that the former leader, Tim Hudak, selected speech pathology as his charity of choice at the convention.

As a youngster, my stutter certainly dampened my confidence as I struggled to get words out. Luckily, I was full of energy and loved sports. I played them all — soccer, baseball, hockey and lots of wall ball. Sports was a great way to compensate for my stutter, build confidence and meet people.

My parents enrolled me at the Toronto French School for Grade 1. The Toronto French School is a private school, and all instruction was provided in French. I later attended Hawthorne Public School in Toronto, where courses were taught half in English and half in French. My parents finally took me out of French completely. Mom thought it was too hard on me to attempt a different language, given my stutter. I was enrolled at Brown Junior Public School. My younger sisters continued instruction in French at Brown, but my courses were in English.

I was always extremely close to my siblings. Stephanie is two and a half years younger than me, and Fiona is seven and a half years younger than me. I was careful to treat them both the same, even though I am much closer in age to Stephanie. If I did something with one, I did it with the other. We did everything together, including summer camp, ski lessons and tennis. But not hockey. That is something I did on my own; although, they both played briefly.

Fiona was so much younger that I was almost like another parent to her. If Mom and Dad were having an issue with her, they would enlist me to help sort things out because they knew she listened to me. Fiona was really too young to get in a fight with. Actually, I don't recall having many fights with Stephanie, either.

They both emulated things that I did. My mother noticed this and told me when I was in high school that whatever I did, my sisters would copy. For that reason, Mom was clear that I had to watch myself. That is why I didn't drink and still don't to this day. I promised Mom that I wouldn't drink, and I made good on that promise. This took a considerable amount of willpower, especially during the high school years. By my mid-20s, I figured: *Why start drinking now?* I was already an elected politician. I had seen many friends make mistakes while under the influence of alcohol. I had also read political autobiographies, including Brian Mulroney's, in which he explained that one of the best things he did was to stop drinking after the 1976 leadership campaign. George W. Bush also wrote in his autobiography how stopping drinking changed his life. What began as honouring a commitment to my mother became a lifestyle I chose for myself.

My beverages of choice are Red Bull and Diet Coke. Mom's sister tried to bribe my cousin Jenny by buying her a car on the condition that she abstain from drinking. My mother's approach was markedly different. She was all about doing the right thing. Besides, as she pointed out, she couldn't afford to get me a car.

Generally, I wasn't a kid who got into much trouble. If I think back to my childhood and tried to recall the worst incident I was involved in, I can only remember one. While at Brown Junior Public School (no relation to me), my friend and I played a prank, where we took all the tape out of the classrooms and we made a giant tape ball. Our punishment was that we were not allowed to share a room at our class trip to Ottawa. That was pretty much it. I know, big deal.

What would get me in serious trouble was if I got a bad report card. Mom insisted on good grades and was very strong on academics. Unfortunately for me, before I was nine, my marks were mediocre. I did pick up my game significantly by the time I was 10.

It was at the age of nine that I became politically aware. My father always encouraged political discussions, despite the fact that by the time I started to take an interest, he was no longer involved directly in the NDP movement.

It really all started when my teacher gave us an assignment to write a letter to the prime minister. So I wrote to former Prime Minister Brian Mulroney on the issue of acid rain, something else I had been studying at school. I was gravely concerned about the issue, as much as any nine-year-old could be. What I didn't expect was to get a letter back. The letter sent from Mulroney's office talked about what he was doing about acid rain, and attached there were articles and documents related to the subject. I was quite excited to get this letter and very impressed with what Mulroney had accomplished on both acid rain and free trade. I have that letter to this day.

It was during what has been referred to as the federal "free trade" election of 1988 that I decided, at age 10, I was a conservative. I'd read the papers as a young kid over breakfast, something my dad also encouraged. And at 10, I really got involved emotionally in the issues of the day. I thought free trade was the right decision for Canada, and I was a huge supporter. That's when I informed my dad that I was pretty sure I was a Progressive Conservative. Dad was just happy that his young son was taking such an interest in politics. I may have defined myself as a conservative at age 10, but I didn't get active in politics until I was 15.

So it was that in the 1993 federal election, Dad ordered up his NDP sign, and I ordered up my PC sign. I was rooting for Isabel Basset, the PC star candidate, and my dad was supporting David Jacobs, the federal NDP candidate. As it turned out, both of our candidates in the St. Paul's riding lost to the Liberal, Barry Campbell.

In fact, the election was a disaster for the federal PCs, now led by Kim Campbell, who replaced Brian Mulroney. To say they "lost" the election is a gross understatement. The party was reduced to only two seats; one seat was held by Elsie Wayne and another by Jean Charest, who would eventually be the next leader of the PC Party in 1994. This was a hugely disappointing outcome for me.

I started high school at Forest Hill Collegiate Institute and then in Grade 10, I enrolled at St. Michael's College School, run by the Catholic Order of the Basilian Fathers. My mother liked the school because it had a strong focus on academics. I liked St. Mike's, as it was called, because it had a strong focus on hockey. Alumni includes NHL greats such as Red Kelly, Frank and Peter Mahovlich and Jason Spezza. Incidentally, Kelly went on to become a member of parliament in Lester Pearson's government and voted in favour of the new Canadian flag. So I was in good company and in the right place, as far as I was concerned.

My grades took a beating. St. Mike's is a private school. To get accepted, you needed to write entrance exams. Though I had made it to an A-student ranking and had been put in the gifted program in math at Forest Hill Collegiate Institute, I was now competing against others for a spot, and they were all A-students. I passed the exams all right, but once in, I realized that everyone was more advanced than I was academically. My first report card at St. Mike's wasn't stellar. I managed a meagre 59 per cent average. It was tough. Grade 10 was my wake-up call, and I was regularly in trouble at home because of my grades.

I realized I was too far behind in math, and it was really too late for me to catch up. I saw that the classes in which I excelled were history and English. I believe that my interest in politics was why I read so many history books. So in Grade 11, I switched my course load as much as possible to these courses, and I got my grades back up to A status.

In high school, I had my first true love relationship with a girl I dated for two years. This ended when I went to university. She was finishing up high school, and things sort of petered out.

My other true love during high school was politics. And if Brian Mulroney was a catalyst for my self-identification as a PC supporter at the age of 10, Jean Charest solidified that certainty.

After the 1993 election, while I was in high school, I became impressed with Charest, the new leader of the federal PC Party, despite the fact that he could hold a caucus meeting in a phone booth since the party had been all but wiped out.

I had heard his speech on TV at that 1993 leadership convention. I remember the speech where he was saying, "the Bloc is a crock," and I really connected with the message. At the time, the separatist movement in Quebec was gaining steam. After the PC Party was all but annihilated in 1993, the Bloc Québécois was surging and would plunge the province of Quebec, and the country, into another referendum on separation, on October 30, 1995.

I was impressed with Charest and the way he could speak about a united Canada with such passion. I really believed this was a guy I could get behind and I wanted to volunteer for him.

As it happened shortly thereafter, I was visiting my Aunt Alice (Tascona) at her home in a little town called North Hatley, just outside of Sherbrooke, Que. I was talking to her about how great Jean Charest was. Aunt Alice asked me whether or not I was aware that Charest was, in fact, her next door neighbour. Of course I knew that! I told my aunt that I wanted to meet him.

So off I went and knocked on his door. I explained to him that I wanted to volunteer for him. Now Charest, being the head of a party with only two seats, was, I believe, quite surprised to have a 15-year-old knock on his door, eager to volunteer. So he invited me in and sat me down. He told me that his sister Carole Charest lived in Snow Valley, just outside of Barrie. That would be easy to get to from Toronto, where we lived. He told me to speak to her and, she could get me involved. That was it. That was the first step. I was now in the game for good.

Carole Charest advised me to attend a delegate selection meeting and get a delegate spot, so that I could attend the PC Party of Canada convention called Jump Start. Once this was done, she promised to drive me to the convention. I became a youth delegate for the riding of Barrie-Simcoe-Bradford or Simcoe Centre, as it was called back then.

Carole Charest did drive me to my first party convention in Ottawa, in 1995, and I loved it. I met a lot of people. My career in politics had begun. I became involved helping out with PC candidates while I was a high-school student at St. Mike's. I worked on my Uncle Joe's campaign for MPP in 1995. I helped out with Isabel Bassett's campaign, also running for MPP in the provincial Ontario riding of St. Andrew-St. Patrick, as it was then called.

Being athletic, I hit a few home runs at the PC baseball tournament at Centre Island in Toronto. It was there that I met and bonded with Walied Soliman. Walied would become a lifelong friend. He was raised in a large family of five boys and grew up in Mississauga, Ont. His dad was a nuclear scientist.

Walied eventually married his high-school sweetheart, Deena, and once married, he started a family, which is a bit of an understatement — they have seven kids. His mother told him after the last kid was born, "Walied, ENOUGH."

Starting in 1995, Walied and I went together to just about every single political event. We caught the political bug, big time. At the time we met, he was running to be president of the PC Youth, Association and I became his recruitment director and vice-president. Years later, the roles would reverse themselves, when I ran for leader of the Ontario PC Party. Walied would serve as my campaign chair.

Mike Richmond is another dear friend I met in 1995, while attending an Ontario PC Campus Association convention. Richmond was then director of the PC Youth Association while I was a high-school student at St. Mike's.

We became close friends, and as I travelled the world and became more involved in politics, Richmond, now a lawyer and the co-chair of energy law at McMillan LLP in Toronto, was involved in every campaign.

I introduced Richmond to his wife, Kaydee, who was from Windsor, Ont., and she was also involved in the Ontario PC Youth Association. Kaydee and I hung out together, but I knew that Richmond was enthralled with her. So at a Toronto Blue Jays game, I told Kaydee, "You know, Mike's got way better tickets than I do, so if you want to go sit with him, that's fine."

Mike and Kaydee Richmond were married in 2009. I organized his bachelor party and I was in the wedding party. Walied, Mike and Kaydee were a central part of my posse. They were always there to back me and travel along the road of my political aspirations.

Back at high school, I created a Progressive Conservative Club at St. Mike's, which became the largest in the country. And, I managed to convince 250 people in a school with a student body of 1,000 to join the PC Party. Being on the St. Mike's hockey team made it much easier to enlist people to join. It became a cool thing to be politically involved. It was at that point that I called Charest and I said, "Jean, we got the largest high-school youth club in the country at this Toronto school called St. Mike's. And I want you to come and speak to the school."

"Well, if it's the largest in the country, I should come and see them!" Charest agreed.

I then spoke to the principal at the time, Father Tom Mohan, and I said, "I wanna have Jean Charest come to our school." He agreed to it.

I really wanted to impress Charest. That's one thing about me; I don't do anything half measure. I knew what motivated 17– and 18-year-olds: beer. Being young and enterprising, I managed to get my hands on two cases.

My first stop was the Audio Visual Club, where I announced, "If you guys put on a real show, like lighting, music, you know, the works … I want this to be treated like a rock concert … I'll give you a case of beer."

This was truly motivational for a bunch of AV geeks. Instead of them working on hooking up microphones, they were now actually putting on a major rock concert. And all for a case of beer.

Next stop: the hockey team. Then the football team and so on. I spread the beer challenge far and wide: "Whichever team cheers the loudest gets a case of beer."

Charest arrived at St. Mike's and walked into the gym. The lights were out. Suddenly, strobe lights burst on, the music was blaring and you could feel the base reverberate in the soles of your shoes. He walked out into this rock concert —a concert in which he, Charest, was the star. Entire sections of kids were jumping up and down, and screaming, not for him, but for that case of beer.

It worked. When Charest left, he said to me, "Wow, Patrick! That really was the most incredible youth event I have ever been to! How did you every manage to get everyone so motivated?"

"Well," I responded, "they really believe in your vision."

I suppose in fairness I had won over a lot of converts to conservatism and Charest and politics. But the beer definitely helped.

Since my marks were now very good, and I had maintained an A average, my possibilities for entrance into any Ontario university were unlimited. I chose the University of Toronto (U of T), so I could be close to Queen's Park at the same time.

During the Mike Harris PC government in Ontario, Walied and I both held down part-time jobs at Queen's Park. In 1997, I worked for Toni Skarica, MPP riding of Wentworth North, a riding that no longer exists. Brett McFarquhar, another backroom guy, also worked there. McFarquhar later became my pollster.

Skarica was a great boss to have and very principled. He never became a cabinet minister; although, he was a parliamentary assistant to a number of ministers. Ultimately, Skarica resigned in 2000 over the Hamilton megacity issue. He had promised that he would not support a "super city" in Hamilton — an amalgamation of Hamilton, Dundas, Stoney Creek and Flamborough, in Ontario.

Ultimately, when Harris moved ahead with this amalgamation, Skarica resigned his seat. Harris told him that we would win the by-election. He could resign if he wanted; however, if he stuck with it and remained in the race and took one for the team, Harris would make Skarica a minister. I remember Skarica sitting with us. He explained that he just couldn't go back on his word. He had promised not to support an amalgamation, and so, to be true to his word, he resigned. The timing was good for me because I was in my fourth year at university and I had been thinking about running in the municipal election.

During my earlier university years, I ran to become the national youth president of the PC Youth Association. That was big potatoes. In those days, the youth wings were gigantic. Along with the presidency, you were provided with an assistant and a good budget. Today, the youth federations have become diminished, and they conduct most of their work on the Internet. But back in the day, youth delegates accounted for one-third of the party, and it was because of their vote that Brian Mulroney won the leadership. Mulroney had served as the president of the PC Youth Federation of Canada, as had Joe Clark. It was a big deal to be one of the presidents of the PC Youth Association.

Getting there was my first experience with the realities of the behind-the-scenes nastiness of politics that most people don't see. The credentials committee was an executive committee that vetted the delegates and determined who would be allowed to represent their riding at the convention to vote on the leader. Walied tipped me off that the executive was trying to screw me over by disallowing the participation of delegates who would come to support me.

Each riding was allowed three delegates and three "alternates" in case the one delegate was disallowed by the credentials committee. We knew who was on the credentials committee, and we knew that they would knock out just enough of my delegates to ensure that I didn't win, but not enough to raise eyebrows. So we had to be in a position that we could see where we thought the executive was going to disallow delegates, and we needed to have alternate delegates who would support me to replace them. The way to get around this was to register alternate delegates who would vote for me.

This wasn't easy or cheap. It meant flying in some people. Mom very reluctantly gave Walied her credit card to use for these expenses. I won a hotly contested race, becoming the president of the Ontario PC Youth Association in 1998. I was 20 years old.

Victory came at a price— $10,000, to be exact. That was the debt loaded onto my mother's credit card. I assumed that when Mom lent Walied her VISA card, she probably thought she was looking at about $500 to $1,000 in costs. Just to add to the bad news, my sister, Stephanie, crashed my car on the way up to the convention.

And the bad news just kept coming in. My hero and mentor, Jean Charest, was about to make a move that would rock my world. I had been elected in February 1998, on a Sunday. It was that weekend during which it was announced that Daniel Johnson was resigning as leader of the Quebec Liberals. There was talk that Charest was the odds-on favourite to take over as Liberal leader of Quebec. Liberal leader? Liberal?

I spoke to Charest on the Sunday of the weekend I won the youth leadership. He told me that there was no way he would consider jumping from being the federal PC Party leader to lead the Quebec Liberals. He was in politics to run federally, not provincially, and his dream was to be prime minister, not premier of Quebec, let alone for another party. This talk was somewhat reassuring.

But the pressure on him just mounted and mounted because of the separatist threat. Quebec was once again struggling with a large contingent ready to separate from the rest of Canada. The issue that had been percolating over the course of my lifetime was rearing its ugly head again, only this time, separation seemed imminent. The pressure on Charest to run to replace Johnson came from everywhere in Canada. The Toronto Star ran an article calling Charest "Captain Canada." People thought Charest was the only one who could beat Lucien Bouchard, the leader of the Bloc Québécois. But, he'd have to do it as a Liberal.

I remember speaking to Charest about two weeks after my youth president win. It was then that he told me, "Patrick, I've been defined in politics as someone who has put national unity before everything else. And if I don't do this, then people are going to say, 'He's not really about national unity.' And, the polls show that I'm the only one who can beat Lucien Bouchard." He added, "My dream was to become prime minister, and you know Michou [the nickname he had for his wife, Michelle] doesn't want me to do this either, but…"

When Charest decided to take on the leadership of the Quebec Liberal Party, that was a hugely difficult moment for me. Of course, I supported him. I had joined him years earlier in 1995, while I was still in high school, at a referendum campaign in Quebec in which he was promoting national unity. A bunch of PCs went down to Quebec as volunteers to basically follow Charest around at his speeches. I took my sister Stephanie with me.

This was the referendum in which the people of Quebec voted *oui ou non* — yes or no, for or against, Quebec separating from the rest of Canada. People from all over the country poured in to Quebec, to try to encourage our fellow citizens that they were loved, and we wanted them to stay in a unified Canada.

The *non* side won against separation, but barely. In my opinion, Charest made the difference. I watched him make speeches, and he was the best spokesperson for national unity.

Prior to accepting the job of leading the Quebec Liberals in 1998, Charest had agreed to do a fundraiser for me to help me wipe out that credit card debt incurred during my election campaign. He had agreed to attend a Toronto Blue Jays game in a private box, and we would sell tickets to participants to raise the cash.

In April 1998, Charest was acclaimed leader of the Quebec Liberal Party. He still managed to come to Toronto, to honour his commitment to me. At the Blue Jays game, I remember everyone was so proud of what Charest had done for Quebec by agreeing to accept the leadership of the Quebec Liberals and try to hold the country together from within.

So many people were coming up to him saying, "Thank you from all of Canada for doing what you did." They certainly weren't just party activists who had encouraged him to lead the Quebec Liberals. The support came from everywhere. It was broad based. If you look back at the newspapers at the time, everyone in the country was routing for him to slay the separatists.

In November 1998, Charest lost his first Quebec provincial election, while I was in university. He got almost 30,000 more votes, but lost the seat count 76 to 48, to Bouchard's Parti Québécois. But in 2003, he did become premier of Quebec, a position he held until 2012. He was the first Quebec premier in 100 years to win three elections in a row.

Armed with my love for politics and public service, in 2000, I threw my own hat in the ring and ran for Barrie city council. At the time, I was in my fourth and final year of undergrad school at U of T. I was 22 years old.

My grandparents lived in Ward 1. You'd think that is where I might have considered running. Instead, I did something a little different. I noted that the president of the Liberal riding association, Jean Sweezy, was the alderman in the north end. (Incidentally, one of my first moves on city council was to change the name "alderman" to "councillor," which was more reflective of the fact that all genders were elected to that position.) Anyway, I decided that I would run against her. I didn't feel we needed a big Liberal who would be more concerned about the Liberal Party than she would be about Barrie city council. That's how I selected to run in Ward 3 (now Ward 9).

My victory was sweet for a 22–year–old. However, while I did win, it was by the thinnest of margins, only about 22 votes. Still, it was a story since no one that young had been elected to Barrie city council. In fact, most everyone was much older. The previous mayor, Janice Laking, was around 70 years of age.

My victory and my age shocked everyone to the point that the publisher of the local paper, Joe Anderson, asked to take me to lunch because, as he put it, "There's something interesting about you, Patrick." At lunch, he told me he never thought I had a shot. We've became great friends since that lunch, and together we got stuff done, like the building of the downtown performing arts centre in Barrie.

How did I manage to win? Good old-fashioned hard work —the ethic I inherited from my grandfather, Joe. I door-knocked non-stop. I was still a student, so I would go to classes during the day and door-knock at night. To do this and to keep my grades during the municipal election, I eliminated all extra-curricular activities, including hockey. That was a real sacrifice. I didn't watch television, and I didn't hang out with friends.

In an iChannel documentary, "Playing with Giants," that was produced on my life as a politician, Barrie city councillor Barry Ward credited my victory to the fact that I brought a first-class "big city campaign" to Barrie. Since then, he noted, everyone running has had to step up his or her game. I literally blanketed my ward with literature.

I made only three promises during my municipal campaign: I was going to be the conservative voice on council and push back on tax increases; I'd weed out waste at city hall; and I'd return people's calls within 24 hours.

I took some steps to bring my promises to life. First, I noticed a bunch of city staff was being sent to Florida for conferences. I immediately used this as an example of wasted dollars and signalled that I would work to end this practice. When the mayor of the day was about to bring in a big tax increase, I brought in a big wheelbarrow of petitions, saying that people in my ward couldn't afford it. That may have been theatrical, but it did get attention and it made the point. (I was probably more into theatrics back then than I am now.) In order to facilitate my ability to return calls on time, I gave everyone a magnet with my cellphone number on it. Of course, this is something you can do in municipal politics, but not in federal or provincial politics, as the volume would be too great to manage.

Now that I had won, I was fully dedicated to my two full-time jobs: my new law school career and my career as a city councillor. I had just entered the University of Windsor for my law degree and managed to schedule all my classes into two days, Tuesday and Wednesday. My council meetings were Monday nights, so I would leave on Thursday evening for Barrie and fly back to Windsor on Tuesday morning.

Each trip to Barrie cost $200, which I'd book through a company called Travelcuts; it catered to the university crowd. That means I spent about $800 a month. As councillor, I made about $2,000 a month. My mother was helping me out with tuition, but I had a contract with her which stipulated that I needed to get top grades, and if I didn't, I'd owe her.

Back in Windsor, I had a student apartment. This made no sense because I was only there for one or two nights a week. The next year I said to two of my buddies, "I'll tell you what. I'll give you a bit of extra cash if you let me sleep on your couch a couple of nights a week."

I also bought a home in downtown Barrie, at 138 Collier St. Though it wasn't in my ward, it was still in Barrie. After all, if I were a city councillor, I should own a Barrie home. For a guy in his early 20s and still in school, that was a big deal.

My parents loaned me $20,000, and I put in $20,000 for a home that cost $157,000. They helped me out a great deal. I renovated it into four apartments and I rented out three. I lived in one. The renters paid the mortgage, which was in my name and guaranteed by my parents. This was the house I lived in at the time that the first accuser was in high school, as she claimed. Instead, the sexual misconduct allegations brought forth against me described a home I lived in after the accuser finished high school.

My quarters were small —really small. Over time, I lived in all the apartments I had carved into the house. But the apartment in which I lived the longest had a bedroom the size of a closet, a kitchen, a bathroom and a TV room.

I learned the ropes quickly. I recall there was a front page headline "Axe the Tax." As a conservative, I tend to be against excessive taxation, a position I maintain. But I also realized early on that taxes were necessary for investment. And if there were to be investments, I wanted those investments in my ward. We didn't have a recreation centre, so I worked non-stop to build the East Bayfield Community Centre, which opened in 2003, right before the municipal re-election. My name is still on the plate at the entrance.

Because I had delivered on my key promises, my re-election in 2003 was a cakewalk. I had a former city councillor run against me, along with another candidate. The lawn signs foretold the election outcome. There were 5,000 homes in the ward, and my campaign had up 3,000 lawn signs. On some streets, where I had door-knocked, there might have been 20 houses, and I had up 18 signs.

Throughout the campaign, local television broadcasts kept reminding people that in elections, signs don't vote. Well, these ones did. Typically, municipal races tend to be close. In this election, I got 72 per cent of the vote, which was the biggest margin in the city at the time.

The way it worked in Barrie was that those elected with the highest victory margins got the most senior positions. So the new mayor, Robert Hamilton, asked me what I wanted.

I responded, "Well, the most senior positions in the city are the chair of the finance committee and Barrie Hydro." I served on the finance committee.

During my tenure as city councillor, I focused on health care, despite the fact that it was largely a provincial portfolio. In response to the doctor shortage, together with the Royal Victoria Hospital, I founded the Physician Recruitment Task Force to help attract more physicians to Barrie.

In 2004, I was called to the bar, and in spring 2005, I set up a general practice in Brampton, where I did a bit of everything, including some family, criminal and real estate law. I continued to serve my ward as a city councillor. Now I needed a small office in Barrie. I renovated my home again, so that half of it was my law office. My living quarters were on the main floor apartment, where I occupied about 600 square feet. I had one tenant in the other apartment.

I was a real go-getter. I got busy very quickly. I hired two law clerks and even another lawyer. I had about 300 clients who were proceeding to trial. Had I continued the practice, it would have been very lucrative.

I would call up companies and ask, "Which lawyer do you use to oversee your collections?"

They'd say, "So and so."

So I'd say, "Well, I'm doing that now."

I called up my buddy Larry Pomfret at a collections agency. He asked me if I dealt in the area of collections. I did not, but I told him I'd learn. "Can you give me your business?" I asked.

"Of course," he said, and he sent me over an $80,000 contract to oversee collections for their company.

I would secure the business first, then I would build up a legal team, as required, to help fulfill the contracts. It was lucrative, but I must say that being a politician far exceeded being a lawyer in terms of satisfying my sense of self and of accomplishment for making a positive difference to my community.

It was a very short-lived practice, which ended when I got elected federally. One of the people who worked at the law office for me as an agent was Alex Nuttall, who eventually became the MP for Barrie in 2015. Nuttall was a student, and he was the guy who booked court dates for me. I mentored him, and we remain friends.

Later in 2006, when I was elected as a federal MP, I resigned from city council and I shut down my law office. I gave all my clients away. I couldn't practice law and be an MP, travelling to Ottawa.

I always I knew I wanted a job that I loved — something that excited me and gave me a sense of meaning and purpose. Something that would put me in contact with many people. And frankly, being a lawyer and making lots of money just wasn't it.

Public service was. It was my calling, my purpose and my vocation. And, I intended to pursue a life in public service with full force. From the St. Mike's PC Club, to youth president, to Barrie city council, the pond just kept getting bigger. Now I set my eyes on the river – the Ottawa River to be precise.

CHAPTER 2

WHEN YOU GOTTA GO, YOU GOTTA GO

I respected Harper and always felt he was brilliant. But we did not see eye to eye.

I was more of a "Red Tory" and I frankly didn't get why there were certain issues that the Harperites were so preoccupied with and opposed to, such as gay rights.

It was now 2004, and my Uncle Joe Tascona was an opposition MPP for the Ontario PC Party. The party had gone from a majority government to the opposition benches with few seats in 2003. It was the Liberal Party that was now enjoying a majority government under the stewardship of Dalton McGuinty. The Ontario PCs were definitely in a downward cycle.

I always thought that I could do bigger things for Barrie if I were a provincial or federal member of parliament. I had watched the tides of history and I had seen the cycles. I strongly believed this was our cycle — a conservative cycle —not provincially, mind you, but federally. That was where the opportunity lay.

The timing wasn't great because I had just been elected to municipal office again and I was still a law student. But, the two federal parties on the right, the Reform and Progressive Conservative parties, were uniting under one banner, the new Conservative Party of Canada. I had been pushing hard for this, as had the conservative youth wing. I never expected that the two would unite so quickly. But both Canadian Alliance leader, Stephen Harper, and Progressive Conservative Party leader, Peter MacKay, managed to get the deal done.

The Liberals were in government in Ottawa and had been since 1993. In 2004, Paul Martin called an election.

I figured now was the time to run for the nomination in Barrie. But with little lead time, I was rushing to put it all together. Once I declared my intention to run, I stopped receiving payment for my job as city councillor, as is the custom. I ran and won my party's nomination in Barrie, defeating my fellow candidates, Rod Jackson and Douglas Edwards.

The Conservative Party lost the election, and the Liberals returned to power with a minority government. I, too, lost in my riding of Barrie by a razor-thin margin of two per cent, or 1,295 votes, to Aileen Carroll, a Liberal backbencher.

My team was heartbroken. In a meeting afterwards, I said to them, "You know what? This is a minority parliament, so we're going to get back to work. And when they call an election again, then we're going to win."

Next time came sooner than expected. It was only a year later, 2005. My competition, Carroll, was now a sitting Liberal cabinet minister. She had also served Barrie in the past as a city councillor and was loved by the community. This time would be harder.

I recall that in the debates, Carroll would refer to me as "the student" or "the young boy for the Conservatives." I found this rather insulting and likely intended to be so. So I just doubled down and worked harder than ever. This time around, I was much stronger. I raised more money and I had built a good volunteer organization of about 200 or 300 people.

The election was January 23, 2006, and there were snowstorms galore. Sometimes a storm could dump three feet of snow. While no campaign welcomes lousy weather conditions, I saw this as a great opportunity.

I would tell my team, "On sunny days, everyone will be out door-knocking, but on those horrible days, who will be out? We will. And that'll show the residents of Barrie how hard we'll work. With this amount of snow, no one else will be out door-knocking. That's what separates us from her. So let's hope for snowstorms, 'cause that means we'll be going uncontested."

I won the riding by a little more than I had lost in the last election. The vote count was in my favour by 1,523. With such a slim margin of victory, I committed to myself that now that I was elected, no one would defeat me again because I was going to work as hard as it took to make a positive different for my community and keep my seat. I realized that since the Conservatives won with a minority, an election could happen any time. So I identified the projects that I wanted to work on, and they would be my sole focus and my sole priorities.

Carroll went on a year later to become an MPP in the Liberal government of McGuinty. She was appointed minister of culture in 2007.

My relationship with then Prime Minister Stephen Harper wasn't great. He had won the leadership over MP Tony Clement and businesswoman Belinda Stronach on March 20, 2004.

I had started part-time work for Stronach's company, Magna, in 2000. At that time, I had no idea that Stronach had political ambitions. While I was working there in early 2004, Stronach decided to run for leadership of the Conservative Party against Harper. She told me that she was having Mike Harris, then premier of Ontario, and William Davis, former premier, nominate her on stage as a leadership candidate. Since in 2004 I was the youngest candidate for the Conservative Party, she also wanted me to be on the stage to nominate her. So there I was, a 26-year-old guy, onstage with Bill Davis and Mike Harris —two veterans.

Successful politicians have good memories. They remember faces, names and events. I believe that Harper, a formidable politician, remembered my name, my face and Stronach's nomination event, despite what he might say now.

And so, when I was elected to Ottawa, I wasn't part of the Harper group and I didn't get many opportunities. But, that was OK. I had made that commitment to concentrate on being the best MP Barrie had ever seen, so that I could keep my seat come hell or high water, including if the government was defeated.

I respected Harper and always felt he was brilliant. But we did not see eye to eye. I was more of a "Red Tory" and I frankly didn't get why there were certain issues that the Harperites were so preoccupied with and opposed to, such as gay rights.

One thing I did respect about Harper was that he always had time for caucus. He took time to listen. If you wanted to speak to the prime minister, you would send a note, and he would call you back. I would send a memo to him every six months with a Barrie update, and I would get a call back at 10 p.m. on a Saturday from Harper, who would tell me what he thought of my memo. I give Harper credit for that. He was a hard worker, and that is something I can appreciate.

While other more senior caucus members would be sucking up to him, I remained focused on my riding and not on climbing the ladder. I'd go to Ottawa from Barrie on Monday morning and I'd return to Barrie on Thursday. Focused on all the Barrie projects, I spent much of my time harassing ministers to death, until I got the funding I needed.

Of course, I would attend as many community events as possible — pancake breakfasts and chili cook-offs. But when it came to delivering on projects, I was focused.

I set up a physician scholarship fund, which would give scholarships to physicians willing to come to Barrie, and I set up a scholarship fund in the name of a Barrie firefighter, Bill Wilkins, who passed away when a house collapsed on him while he was in the line of duty. He died without any end-of-life benefits. His kids and wife were left with nothing. This fund would help families like his. I got some big wins on projects such as the expansion of Georgian College and the cleanup of Lake Simcoe.

The publisher of the local paper, the Barrie Advance, was Joe Anderson. His passion was to create a downtown performing arts centre. He lobbied Minister Carroll at Queen's Park for funding. I'm not certain what she was thinking when she turned him down flat because she said it was a conflict for her to help the community establish a performing arts centre that would be located in her riding. That was simply crazy!

Anderson was *so* pissed off! I mean, this is the publisher of the paper. You get a win for him and you're golden. Furthermore, there were great arguments for the establishment of the arts scene in Barrie. *The community should not be discriminated against because it happened to be in the riding of the minister of the day*, I thought. So I promised Anderson, "I know that Aileen didn't get this done for you, but I will."

In Ottawa, I harassed the hell out of the federal Heritage Minister James Moore, and got the funding. Normally, government funding requires a third from the city, a third from the province and a third from the feds. But this deal was 50-50 between the city and the feds. We got it done and we built the downtown Centre for the Performing Arts.

While my great uncle, Tony Tascona, a well-regarded Manitoba painter, received the Order of Canada for his art contributions, I'm more of a hockey guy. But here I was, now involved in the arts scene. I knew it was important to the people of Barrie, and they convinced me of the many spin-off benefits that a robust arts community would bring to Barrie, notably, more businesses and more physicians. I became a champion for the arts in Barrie.

When I ran for re-election in 2008, the Barrie Advance newspaper, which was owned by Torstar Corporation, endorsed me. It endorsed me again in 2011, when the Conservative Party, under Harper, finally won a majority government.

In Ottawa, all MPs were ranked in caucus according to our margin of victory. The thinner the margin, the lower the ranking. I had won in 2005 by a thin margin, so I was ranked near the bottom, 38th of 40 Conservative MPs. Still, in the 2008 election, my seat had been targeted by the party for victory, even though it was considered to be a really tough fight. And although the Conservatives still only won a minority government, I won my seat by 15,000 votes, and my ranking took a giant leap from 38th to eighth.

I began finding ways to raise money for Barrie and have fun at the same time. For example, I started the Barrie marathon, being an avid runner myself. I always wanted to have a half marathon in the city. One day, I went to a store called the Running Room in Barrie and asked why we didn't have a half marathon. The answer I got back was that city hall would not allow it. I couldn't get over that. So I called up city hall and said I wanted to do a charity half marathon together with the Running Room. The response swift and positive: "Sure!"

Job 1 was to get some sponsors to pay for barricades and portable washrooms. I got Red Bull and some friends to sponsor the event. Through these efforts and their generosity, I was able to cover all the expenses. Every runner paid $40, which went to cover a T-shirt and a medal. The rest went to the charity I selected.

The charity I chose was the cardiac unit at the Royal Victoria Regional Health Centre in Barrie, where my late grandmother, Edna Tascona, had volunteered for many years. I actually took her volunteer certificate and put it up in my office as a reminder to me of what communities were all about. The head of the cardiac program, Dr. Brad Dibble, a cardiologist, was also a very close friend of mine, so this was a great cause for me. I was committed to making this event the biggest fundraiser for the cardiac unit.

The charity half marathon typically raised between $30,000 and $40,000. Not bad! In its first year, we had 500 runners participate. This grew to 800 runners and again to about 1,200 runners. It became a big deal. When I became leader of the Ontario PC Party, it was too much work for me with my other commitments. So I passed it off to other organizers. Unfortunately, it has since fizzled.

Apart from running, my other love is hockey. The idea for Hockey Night in Barrie began years earlier with a one-time event. Benefiting from the NHL strike, Barrie organizers managed to get Shane Corson, a famous NHLer, to participate in a hockey game in Barrie. People came to watch. It was a hit, to say the least, and all the proceeds went to the hospital.

Then in 2008, the idea came to me. I thought, *Hey, I know a bunch of hockey players. Maybe I should bring this event back on a regular basis?* I called the head of the hospital and the chair of the foundation, David Blenkarn, and took him to lunch. I told him that six or seven years earlier, we had this fundraiser for the hospital, and I wanted to make it an annual thing. I promised to pull out all the stops and make it a kick-ass event. I knew I could. After all, I played hockey everywhere, so I knew guys who knew all the famous hockey players.

We called it Hockey Night in Barrie. We filled the Barrie Molson Centre and brought in NHLers to play in front of Barrie fans.

In its first year, I called big companies in Ottawa to donate. Quickly, I was able to raise $100,000 in sponsorships. The challenge was to sell 4,000 tickets to a new event. Working hard, I think we managed to sell around 3,000 tickets or so in its first year.

I landed a bunch of retired NHLers. But I also managed to get present-day superstar Rick Nash. Nash was about as famous a player as you could get. He'd played hockey with one of my buddies in Barrie, and his participation really kicked the event up several notches.

Everyone had a blast. People would purchase tickets just to watch these NHLers play. In a small town, that's a very big deal. Hockey Night in Barrie was held each summer, and it got easier to put together over the years as the event became more established. Numerous NHLers had their cottages near Barrie, which also facilitated their participation. Over the years, Ron MacLean, Don Cherry, Steven Stamkos, Connor McDavid, Corey Perry, Matt Duchene, Mark Scheifele and Aaron Ekblad all became regulars.

For those of you who aren't hockey fans, those names will mean little. But to those who are, those names carry a lot of weight, which is why Hockey Night in Barrie became the biggest charity hockey game in Canada. One year it was featured prominently on the front page of The Globe and Mail. And, my good friend, TV celebrity Alan Thicke, not only participated regularly, but also did a television show on the event.

The half marathon was in May, and Hockey Night in Barrie was in August. So, while many MPs would take it easy over the summer, I would work like a dog in the summers putting these events together. I had a blast.

Then there were other hugely serious and controversial initiatives in which I became involved. These initiatives would educate me, shape me and my thinking and bring me into cultural communities in which I had never before been active. They would also put me on a collision course with my own party.

When I won the leadership of the Ontario PC Party in 2015, I was proud at the diversity represented on that convention floor in Mississauga. I brought that diversity to an otherwise disproportionately white, male party. But my relationships with these cultural communities started years earlier, while I was a young MP in Ottawa.

Many people wonder why the Tamil community came out in huge numbers to support me in my leadership bid. I heard the rumours that I signed people up from these communities without their knowledge or that I bussed in people during my election runs — people who had no idea who I was. That's all bullshit. These communities supported me because I had supported them.

A good example of a community that was instrumental to my political success is the Tamil community. I continue to have a great relationship today. But it began many years ago.

For years. Sri Lanka was plunged into civil war between the Tamils, headed by an organization that sought to establish an independent Tamil state, and the much larger Sinhalese community. In 2006, then President Mahinda Rajapaksa announced his intention to eradicate the Tamils.

By 2009, after the civil war, the military forces conducted a cleansing of the Tamil community. Tamil families were hunted down, put in internally displaced persons (IDP) camps and slaughtered. Tens of thousands of bodies were being thrown into mass graves. But these reports hadn't really been broadcast internationally. It was only people from Sri Lanka who were screaming about what was happening there.

The Tamil community in Canada is large, around 300,000. And this community began to organize. They began a Tamil movement here in Canada and other Western countries to raise awareness about the genocide of their people and to hopefully garner support to stop it.

Tamils marched on the Gardiner Expressway in downtown Toronto, and the city was forced to shut it down as a result. They staged a big protest in Ottawa, but still no one was listening or paying any attention. I find it extraordinary that we had 100,000 people in Ottawa protesting, and no one was hearing them.

In my riding of Barrie, I had no Tamil community to speak of. In fact, I had I only two Tamil families in the entire riding.

But one day, I got a visit from a constituent who was from one of the two Tamil families in my riding. She walked in and just broke down in tears. I will never forget that moment as long as I live. She said I wouldn't believe what they were doing to her uncle and family in Sri Lanka. And she explained what was going on. Normally, a politician gets lobbied on many issues, and to be honest, sometimes you really don't know what to believe.

I believed her. I believed her tears. I believed her emotions, and what she was telling me was disturbing. I promised to look into it.

When the Tamils launched the big protest on Parliament Hill in Ottawa, the Conservative MPs had been ordered not to attend. In 2006, our government had listed the Liberation Tigers of Tamil Eelam as a terrorist organization and was treating all Tamils as terrorists.

But I thought something didn't sound right. So I decided to attend the demonstration and see what was happening. Naturally, in 2009 as a backbencher, no one really knew who I was. I started shaking hands and asking people to tell me their story.

That's when I bumped into one of the main organizers, Babu Nagalingam. That was a fateful meeting; although, neither one of us knew it at the time. He would become one of my chief organizers when I ran for the Ontario PC Party leadership.

Nagalingam was surprised to see me. He told me that they had members from the other political parties show up at their demonstrations in the past, but to date, never a Conservative. In fact, Nagalingam reminded me of my own party's edict: I was not allowed to be out at the demonstration at all. I suppose his lobby efforts with the Conservatives had yielded knowledge about that directive imposed on MPs by the party and probably had not yielded much else.

I told him the story of my constituent and how I'd promised her I would look into it. Nagalingam offered me the opportunity to view a Channel 4 British documentary of the horrors of the Sri Lankan killing fields. I was disgusted.

I decided that I wanted to see this reality in person and that I would help my constituent bring her uncle to Canada. She wanted him to apply for residency. But along with many others, he was in the IDP camp. To get to Canada, he needed the Canadian sponsorship papers. And the paperwork was located in the embassy, in Colombo, the capital city of Sri Lanka. So if you're in an IDP camp, you obviously have no access to the embassy.

I committed to going to the embassy in Colombo, where I would get the forms. I would then travel to the IDP camp and bring this man the paperwork. It would also enable me to see what was behind the curtain, so to speak.

I called my friend and fellow MP Paul Calandra, in Markham, Ont., who had many Tamil constituents in his riding. He was hearing about the atrocities on a regular basis and he, too, believed something sinister was happening.

"Paul," I told him, "we're going to go to Sri Lanka, you and me. We'll go there and we'll take care of the constituents. Trust me, this will be good."

He was caught completely off guard. "Patrick, what are you getting us into?" Calandra didn't really know what I was doing, but he was prepared to go along with it.

I booked the cheapest flight I could, and I applied for my travel visa. On the application I listed that the purpose of the trip was to visit an IDP camp. The application was turned down by the Sri Lanka High Commission.

This not only pissed me off, but also tipped me off. Why would the commission turn down a visa from a parliamentarian, unless they had something to hide? I began attending Tamil events in Toronto and telling my story: that I was denied a visa as a parliamentarian, and that in my view the only explanation for this was that the Sri Lankan government was hiding something.

Here I was, a Conservative MP speaking out against the Sri Lankan government. This made me a hero in the Tamil community. Many YouTube videos of me from 2009 and 2010 are accessible online if you google "Patrick Brown and Tamil." I became an activist, and for the first time, the Tamil community finally had an advocate within the Conservative government.

I realized that I needed support on Parliament Hill. I was going to hold a movie night and I was going to show the Channel 4 documentary that Nagalingam had shown me. I told him that I could invite all the MPs, many of whom were from Alberta and Saskatchewan, and most of these folks didn't even know what a Tamil was. I explained to Nagalingam that the reason why they weren't being heard was because no one heard them outside of Liberal Toronto.

After Question Period one day, Harper ran into Calandra and me in the lobby. He told us that we needed to be careful. As he put it, "We don't know about this group. Don't get too close." Calandra's initial reaction was to suck up to the prime minister, so he immediately backed off.

"I'm out, Patrick. I'm not going to these events any more. I don't wanna get on the wrong side of the PMO [prime minister's office]."

By this time, I was completely seized by the issue. I was going to continue to attend the Tamil events and to hold events on my own. I was vocal and I was speaking out against the Tamil dictator, Rajapaksa. And I was getting big crowds listening to me. I flew to Geneva for the weekend to give a pitch to the United Nations on behalf of the National Council of Canadian Tamils. I also went to the United Nations in New York to give a speech there.

I invited MPs from all political stripes to a movie night and reception for the screening of the Channel 4 documentary. This evening was organized by me and the Canadian Human Rights Voice (CHRV), a Tamil-based

TAKEDOWN

organization that was focusing on these Sri Lankan abuses, and the footage is available on YouTube. Naturally, my target was government MPs who had the power to do something.

About 30 or 40 MPs showed up. For the first time, they were listening. I got a bunch of MPs to sign a letter to the prime minister, requesting that government look into the Tamil situation in Sri Lanka.

The Tamils took note. They had no traction at all in Ottawa before me, then here's this guy, Brown, and he's getting them into government. I was fast becoming a hero in the community.

Now I realized that my efforts were putting me offside with the PMO. I briefly considered the associated risk. *Oh well*, I figured. *What are they going to do to me? I'm a backbencher. They can't take away my status as a backbencher.*

I had done some media on the issue. Soon thereafter, I got calls from the PMO, asking me what the hell I was doing. There was definitely friction between me and the PMO. To be fair, Harper had warned Calandra and me, and I was essentially carrying on, anyway, despite the warning.

I finally caught a break. Lawrence Cannon, then minister of foreign affairs, approached me and said, "Patrick, you're on to something." He had attended a Commonwealth meeting and he sensed that something didn't seem right in Sri Lanka. He had been trying to push the Commonwealth into looking into the allegations of abuse.

I was relieved. This was the break we needed, and it started a cascade of interest with the MPs. Bruce Stanton got interested in the issue. So did Harold Albrecht and a bunch of the Kitchener-Waterloo MPs because they had a large Tamil community in that part of Ontario. Now I had a number of MP advocates on my side. Things really turned around with the PMO, as well, when Minister Cannon finally recognized a problem.

The Sri Lankan high commissioner, who never bothered with me in the past, came to see me at my office after movie night. She was livid and wanted to know why I was backing terrorists.

I said, "Look, you're spreading your propaganda to every MP. You're accusing every Tamil of being a terrorist. The ones in my riding are just good people whose families are being murdered. So for every MP office you visit, so will I."

I'm not sure that any high commissioner is accustomed to having an MP be so combative. She was not amused. She had also accused me in a speech of taking the positions I did out of political expediency (that's a fancy way to say getting votes).

I asked her at the time, "How many Tamil families do you think I have in my riding? I have only two."

"Two?" She expressed surprise, then her face softened. "You mean 2,000?"

"No. I mean two — as in two families."

I would talk about my encounter at all these Tamil events. I'd say, "You know what the Sri Lanka high commissioner told me? She said I can't have a movie night, and I told her that for every door she goes to with her propaganda, I 'm going to follow up and I'm going to tell the truth. She's been able to push a myth that Tamils are terrorists, and no one has pushed back. Well that party's over." The Tamil community was ecstatic. I was their champion,

Finally, in 2013, Canada became the first G7 country to call for the Commonwealth to boycott Sri Lanka. Ultimately, the boycott raised awareness, and Rajapaksa was pushed out. The United Nations agreed to investigate him for war crimes.

Unfortunately, despite all this, I wasn't able to get any of my constituent's family members out of the country. Even so, the Tamil community credited me for changing the government's position, and to some extent, the international position. In 2013, the CHRV presented me with its human rights award at a gala attended by about 2,000 Tamils. Coming through this awful ordeal together, the Tamil community had become like family.

Tamil organizers told me that in 2009 I had backed two Tamil families in my riding and by doing so, I backed the entire community. They promised me when I was running for PC Party leader in Ontario that they would be help me sweep the Greater Toronto Area (GTA) by mobilizing Tamil families.

"You didn't help us because it was politically smart. You did it because it was right," they said. And they never forgot. I owe the Tamil community a great deal for my PC leadership victory in 2015.

Then there was my relationship with the Indian community — another set of important activities that alienated me from the office of the prime minister and the party whip.

It all started when Liberal MP Ruby Dhalla decided to run for chair of the Canada-India Parliamentary Association, which was focused on Canada's official friendship with India. Our caucus was looking for a Conservative MP to run against her.

My friend Naresh Raghubeer thought that being the chair of the official association of such an important and prominent ethnic community would make me a pretty important guy. I'd be "Mr. India." While I was no expert, I loved the people, the food and the culture. Growing up, my dad was the designated "family cook" on Fridays, which meant he ordered in. Friday dinners were great since he'd bring back food from a restaurant called Sweet India on Airport Road. And hanging out in Brampton, a city known also for its strong Indian community, I developed a fascination with Indian culture. However, I was now MP of Barrie, and as was the case with the Tamil community, my riding really didn't have much of an Indian community.

All the same, I agreed to run as the Conservative MP against Dhalla. There were about 200 MPs present at the vote. And I won. I owed this victory essentially only to the fact that there were more Conservatives than Liberals or NDPs at the vote.

You can imagine the big brouhaha that ensued. After they announced the results, Dhalla started screaming, "You guys are so spiteful! You ran Patrick against me? Patrick *Brown*? He's not even Indian! He's not even Indian!" Deepak Obhrai, who was chairing the vote, banged his gavel and yelled out, "His last name is Brown, and that's good enough for me!" Everyone laughed, except Dhalla.

I now held a position that was well respected by the government of India, as well as the Indian community in Canada. I got the VIP treatment at all their events. I found myself attending many Indian events in the GTA. This was an area in Ontario where the Conservative Party really had no presence at all.

I told Harper that since we didn't have much presence in the GTA, I wanted to concentrate on two things. First, I wanted to build my own relationship with India, but second, I also wanted to build our party's presence in the Indian community and help our candidates forge better relationships. This would build the party. Harper liked that.

I got very close with groups such as the Indo-Canada Chamber of Commerce and the Canada India Foundation. I became good friends with the key officials to the extent that I was often a dinner guest in their homes. We bonded. The officials and representatives in these Indian organizations tended to be heavy hitters in the community. Many of these people were worth hundreds of millions of dollars.

One day, they approached me with an issue they needed resolved. They told me of a politician in India by the name of Narendra Modi. He's was the chief minister in the Indian province of Gujarat. A chief minister in India is similar to being a premier in Canada. My friends told me that they believed he was the future of India. However, the United States had turned down his travel visa as a result of the Hindu-Muslim riots that had broken out in his province. The perception was that Modi had tacitly allowed the riots to develop and failed to handle the situation. People were referring to him as "The Butcher of Gujarat." Modi insisted that he had nothing to do with the riots, but it didn't matter. The U.S. Department of State opinion had been formed.

Thanks to this perception, Modi had been organizing a trade conference in India, and now all the delegations from other countries were cancelling their participation. It was an embarrassment. Modi's staff had asked the various Indian associations to ensure that a Canadian MP attended the trade conference. The community needed me to go. So I called Senator Consiglio (Con) Di Nino, who was the Senate representative on the Canada Indian Parliamentary Association, which I chaired. I told him that he and I should attend the trade conference to be held in Gujarat. Di Nino was totally up for it. He, too, loved India and had visited about 20 times.

However, per usual, nothing came easily. The call came swiftly from the Department of Foreign Affairs and International Trade (DFAIT), advising us not to go because Gujarat was on the banned list. Di Nino and I went, anyway. We were already en route when we received another call, this time from Canada's high commissioner, ordering us to turn around and come back to Canada.

By now, we were also getting calls from the PMO. *Here we go again*, I thought. The PMO was essentially telling me that I was not allowed to participate at the Gujarat trade conference because Canada had not yet taken a position on Gujarat. The government did not want the optics that Canada was condoning Gujarat, Modi or the events in that province at this time. Senator Di Nino's advice to me was to proceed. After all, he argued, it was often better to ask forgiveness than permission. I have always remembered that advice. It would come in handy very soon thereafter.

We also received a call from the office of the party whip, Gordon O'Connor. The message was simple enough: if we continued on to this conference, the first thing I would need to do upon my return to Canada would be to present myself to the party whip, where I would undoubtedly be in Big Shit.

We went, anyway. My buddies in the community told me that I had to do this. I had to speak on behalf of Canada. It was important for them.

Thank goodness we went. At the conference, the government had ordered a 200-foot Canadian flag. They wanted to send the message to Canada that this guy, Modi, was *not* a pariah. As it turned out, only two countries attended — Canada and Japan. Every other country boycotted the event. But unlike Japan, we didn't have backing of our government.

Modi greeted me for the first time. "I know you were under a lot of pressure not to come, and I really appreciate your being here."

When I got back to Canada, O'Connor called me into his office. He told me that I would not get any promotion within the party. There would be no chance of me ever being a parliamentary secretary or a minister. He might have threatened to kick me out of caucus, but he didn't. In any case, I was already in their bad books, and if they really wanted to throw me out, they likely would have done so by now. I figured I'd be good on that front.

As if that weren't enough, I was now being placed on the official travel ban list for one year. This did not mean I wasn't technically allowed to travel for official purposes. I was, that is, technically speaking. However, it meant that government wouldn't pay. That wasn't so bad, either. I mean, I knew that I could get the Indian organizations to sponsor my flights.

But then came the kicker. The travel ban also meant that government would not approve my application for any time off that was required for official travel. Of all the slaps on the wrist, this one was a real problem.

Soon after, in 2009, and while I was still very much in the government penalty box, I received a call from Modi. By now, we had each other's cellphone numbers. He told me that he was building a convention centre dedicated to Mahatma Gandhi, and he was asking for countries all around the world to participate in the "water-pouring ceremony." This ceremony would have delegates from around the world pour water into the foundations of what would be the new convention centre. "Would I come?" Modi wondered. He added that they would make me a guest of the state, which would be certainly better than the treatment I was getting by my own government. Sounded great!

I looked at my schedule. It was pretty impossible. Parliament was sitting, and Modi wanted me to be there on a Friday. That meant that I had to leave Ottawa on the Wednesday. And then I would need to be back for Monday. Thanks to my travel ban, not to mention the schedule, I knew there was no way that I would be allowed to go.

Indian community reps were calling me. They were astounded. I could not possibly turn down Modi. It would be a real slight. And besides, "He likes you," they reminded me. "You gotta go."

I tried to explain my predicament. "Look, guys. I'm already in massive shit with my own government whip. If I ask to take time off, he'll say 'No.'" I tried to convince them of the impossible nature of their request, but deep down, I was considering it.

My Indian community friends told me that the Canada India Foundation was prepared to fund two tickets, one for me and another for an MP of my choosing. I knew exactly who that would be. I approached a new Conservative MP from Calgary, Devinder Shory. Shory was an MP, he was Indian and he absolutely loved Modi.

Shory was so excited when I asked him if he would accompany me to India. "Sure! I'll go with you!" he said in a heartbeat. "Do we have to ask the party whip?"

Di Nino's advice played out in my head. "Devinder, we are *not* going to ask the party whip because he'll say 'No.'" I was the veteran MP of the two of us, so I told him in as resolute a voice as I could muster, "Just trust me on this one. We won't ask permission. We'll just apologize afterwards. I've done this before."

It all looked possible, then the party called a marathon of votes for the Wednesday night — about 30 votes. Our flight was at 9 p.m., and we would need to leave midway through the votes. *How would that possibly go unnoticed?*

I came up with a plan. "Devinder, you and I, we're going to go to the washroom. They can't deprive us of that. After all, when you gotta go, you gotta go. Right? And they're going to be too focused on the votes; they won't notice."

About 15 votes into the process, I said, "I gotta go to the washroom." Shory did the same. We were out the back door with our bags to catch out flight.

The next day, there were many missed calls on my phone from the whip's office. "Where are you? You missed all these votes!" I told Shory not to respond.

I poured the water over the foundations of the convention centre. And I gave Modi a very big hug. He was so happy. And Shory was thrilled.

On Monday we returned to Canada. Back in the office for more shit. I was informed that they knew I had been in India over the weekend. I was told that the whole thing played out on social media. Busted!

"That's a very long way to travel to go to the bathroom," the whip stated. Clearly, he was not amused. "How is it that two or three MPs give me more work than the other 160? It's clear that you just don't respect me." Bingo. That was the real issue. I have come to appreciate that there is nothing worse than a guy in a position of power who thinks he's been dissed. My punishment may have been more about disrespecting his office than about Modi or Gujarat or the riots.

I later spoke with Conservative MP Jason Kenney, who was also very intertwined with the cultural communities. Kenney and I were never close. He was a social conservative, and I wasn't. He was upset when I marched in the Toronto Pride Parade. And he was upset when I said climate change is man-made and irrefutable, and we have to do our part. I am a Red Tory, a more progressive conservative, and he is from the religious right.

However, when it came to this issue, Kenney said to me that if he had been in my shoes, he'd have done the same thing. He appreciated the work I did in cultural communities, even though, according to his friends, he would get jealous when I was referred to as best cultural organizer that Ontario had ever seen after my Ontario leadership win in 2015.

Where we were alike was that we both understood the importance of cultural engagement. We knew cultural communities and we understood their complexities and their intricacies such as the differences between Sikhs, Hindus and Malayali.

Modi and I continued to bond. I would go India every six months. We got an awesome new high commissioner in India, Stuart Beck. He believed strongly that Modi was "the real deal." He told me that the matter of the riots in Gujarat that had sparked the international shunning of Modi was being referred to the Supreme Court in India. That process cleared Modi of any wrongdoing and confirmed that Modi had absolutely nothing to do with the riots.

Modi went on to win a third term as chief minister of Gujarat by a massive landslide. He also won the Muslim community vote. Having had his name cleared, and on the heels of a massive victory, all the countries that had boycotted his trade conference began attending events in Gujarat, the economic engine of India.

But Modi never forgot who was with him when he needed support. And while back home, I was having trouble getting permission to go to the bathroom, in India, Modi began promoting me as a friend. He'd invite me to lunch with Bollywood stars, including Priety Zinta, and with billionaires such as Ratan Tata (who has a net worth of about $70 billion US and the Ambani brothers. He had me sitting at tables at events with the who's who of India. When I returned to India with Canada's high commissioner, I was walking around with a big stick. I was given state status. I would travel around with three vans in front of me and three vans behind. There were guys with machine guns to protect me. They even had my photo on banners at the convention. The speech I delivered has since been posted to YouTube. But the word that spread was that Patrick Brown from Canada is friends with Chief Minister Modi.

Kenney agreed that Modi was the real deal, and he was pushing the government to open up a trade office in Gunanagar, India. We already had one in Gujarat. In 2012, Canada opened a new trade office in Gunanagar. That was Kenney's doing, not mine. Despite that fact, Gujaratis continued to give the credit to me.

Once Modi was elected prime minister of India, the PMO was very keen to have him visit Canada. Modi was not the likely victor, but his victory was facilitated by a massive lapse in political judgment by the congress of Gujarat. In a gross error, the Congress Party made comments about how Modi's family was nothing more than tea sellers on the streets of Gujarat.

This was very offensive to many Indians who held similar jobs. The voters rallied around him, and he won a majority in a country where typically governments are "pizza parliaments" —minority governments made up of many different factions.

After this victory, I had DFAIT and folks from the PMO waiting for me in the lobby of parliament, asking me how to deal with Modi. I was asked to assist in getting him to the country. Though I never checked with the whip's office, I was quite certain that I had gone from being the black sheep to being a very valuable asset. After all, I had been invited to see Modi take the oath of office when he became India's prime minister.

Now I wanted to play a big role in Modi's first official visit to Canada. Typically, the PMO reserved that role for ministers. But I got around that.

When Modi had been first minister, we would text each other directly. Once he became prime minister, I was instructed to text his principal secretary, AK Sharma. So I did, and I asked Sharma, if possible, for Modi to tell the Canadian side that he wanted me around when he arrived in Canada. The Indian officials messaged the Canadian officials that Modi expected Patrick Brown to be there when the airplane landed in Ottawa. There I was on the tarmac with Kenney and Foreign Affairs Minister John Baird. I was going to shake Modi's hand when he landed.

I was also invited to the private dinner taking place in the Senate Chamber dining room, a venue that was reserved for dinners with foreign dignitaries and the like. The dinner was attended by about eight or nine of us, including Harper, a few of his senior ministers, Modi and some of his senior ministers.

The Canadian delegation arrived first, and we were waiting for the prime minister of India to arrive. When he did, Modi shook Harper's hand. Harper said, "I understand you know Patrick very well." Modi smiled and responded, "Patrick Brown is a friend; he has been to India many, many times. If he wanted to run in India, he would win as an MP there."

I said, "You know, prime minister, if I were to run India, I would run in Baroda," which was Modi's home town. He chuckled at that.

61

Harper said to Modi, "You know, we have always encouraged Patrick's work in India." Hmm. *Excuse me?* I thought maybe Harper was not aware of the royal ass-kicking I got at the hands of the party whip, or how he threatened me, disciplined me and essentially blackballed me over my work. As I mentioned before, great politicians tend to have very, very long memories. On the other hand, here's an example of when great politicians need to have very, very short memories. To be fair, I suppose I wasn't always a team player. But I don't regret it.

The Globe and Mail published a front page story of the top 10 MPs who voted against their own party. I made that list. The fact that I never made cabinet might be attributed to my voting patterns, along with my lengthy bathroom break to India and other somewhat rebellious moves. The fact that I ended up being on the right side of these issues didn't matter much.

But what I found most galling was how I was chastised in my run for the Ontario PC leadership because I never made it to cabinet while I was the federal MP in a majority government. And of course, the response I gave at the time was that Harper had a strong bench of talent. But the truth is that I was marginalized because I stood up for some things that just didn't sit well with the whip or with Harper, or both. This is not a reason that can be presented during a leadership campaign, but in my view, it was the truth.

I don't regret a moment of my actions. I am proud that I defied the party whip. I am proud that I defied my government when it came to the rights of the communities I represented.

When it came to votes, the truth is, there were some votes I was proud of and others where I had to hold my nose and voted as most politicians have to do on occasion. As a backbencher, you could only shake the government's will so often. You really needed to pick your spots. One might argue that I tried the prime minister's patience too often, and I suppose the fact that I made the top 10 list of The Globe and Mail could be proof of that.

One of votes that I was most proud of was when I voted against my party and sided with the Liberals on a private member's bill that would provide end-of-life benefits for firefighters' families. In 2004, the Conservatives promised in the platform to set up an end-of-life benefit for firefighters. I had become very close to the Barrie firefighters. I had organized hockey tournaments: MPs versus firefighters and MPs versus police. Both these groups loved me. I campaigned on this promise. But when I was elected to government, I tried to put forth a private member's bill to create an end-of-life benefit for firefighters and was told by the house leader that we were not certain as a government of where we stood on this issue. I was not allowed to put forward my bill.

Instead, the Liberals' Ralph Goodale did. And, guess what? The Conservative caucus was instructed to vote against his bill! I mean, we campaigned on this very item in 2004, and now we're voting against it? Gimme a break! I made it clear that I wasn't going back to Barrie, having voted against something that I campaigned on. I just wasn't.

I went around to petition other MPs to vote against government and to support the Goodale bill. I tapped the firefighters' union for support, and wherever they had good relationships with the MP, we'd pay them a visit. I got 30 Conservative MPs to vote against government. Government lost that vote, and Goodale's bill passed.

At its national conference in 2012, the International Association of Firefighters handed out two honorary firefighter badges. The two recipients were me and former Ontario Liberal Premier Dalton McGuinty, who had championed firefighter causes in Ontario.

This would be another unlikely constituency that would back me in my 2015 bid for Ontario's PC Party leader. In fact, at my leadership launch I had three unions nominating me — the nurses' union, the police union and the firefighters' union. People couldn't believe this was a bid for a Progressive Conservative leadership with three unions nominating.

There were other votes I was not proud of. The vote I regretted the most was on gay marriage. We had made a 2004 platform commitment on gay marriage that Harper would reopen the debate on for same sex marriage and only after debate, and pending the results he would he put the issue to bed if it had no support. The Conservatives lost that election.

Early in 2006, when we had just been elected MPs, we were told that this previous election promise still held, and that we were expected to vote in favour of reopening this debate. I was new and very young. I was not about to rock the boat and so I voted with the party.

I regretted this because I had friends who were gay, a family member who was gay and this made no sense to me at all. This was the part of conservatism that I disliked. My family didn't like it, either. They wondered what I was doing supporting this vote, but I explained that I had to because there was an expectation to vote for platform commitments.

It was explained to me that the commitment was limited to debating the issue of gay marriage. And that in a minority government, any proposed changes to gay marriage were sure to fail. So the issue would be done. We would have honoured our commitment to the religious right, but no real changes would ensure as a result. I supposed this thinking was what was considered clever political thinking. I understood that Harper was trying to maintain the conservative coalition that was still young. And so was I. I was a 27-year-old junior MP, so I held my nose and went with the flow.

A few years later, Winnipeg MP Rod Bruinooge, who often sat beside me in the House when the seating arrangement was alphabetical, put forward a bill to have a committee study when life begins. Bruinooge was someone I got to know well, given that sometimes you were subjected to eight hours in the House, sitting side by each.

Bruinooge headed up the pro-life caucus. In his pitch to caucus, he argued that the committee would be a bone to throw to the religious right. Again. He emphasized that they really wouldn't have any power to act. Again.

I knew that the prime minister didn't want these religious issues resurfacing at that point. But unofficially, the leaders of the party were pushing it. Kenney was campaigning in caucus for it, and at the time he had a big following. Kenney is a devout Catholic, who had considered priesthood. For him, abortion is a big issue.

I had people telling me that if I didn't vote the right way on this, my nomination in the future could be challenged. There was a huge pressure campaign. So I devised a plan. I put together a House of Commons newsletter to my riding that included a survey to see what constituents in my riding wanted.

I recall receiving about 2,000 responses. Interestingly, about 98 per cent of the votes came back in favour of the motion to strike the committee on when life begins. I believe that was because the majority of people for whom abortion was not a big issue didn't bother to vote at all. But for those who did care about this issue, they organized responses. Many of those voting in favour of the motion were the result of church- organized efforts, not so much the Catholic Church, but evangelical churches. I now had to honour a vote that I personally did not believe in. Again.

I was very clear with the local media that while this vote did not represent what I personally felt, I had to honour the response I received from my constituents. This also happened to be the easier route to take. I wouldn't be pissing off Kenney, I wouldn't be putting my nomination at risk and the issue would just go away. I held my nose — again.

Of course, during the Ontario PC Party leadership race, my opponents in the party and the Liberals were quick to position me as some type of social conservative who was against choice for women. When I won the leadership, the Liberals smacked their lips thinking that the PCs had just elected a "SoCon" (social conservative). But that was far from the truth. In fact, on the public record, I was the first Barrie MP to participate in the gay pride flag-raising event in 2012.

I suppose my time in Ottawa helped define me, for better and for worse. It also branded me inaccurately or accurately. Armed with the celebrity and baggage of my days on Parliament Hill, I now set my sights on Ontario.

CHAPTER 3

THE UNLIKELY CANDIDATE

I knew one thing: politics is about numbers.
The existing party members were the diehards. They
might have favoured other candidates, but they were
few...They didn't reflect the fabric nor the views of the
general electorate of Ontario.

It was 2014, and Ontario was headed into a provincial election. In May, I was headed to India, to attend Modi's swearing in. As the plane took off, I remember thinking to myself that Tim Hudak was going to blow the election again. After I arrived back, Hudak would, in fact, blow the election — again.

This was an election that should have been won by the Ontario PC Party. I won't say an easy win because that connotes an arrogance that is dangerous in politics. Politics is certainly a game where anything can happen and often does, as my story indicates. But by 2014, the general feeling was that Ontario needed a change in government and this election was winnable.

In February 2013, Kathleen Wynne had become leader of the Ontario Liberal Party, taking over from Dalton McGuinty, who had stepped down as party leader in 2012. Despite winning the 2011 election, McGuinty lost the massive majority the Liberals had enjoyed by one seat. During the course of that election, McGuinty cancelled two gas plants that had been foisted on certain communities during the course of his administration. Now, understanding that these gas plants stood in the way of a victory in those ridings, McGuinty cancelled them.

People saw this as a massive abuse of taxpayer dollars for political gain. The gas plant cancellation and associated costs (which the auditor general estimated at $1 billion) would eventually balloon into a major scandal and send one Liberal to jail for an attempted cover-up. Still, McGuinty won.

People were tired of him (he only beat Hudak by two percentage points), and the economic recovery that was still in its infancy had stalled. People were worried about jobs. But Hudak, leader of the Ontario PCs, and his campaign team decided to run on issues such as discouraging affirmative action for foreign workers and bringing back chain gangs. These distracted from the bigger commitments to jobs that Hudak was also promising. And at a time when people were very concerned about the health of the economy, these "red meat for the base" promises seemed like small thinking.

In addition, people didn't really connect with Hudak. Many said the party failed to brand him properly in the election. Whatever the reason, the PCs lost.

That was 2011. Now it was 2014, and Hudak would meet Wynne, his new opponent. For Wynne, it was her first general election.

The Liberals had been in power since 2003. Wynne had been left holding the bag on the gas plant scandal for which McGuinty's chief of staff, David Livingston, was eventually found guilty of destroying emails in an attempted cover-up. There had been other scandals as well. Teachers, always a big constituency, had felt that they had not been fairly treated by the McGuinty Liberals, and the courts agreed, finding McGuinty's unilateral clawback of their collectively bargained benefits to be unconstitutional.

But there it was. The PCs went down to a stunning defeat, and Wynne and the Liberals were returned to power and even managed to get their majority government back.

Hudak had stolen defeat from the clutches of victory when he promised to cut 100,000 jobs in the broader public sector in a province where only four million of 14 million people vote. Many of these voters worked in the broader public sector. Everyone saw themselves as a potential target for the cuts — nurses, firefighters, paramedics and teachers, along with government officials. Unions saw their bases eliminated.

In addition, party members felt completely shut out of the creation or vetting of the party platform. It all seemed to be orchestrated from a small group around Hudak. I suppose if the platform had been a success, these complaints would not have found wings. But the 100,000 job-cut promise was a glaring mistake, and one that allowed members to point fingers at an elite process that sealed the fate of an entire party. It was certain that Hudak would step down as party leader.

The night that Hudak and the PCs lost the 2014 election, I got three calls. I had just finished watching the results with Barrie MPP, Rod Jackson, who lost his seat. The first call was from Naresh Raghubeer, my friend and colleague who had accompanied Senator Di Nino and me on that first trip to India. Raghubeer simply said: "Patrick, this is your time."

The second call came from Walied Soliman, my buddy. He said simply: "Are you ready?" And my third call came from my good friend Mike Richmond, who also encouraged me to run. If this sounds as though I hadn't considered running for Ontario PC Party leadership until these calls came in, that would be accurate.

A few days later, I was going to a Canada-India gala. I was heading down the escalator with Parminder Gill, MP for Brampton-Springdale, and I turned to him and said, "You know, Parm, I'm getting people encouraging me to run for the Ontario PC leadership. Isn't this crazy? I'm probably too young for that."

He responded, "No, it isn't crazy. And in fact, if you run, I'll be the first MP to endorse you."

I was surprised at how emphatic he was. I began to take this idea quite seriously and started speaking to other MPs to gauge their reaction.

I spoke to one of my best friends in caucus, MP Gordon Brown, who tragically died of a heart attack in May 2018. He told me that as far as he was concerned, I could do this 100 per cent. I had received the support of about two dozen MPs, which was pretty significant.

In October 2014, I threw my hat in the ring. My main adversary in the race was Christine Elliott, the MPP for Whitby-Oshawa. This was her second time running for party leader; she had run and finished third to Hudak in 2009. Though we were not close, I had worked with Elliott's late husband, Jim Flaherty, who was the federal finance minister until his untimely death earlier in 2014.

Elliott is a class act and was loved by many in caucus. She's intelligent, elegant, honest, articulate and had much experience in the opposition benches. *Was I crazy to be entering this race?*

Maybe I was. But I ran, anyway. I knew one thing: politics is about numbers. I felt I could get the numbers needed by expanding the party membership, which was at a meagre 10,000. The existing party members were the diehards. They might have favoured other candidates, but they were few in number and homogenous voters. They didn't reflect the fabric nor the views of the general electorate of Ontario. The PC Party was not where it needed to be to heading into a general election.

Before I ran, I reached out to Bob Stanley, a long-time friend and veteran political organizer. Stanley ran Frank Klees's second-place campaign against Hudak for leader of the PC Party. He was also my campaign manager when I ran federally in 2008 and 2011, and he did a great job. He had always been a real war horse of the PC party since the '70s and was generally liked by everyone. Stanley was someone who I thought could be very helpful to me.

When I asked Stanley what he thought of me running for leadership, he responded, "No one works harder than you. I think you can do this."

I put together my leadership team. Bob Stanley was my campaign manager. I added Walied Soliman, Mike Richmond, Babu Nagalingam, John Mykytyshyn, Rick Dykstra and Brett McFarquhar, my pollster.

Dykstra was one of my good friends in Ottawa. His office was next to mine in the old West Block, and we had both won by very narrow margins, me in Barrie and he in St. Catharines, Ont. We both liked hockey and played together once a week. We went to the gym together and played sports. Dykstra has a Dutch background, and I travelled to Holland with him in 2010 to visit some of the Canadian war cemeteries there. We both shared common views and we'd walk together to Question Period. We really hit it off. I knew his wife, Kathy, and his kids. I hired Dykstra's son Zack to work for me during the leadership race.

Dykstra brought with him a good network, including Andrzej Kepinski, a minority owner in Fallsview Casino Resort. This would be significant because it was my friendship with Kepinski that would set me on a collision course with Great Canadian Gaming Corporation. But that's for later.

Then there was John Mykytyshyn. I loved to bounce ideas off of him. Mykytyshyn had a background in polling and was very politically active when he wasn't working on theatre concerts with his sister. Like me, Mykytyshyn was always up until about 1 a.m. We both kept crazy hours, and I knew that I could call him at midnight and ask him what he thought about this or that. Many on the campaign never understood my friendship with him and were surprised that I would put him on the campaign.

Mykytyshyn loved to tease people. A fun quality, but politics isn't always fun. People get bruised easily. He was also honest, and at times, too honest. Up until that point, Mykytyshyn would leave a campaign effort having turned his friends into enemies. When Rob Hamilton was running for mayor of Barrie, I put him in touch with Mykytyshyn, and Mykytyshyn got a job managing the campaign for Hamilton, who won that election. And Mykytyshyn made enemies.

I was pretty clear with him. I said, "John, you're gonna have a job on the campaign. Promise me this: you are going to leave this campaign without making new enemies. You'd leave every campaign that you've worked on, and there'd always be someone who had been your best friend whom you now hate. So you're going to promise me you aren't going to create any new enemies. You're going to be nice to people. You can't make jokes at someone's expense. John, if someone's fat, you can't say, 'You're fat.' Only say nice things."

It worked for a time. Mykytyshyn worked on the campaign, and he didn't make any new enemies, which in his case was unheard of. Everyone tolerated him because they knew I liked him. Mykytyshyn had a reputation; they called him "The Knife." He's actually a really decent guy, and I had and have a lot of time for him.

Unfortunately, his new persona lasted until after I won leadership. I brought Mykytyshyn in to run the Conservative Leadership Foundation, the training school for youth. Personally, I think youth training is terrific, and we don't do enough of it. Everything was going smoothly until there was the front-page story in the Toronto Star about Mykytyshyn throwing a shoe at some young delegate. The foundation is supposed to be about mentoring upcoming leaders and training them for the election. I didn't get how throwing a shoe fit that mandate. I'm not certain if Mykytyshyn had been set up, but we got really bad media.

To this day, I respect him and I think he has mellowed. Like a good wine, Mykytyshyn has aged well, and he's still one of the sharpest minds in politics.

During the leadership campaign, I also had a fateful meeting with someone who would ultimately come to play the most important role in my life. In 2015, I met Genevieve Gualtieri, nicknamed "GG," at a reception her parents organized for me at their home. Her mother was a member of the riding association for Mississauga-Lakeshore.

GG was the bartender at that event, along with her then boyfriend. I, too, had been dating someone. I always kid GG about how she fell hard for me at that event. Truthfully, she didn't; she was otherwise occupied with someone else.

The leadership campaign was challenging because the other candidates were all members of caucus: Christine Elliott, Vic Fedeli, Monte McNaughton and Lisa MacLeod. There would not be much caucus support for me. My first supporter in caucus was Rick Nicholls, who joined my campaign in fall 2014.

Then in January 2015, Jack MacLaren another provincial PC caucus member, came over to me saying that the party was broken and needed real change and that I was the only one to bring in that change. MacLaren's support really got the ball rolling.

Soon after, Toby Barrett, another MPP, threw his support behind me, saying, "You're the only one talking sense." He came over in February to support me as well. Now I was up to three caucus supporters.

Randy Hillier, who had entered provincial politics in 2007 representing the riding of Lanark-Frontenac-Lennox and Addington, had run against Hudak in 2009 and lost. In 2015, he was supporting Elliott. A little-known fact is that Hillier and MacLaren are sworn enemies, even though their kids married, making them family. And Hillier hated me.

I was up to three caucus members supporting me. Elliott had most of the caucus support, but for an outsider to the provincial scene, an unlikely candidate and an unfamiliar name in Ontario — it was a start.

MacLeod eventually pulled out of the race and threw her support behind Elliott. Some of her staffers and the riding association president defected to my camp. MacLeod thought she could deliver her Ottawa riding of Nepean-Carleton to Elliott. But she didn't. In fact, I would win that riding by an overwhelming margin. That would always be a sore point for MacLeod. She hated me for it.

I also called upon Bill Davis, former Ontario premier, for support. I explained to him in a meeting at his office that I was going to restore Ontario's PC Party that he had built.

At that meeting, we spoke for about an hour. I pulled out my firefighter badge and I told him I had the support of the firefighters', the police and the nurses' union on my leadership nomination meeting in Barrie.

Then Davis said, "Well, I can do better than that!" and he pulled out of his wallet his Ontario Provincial Police (OPP) badge and told me that he was an honorary OPP. He explained that he was supporting Elliott for leader and expected her to win; although, he did like what I was saying. He added, "But if you do win the leadership and it doesn't go as expected, know that I will be there to help you."

Over the course of the years after I won leadership, Davis came to a number of my events, including my first Leader's Dinner speech, which had over 3,000 people in attendance. Former premiers Ernie Eves and Mike Harris attended, too, but the only person I really singled out in my speech was Bill Davis, who got a rousing standing ovation for his achievements.

73

As I wrote before, it angered me when I heard the allegations during my PC leadership campaign in 2015 that ethnic communities were being tricked into voting for me. That was false. I have no doubt that these lies were born of the lack of relationship that the PCs had with ethnic communities at that time. But as an MP, I had been going to cultural events and building my relationships. By the time I announced my intention to run for Ontario Party leader in October, I had lined up all sides of each of these communities — the four sides of the Sikh community and the three sides of the Tamil community.

The Tamil community organizers told me when I announced my candidacy that they would be able to sweep the GTA for me. They reminded me of what they said in 2009: I had gone to bat for two Tamil families in my riding, and by doing so I backed the entire community. They reminded me that they believed I didn't do what was politically advantageous, but I did what was right. They reminded me of what they had never forgotten.

No one took me very seriously when I ran. They figured all these people I signed up as members wouldn't actually come out to vote. There is this perception that ethnic communities don't show up. It's not true, and I proved that. They may not typically come out to vote, but as I was told by one organizer, "For you Patrick, they'll walk over glass to vote." They set up a campaign office in Scarborough, Ont., called Tamils for Patrick, which had about 100 people in it at any given time.

During the campaign, we signed up around 10,000 Tamil members, and of that group, about half voted. Consider that in a leadership campaign, a 30 per cent turnout is good. Consider that the leadership race that selected Hudak had a 20 per cent turnout. So a 50 per cent turnout is very strong.

As I said earlier, the PC Party had 10,000 members in all, which worked out to an average of about 100 members per riding. Some ridings had thousands, and many had very few members. In key ridings such as in Scarborough, where there were about 20,000 Tamil families per riding, my campaign team knew it would be a cakewalk for us. But I said to the team that the goal was to find Tamil families in other ridings.

Through their human rights work, Tamil organizers already had strong networks and formidable lists of all the Tamil families in Ontario, including in which ridings they were located. In the weaker ridings, if we could get 500 Tamil members signed up to vote, we knew we'd have 80 per cent of that riding.

In northern Ontario, we looked to find Indians and Tamils. It turned out that in Thunder Bay, there was a 500-member Indian community. In Timmins, the guy who owned the local restaurant was a Tamil community member.

The Tamil organizers would call the families and send them three YouTube videos from 2009 on my advocacy efforts to stop the carnage in Sri Lanka. And they'd tell the families to watch the videos. "This guy's our hero."

Nagalingam would tell them that the *only* guy who stepped up in their hour of need was Patrick Brown. "Well, guess what? Nagalingam explained. "This is now *his* hour of need, and we need to reciprocate."

Most Tamil families already knew about me, but just by sending the video they would say, "What can we do to help Patrick?" They mobilized for me across the province.

We also built a pretty impressive presence in the Filipino community. It wasn't as strong as the Tamil and Indian communities, mind you, but I had done some work to help a family in Canada who had been deported, and during that experience I developed a close relationship with the Filipino community in Barrie. Tobias Enverga, a Filipino senator who has since passed away, was my outreach around the province.

People often asked how was I so competitive in Elliott's backyard, like in Oshawa, Ont.? I won half those ridings and I was getting 40 per cent in others. It was thanks to the support I had in the Indian, Tamil and Filipino communities. They won the riding and the leadership contest for me.

Pollster McFarquhar kept telling me that there was no way I could beat Elliott because I was only at two per cent in the polls, and the margin of error was only three per cent. But early on in the leadership campaign, I said to McFarquhar, "Actually, you know what? You're wrong. It's already over." I knew because I had gone out and visited all the leaders of the Tamil and Indian communities, and each community had a presence in the majority of ridings in Ontario. I had the support of *all* the top organizers in both communities. Anyone Elliott got would be a fourth-class organizer.

Hockey became a real political lever for me. I'm a huge fan, and through Hockey Night in Barrie I became friends with these NHLers and started practicing with them. When I ran for the PC leadership, I got famous NHLers to travel with me.

Up in northern Ontario, where no one would show up for events, now famous people were with me, so we'd get a big turnout. All of a sudden I've got a draw. When I was a backbencher MP from Barrie, I wasn't going to get a good turnout in Ontario towns such as Fort Frances or Timmins. But now I was bringing in Mike Gartner and Dale Hawerchuk and other Hockey Hall of Famers. When Wayne Gretzky endorsed me, that made front-page news.

In Sault Ste. Marie, Ont., I said to Gretzky, "You played minor hockey here for the Soo Greyhounds and you're still a legend. You have your photo on the side of a building. I want to give the top volunteer a signed jersey and a puck." So I got some Soo Greyhound jerseys and pucks, and he signed them, and we gave them out to the top volunteer each week.

Hockey became interwoven into my political strategy, not just during leadership but after as well, when I recruited candidate Troy Crowder, a 10-year NHL veteran, to run in Sudbury, Ont. I remember taking famous hockey players to Ottawa to participate in receptions. I was able to leverage my sporting relationships in a very powerful way.

I don't think that hockey or sporting celebrities have ever figured so prominently in Ontario politics as they have in the last few years. While many scoffed and didn't see any relevance of Gretzky's endorsement, I knew this was a powerful way to garner attention, and in politics, attention is key.

After I won the leadership, Roberto Alomar, the Toronto Blue Jays' National Baseball Hall of Famer, came up to Simcoe North to help me out in my by-election. I also had Mike Keenan, coach of the first New York

Rangers' Stanley Cup-winning team in more than half a century and from Victoria Harbour, B.C., send out a mailer to everyone in the community. I won my Simcoe North by-election by a landslide.

I then mobilized cultural icons, including Modi. He was coming to Canada right before the PC leadership vote. In April 2015, I had rented a hall for a campaign rally across the street from where he was having a state dinner with Harper. I texted Sharma, his principal secretary, and said that I really needed him to give a message to Prime Minister Modi; I really needed him to come to my rally for PC Party leader.

The message I got back was not encouraging. It read that they would "do their best." Everyone around me said there was no chance that Modi, a sitting prime minister attending a state dinner, would leave a dinner, make his way across the street and show up at a provincial opposition party's leadership candidate rally, no matter how close in proximity the venue was.

I disagreed. I spent about $30,000 renting the hall and inviting every influential Indo-Canadian in Ontario. I made a campaign button with the outline of the province of Ontario and the words *PATRICK BROWN FOR A VIBRANT ONTARIO*, riffing on Modi's slogan, *VIBRANT GUJARAT*, which he used while he was first minister of Gujarat. I figured he'd get a kick out of that. Everyone was grabbing these pins.

Modi did come across the street to my rally. He made his way to the stage, and people were in absolute disbelief that the prime minister of India was there. Modi turned to me and said, "You know, your security, the RCMP, told me not to come. My security told me not to come. But I have come. And I am here for Patrick *bhai*. Bhai means "brother" in Hindi.

Then he gave me a big bear hug and held my hand up in the air, as though I had just won the world wrestling championship. The crowd went wild. That was the photo. The press gallery commented on how unusual this was. It was beautiful. There stood Modi and all the signs in the background, which said, *PATRICK BROWN FOR THE WIN*.

I wore a jacket that I called the Modi jacket. It was a jacket style that he liked wearing. And I also donned the button *A Vibrant Ontario*. Modi found that hilarious.

Political races, as I said before, are all about numbers. Everything you do is about signing up supporters and getting them out. I knew that we had signed up around 40,000 members. That was huge for a party that had a membership of 10,000 before leadership. My members were people who didn't care about social conservative issues. These were friends and new Canadians with a personal bond to me.

McNaughton, MPP for Lambton-Kent-Middlesex, who was running against me for the leadership, claimed that his team signed up 14,000, but we think it was closer to 10,000 members. Elliott, the PC Party's deputy leader and health critic, had signed up between 12,000 and 14,000 members. These numbers paled in comparison to mine.

McNaughton saw the writing on the wall and dropped out of the race. We had some meetings with McNaughton, as did Elliott. McNaughton told me that Elliott had offered him deputy leader in writing, and that he had pretty much agreed. I told him that he couldn't deliver his 10,000 to Elliott, and that I had already won. I told McNaughton to do a survey of them. He would see; they don't like her. I also reminded him that he'd attacked Elliott this entire campaign. I, on the other hand, had signed up all the first-string community leaders around the province. My numbers were strong. I wanted his support, but I couldn't offer him deputy leader.

At the negotiation, Walied sat down with McNaughton and delivered my message: I saw him as a senior member of my team, and I would see him in the role of critic of an economic portfolio. This promise would be on good faith, and that if McNaughton had any campaign debts, I would be coming out to events to help him cover these. That is what I was prepared to do. I made good on those promises. I made McNaughton the economic development critic, and I spoke at his functions to help him get rid of his leadership debt.

McNaughton threw his support behind me, as did Bob Bailey, MPP for Sarnia-Lambton. This now brought the number of caucus supporters to five, versus about 18 for Elliott, who was up north that day when McNaughton announced his support for my leadership run. I heard from many that she was quite devastated because he had apparently promised to support her. I think it was then that Elliott realized the game was on. Up until then, I believe she thought she had it in the bag.

I knew McNaughton's people were single-issue members and social conservatives. Had either McNaughton's or Elliott's campaigns been smart, they would have done some research. And they would have discovered that I participated in the Pride flag-raising in Barrie. But no one did. You simply needed to google "Patrick Brown Pride flag-raising Barrie," and there would have been a photo of me on the front page of the Barrie Examiner in 2012. It would speak of how I was proud to be the first MP in Barrie's history to be in a Pride flag-raising. I had done that to turn a chapter on these issues and to set the Barrie record straight on where I stood. There were a number of conservatives in the riding who were upset, but as Pierre Elliott Trudeau famously said, "The state has no place in the bedrooms of the nation." On this point, I tend to agree.

I realized that this would have turned all of McNaughton's people away from me, and I was preparing for that day when someone would out me for being too progressive. But during leadership, it never came. Instead, I was branded a SoCon.

We worked hard to sign up members, figuring that Elliott's people would get hold of that photo and send it to McNaughton's supporters. And I would lose any support from them if McNaughton dropped off the ballot. McNaughton's people would not have voted for Elliott. They didn't like her, but they would not have voted for me, either. They just wouldn't vote, period. However, interestingly, McNaughton's people did vote for me after he left the campaign.

McNaughton gave us his list of members, and we picked up about 50 per cent of his vote or about 5,000 votes. This made my margin of victory much wider than it would have been. If the Tamils were 5,000, McNaughton's supporters rivalled that number. My membership count was now up around 45,000.

Richard Ciano, party president, used to conduct sessions at local riding associations, where he would discuss what went wrong in the general election in 2014. Elliott and I would attend and listen in. There would be maybe six people in attendance. Meanwhile, I'd attend events such as Tamil Fest in Scarborough that had tens of thousands of attendees.

Finally, I said to myself, *Why in God's name am I wasting my time with these sessions of 10 people at the riding associations? Let Elliott have them all. She can get all their endorsements. There were 5,000 at the event I was at last night in this same area. Why not just go sign up a thousand of them?*

That's really when I realized it was over. It's when I saw a pathway, an opening to victory because I saw bigger constituencies from which to draw votes. Everyone said that Elliott had this race locked up. She was polling at about 70 per cent, and I was polling at about two per cent. Almost all the caucus was with Elliott. You might say that that her campaign was playing the traditional game of chess. Meanwhile, I had changed the board.

Throughout my campaign, I was being criticized by Elliott's people and others that I had no policy. I did participate in the debates and had a position on a broad range of issues. But I said that I wanted to have a real policy consultation with the grass roots of the party, and that policy should not be written during the leadership campaign. This was drawing on the Hudak experience and the fallout from party members who felt they had been excluded from the process. I had criticized him for making up policy on the fly, on the back of an envelope, and I wasn't going to repeat that error.

I also believed that policy needed to involve a membership that was much more robust, so that it could be more connected to the province. A membership of 10,000 was not connected to the province, but a membership of 100,000 would be. That was one of the lines I used.

Mind you, I did take positions. And some came back to haunt me later.

McNaughton had made sex education the big issue during the leadership campaign. We found he had traction among some of the membership with that issue. We were careful to use language that there had not been enough consultation with educators, parents and experts. We never engaged in homophobic language that some of McNaughton's hard right supporters would have supported.

We tried to be more neutral: "In the future, we will try to do better with consultations. We want to focus on math scores …" We tried to straddle the line as much as possible. And of course, on whether or not I would march in the Pride Parade, I wiggled my way, saying I would answer that if and when I got invited to the event. I tried not to box myself in. Tanya Granic Allen was the one who boxed me in after I won leadership. A story for another chapter.

What many people forget is that there were two drafts of the sex education policy. The first draft was less accommodating than the second. When the first draft came out, we were told that parents could not take their kids out of the classrooms during the teaching of sex education, and we were told that they couldn't get access to lessons plans that mapped out exactly what was going to be taught. In all fairness to Premier Wynne, in the revised version parents could take kids out of classrooms if they so wished, and they could have access to copies of the lessons plans.

However, in a smart play by Wynne, which I believe was intended to raise havoc during the PC leadership, she released the revised draft just before our convention. Wynne had everyone thinking that the sex education curriculum was based on the original policy that had been formulated under the leadership of Deputy Minister of Education Ben Levin. Levin, a long-serving public servant, was charged and convicted with possession of child pornography in a chilling trial. Some of the evidence related to him coaching undercover investigators posing as parents, to get their young children into sexually compromising situations. I found it all pretty disgusting. The fact that he had been the deputy minister of education (and also a member of Wynne's transition team) added to the sheer anger felt by many parents. It certainly placed the policy in a very different context.

So our leadership candidates were essentially campaigning on a version of the sex education policy that had been altered. Once all the PC leadership candidates had put their stake in the ground that they were against the curriculum, the government released the revised version. That really showed me just how smart the Liberals were at politics.

I believed early on in the campaign that we had won the leadership, and that I was in the 70 per cent range. But I was worried that my party would cheat me out of a victory. And it tried. In the polling stations, sometimes 20 per cent to 30 per cent of the members were being turned away. Party officials knew we had Tamil support, and they were checking every letter of the name to ensure it matched with the official ID. Sometimes on a driver's licence a Tamil name would be truncated. If one single letter didn't correspond, the voter was turned away.

The party also scheduled the first leadership vote on a Khalsa Day, which celebrates the Sikh new year. It happened to also fall on a day that was a Tamil holy celebration. More bullshit. We knew that was Ciano, party president, and his friends trying to screw us over. So, we worked like mad to get out our membership vote on the next voting day. We did.

In the end, they were too clever by half, literally speaking. They had organized two voting days, instead of one. Had they allowed one day to vote, it would have hurt us, for sure.

I felt party headquarters was clearly against my candidacy. I didn't trust Nick Kouvalis and Ciano. Kouvalis was Ciano's business partner and had worked on Rob Ford's campaign when he ran for mayor of Toronto in 2010 and won. Kouvalis also worked on John Tory's campaign when he ran for mayor of Toronto in 2014 against Doug Ford.

These two guys did crazy things. They were actively supporting Fedeli, finance critic and MPP for Nipissing, for leadership. When Fedeli left the race, Kouvalis and Ciano declared they were "neutral." However, we knew they didn't like Elliott, and they were also skeptical of me. Once Fedeli dropped out of the leadership race in February 2015, the relationship between my team and Ciano/Kouvalis was marginally less strained. We still didn't like Ciano, and Ciano didn't like us.

They came to us about six weeks before the vote and they said, "We want to do some polling for the party, and before we do so, we want to make certain that the leadership candidates are on side. It's going to cost around $150,000 to $200,000 [or some ridiculously big number like that] to gauge the landscape of the province."

I remember talking to Walied and Stanley, and I remember saying we were being asked to agree to do this polling at a tremendous cost. But the results of the polling, which would be conducted in April, would be presented to the new leader after he or she won the leadership.

Wow. *Why in the name of God would I pay the company of the so-called party referee of our leadership race $200,000 for results that I wouldn't get until after race?* McFarquhar, my pollster, would be charging around $5,000 to $10,000 for a landscape of the province.

We discussed it, and I said that I believed that Ciano and Kouvalis were testing us. If we didn't agree to pay the money to his company, we would be declared enemies. We were being compelled to agree to this expensive poll. So we did. I suppose neutrality came at a price.

We knew that at this point we handed in around 45,000 party memberships because the person at the front desk at headquarters told us so. We knew that Elliott announced about 14,000 memberships. In 2009, that would certainly have been enough to crown her leader. No one thought 45,000 was even possible.

When we announced that team Brown had signed up 45,000 memberships, Elliott's camp went cold. They didn't respond for three or four days because probably they didn't know how to respond. Then they argued that we were inflating numbers and that we only signed up 30,000. We knew this was wrong because the total membership of the party was now 82,000.

There had been 10,000 memberships existing, and we knew we had put in 45,000, including around 5,000 of McNaughton's members who we believed were going to support me. That left around 5,000 of his members who were up for grabs. The party told us that 8,000 new members had been signed up during the course of the leadership from online sign-ups after debates. These memberships were not ascribed to any particular campaign. We knew that Elliott had delivered around 14,000 memberships because someone at party headquarters had given us all the numbers. So the math indicated that our numbers were absolutely consistent. It was basic math.

My team told Ciano that people were making up numbers in the media. We believed he needed to provide the media with the actual numbers. He was unwilling to proactively or publicly release anything. However, if the media called and asked him, then Ciano committed to providing them with an off-the-record tally.

We were pissed at him. We wanted the party to put out a press release with the actual numbers, as we had been previously told it would. We chalked it up to Ciano trying to play both sides: me, who wanted the numbers out, and Elliott's camp that did not. To be fair, he did provide the media with the real numbers when they asked. In any case, I'm not certain the media believed them, anyway, as I was considered a real long shot.

Saturday, May 9, 2015, was convention day. My entrance into the hall at the convention was grand, even though it had not been planned that way. I walked into a fairly sedate conference room after Elliott's supporters were all seated rather politely. There was a prevalence of white faces.

Then, Team Brown blew into the room. I thought back to Jean Charest's entrance into that high-school auditorium, back at St. Mikes. I marched down the aisle to the front of the room with an army of faces, all different colours. They were cheering, clapping and screaming my name. They carried signs and noise-makers. It was loud and unruly for an otherwise polite convention, and those seated on the Elliot side seemed rather uncomfortable with the whole thing.

We filled the seats on the left-hand side of the room. It was quite a funny scene when I think back. If you took a photo of one half of the room, then the other, and compared the two, it would look as though the photos were taken at two very separate events.

I knew my supporters would give me a stylish send-off. At cultural events, I was absolutely mobbed for photos. It's just the nature of the culture; they are vocal and emotional. It felt great.

On my way to the convention centre, I was pretty confident in my chances because I had seen our tracking numbers, and I thought I knew where we were in every riding. I also knew that our tracking numbers were very conservative. Still, given the cheating and the shenanigans at the polling stations, I was uneasy.

That unease dissipated once the results from the first five ridings were announced. It was then that I knew I would win.

The party wanted to make the leadership event exciting, much like a TV presentation. Their goal was to build the suspense on the convention floor. Because of that, I assume that they deliberately released ridings where Elliott had won in the hopes of keeping the race looking competitive, even when they knew that she wasn't going to win.

At this point, I knew nothing of the results, and I am certain that Elliott didn't, either. But while Elliott's side rejoiced at the first riding results, I realized then that what I was seeing up on the big screen was actually very bad news for Elliott, whether or not her supporters understood that.

The results in the first riding were announced. It was a Kitchener riding, and one in which I was expecting to be clobbered. Instead, I was shocked. *Was this real?* The results were very close. Elliott won the riding all right, but by a vote of about 51 to 49 votes. I remember thinking to myself, *Wow, that's a safe riding for her — and she only won by two points?*

Then another result was announced. Once again, she won by a narrow margin in a riding that should have been a big win for her. So after a few of these ridings were announced, I began to realize that Elliott was barely winning her safe seats.

In each of the ridings that Elliot won, our campaign tracking numbers had us much further behind than what we ended up with. And these were her ridings, not ours. The results of the ridings in which I knew I was going to *kill* hadn't even been announced yet.

As the party was still announcing Elliott's victories, I knew I had won.

I was surprised that she seemed surprised. But I was told that people in her campaign didn't warn her of what was happening out there. Our internal polling had us in the 70 per cent to 75 per cent range. I assume that Elliott had been told the same thing.

That's not uncommon in politics — a wishful-thinking strategy of suppressing the truth takes root in an attempt to protect the leader. (Of course, it also has the unintended consequence of protecting the campaign staff from possibly being fired, but surely that's pure coincidence and secondary to the exercise.) I believe that's what happened to Wynne in the devastating results of the June 7, 2018, election. Her campaign team may have lied to her until the very end. She was possibly told that she could come back, even though no one else's polls showed that.

I also believe that no one expected that my ethnic vote would show up. But it did.

They announced my win without putting up the results in the 12 ridings in which I held the biggest margins. That's because when the candidate is close to the number of points required to win leadership, the party would announce the candidate's own riding results to bring the candidate over the top. In my case, Barrie results were announced, and I had managed to get the points required to be leader of the Ontario PC Party.

After that, they never bothered announcing the results in ridings such as Windsor or Scarborough, where I received 80 points or 90 points out of 100, likely because that would have been overkill, and they wanted to let Elliott save some face. I had no idea they were going to announce the ridings like this. That was all party headquarters and Ciano. Frankly, I think it was degrading for Elliott and showed an interest in theatrics and a tone-deafness in decency. If they wanted to make it more suspenseful, they might have simply sprinkled her victories among mine.

It was when they announced me as the winner that it all started to sink in just how big this was. I hadn't looked at my speech all night because I didn't want to jinx it. On the convention floor, I pulled out the papers for the first time that night and took a quick look at the notes that had been prepared for me by Richmond. I made my way to the stage. I started to speak. I greeted everyone in multiple languages, which was not a common practice for our party. I gave a nod to the unions that had helped me: Laborers' International Union of North America, the police, the firefighters' and the nurses'. That might have been a first for the party as well. I could tell that many in the room were shell-shocked.

From there on, everything was surreal. I was taken back stage to prepare me for a media scrum, and that's when I noticed party security guards around me. I knew then that things had changed.

After, I asked John Capobianco, who had been working on Elliott's campaign, to set up a call with her a few days later. He told me she'd take the call at a specific time. When that time came, she didn't take the call. This happened again.

I then sent Elliott a text in which I told her that she'd done a great service to the party, and I wanted to show her the proper respect. I offered her any opposition critic position she wanted. I offered her the continued role of deputy leader, which she had under Hudak. I told her that I realized party fights were very difficult, but that I was eager to have her involved in any way, shape or form that she liked.

A few days later, I got a very succinct response: "I have no interest in being involved." That was it. I had been told by people that she was very upset about the loss, and that her team didn't prepare her properly. Everyone disappeared on her. She had that big office on Yonge Street for a long time after, and I was told that bills weren't being paid. A former staffer leaked to me that if Elliott accepted a position from the Liberal government, it would happen on a day where it would hurt me politically.

The day before my Simcoe North by-election, it was announced that Elliott had resigned and had accepted a newly created position of patient ombudsman, which overshadowed my by-election victory.

Do I blame her? No, I don't. Politics is emotional and visceral. You're all in one day, and the next day you have nothing. I can relate. Her response, however unappreciated by me at the time, was human.

Right after my leadership victory, I named Bob Stanley to be executive director of the PC Party. He ran many campaigns, and I always felt that he bore the brunt of the disappointment felt by unsuccessful candidates because he was managing that process. In retrospect, I wish I had kept the position of executive director further removed from the candidate nomination process in the various riding wars that were to develop, so as to reduce Stanley's exposure. But he was a hands-on guy, an honest person.

I was now going to build a new PC team, my team — or so I thought.

My victory was in May, and by fall 2015, GG and her boyfriend had broken up. I was also available. Our relationship began in January 2016. Little did we both know that some on my team would undermine this relationship, as well as my new-found leadership role.

CHAPTER 4

GROWING PAINS IN THE BIG BLUE TENT

My meeting with Wynne was the most hostile meeting I could ever have anticipated. I believe that she wanted to send me the message not to waste her precious time. That was the first and last meeting in private.

My new office was located on the third floor of the legislature building also known as "The Pink Palace." The Pink Palace is situated on a kind of island of land surrounded by Queen's Park Crescent that turns into a majestic tree-lined boulevard, University Avenue. To the south of the building is a lovely park that is used for many official events. The large limestone stairs lead up to big, brass-fitted oak doors. A massive driveway circles the building, and parking there is generally off limits to the public.

I opened the door to my new office and looked around for the first time. It was massive, compared to any office I had previously held. The entrance had a reception area with some workstations and offices for staff. To the left was my large corner office, which connected to another large office for my chief of staff. To the right of reception was a large boardroom with a table that could easily host 24 guests. Off to the side of the boardroom was an access door that led to a vault, where sensitive documents could be housed.

The building was old and grand, with high ceilings, fireplaces and lots of oak trim. I made sure to give my office a welcoming feel by hanging my choice hockey memorabilia and other items that reflected my interests. It was great to see my name on the glass door as the *Leader of the Official Opposition*. I had no idea that in January2018, cameras and the media would be there to watch maintenance staff scrape those letters off on national television under a very different set of circumstances than I would have imagined.

I tasked Mike Richmond with setting up my Queen's Park office. This included conducting all the inaugural interviews and creating all the confidentiality agreements. Soliman was in charge of building a campaign team.

In the early months, I went through a few chiefs of staff: first, Pina Martino, who'd had the job with Jim Wilson (who was interim party leader after Tim Hudak's departure). We asked her to stay on as long as she wanted. After she left, Nick Pappalardo filled the role for a while.

Alykhan Velshi approached us after Pappalardo left. Velshi had this reputation of being a master strategist in Ottawa, where he worked for influential Harper cabinet minister Jason Kenney. His pitch to us was simple: he had been earning $300,000 at the consulting firm of McKenzie, but he'd be willing to take a pay cut on the following condition — that the PC Party would agree to pay him $50,000 in addition to the standard salary of the job, $100,000. We agreed, and with that bump in pay he was in.

We were all impressed with Velshi. He seemed to know every file and he understood the cultural community, which was hugely important to me. After working for Kenney, Velshi moved into Harper's office. In fact, it was Kenney who placed Velshi in the PMO. (Harper gave Kenney free reign to put people in places.) I personally hadn't had any dealings with Velshi during my time in Ottawa, but I had heard he was one of Harper's top guys. After he left the PMO, he went off to work for a company called Ethical Oil.

When we sat down for the first time, I said, "You've got this great reputation as a master organizer. Just tell me this. I have very different positions than Jason Kenney on gay rights and on climate change. What do you think about that?"

His answer was exactly what I wanted to hear: "Very smart moves; it's very shrewd. The way you've been able to modernize the Ontario PC Party is brilliant."

I pressed him further. "So you mean to tell me you have no problems? Because your Ethical Oil friends may have problems with a guy who believes in climate change and carbon pricing."

He textbook response was: "Not at all. My job is to make you premier."

He really did give a great interview. I now believe that Velshi played us in that interview to get the job. And I often wonder if he was there all along to undermine me.

We added Logan Bugeja to the office in the role of personal assistant. Bugeja had been on my MP team as a summer student. Her mom worked in my MP office and MPP constituency office in Barrie, and her sister worked in my Barrie restaurant, Hooligans. Bugeja met her husband, Jim Ross, during my 2015 leadership campaign. I was confident to have her on board.

Another addition to the team was Dan Robertson. We brought Robertson on as chief strategist. So many told me he was brilliant during his time in Harper's office. He was the protégé of Patrick Muttart, a political strategist and one of the key operatives behind the Conservative Party and Harper's rise to power. Robertson was certainly an outside-the-box thinker. He was also stubborn and emotional, and as this story will show, totally unable to handle the crisis of January 24, 2018.

When I won leadership, I made Bob Stanley the party's executive director. Rick Dykstra would become the new party president later at our annual general meeting (AGM). The last hire was Andrew Boddington as campaign manager for the 2018 general election. Boddington had been recommended by Robertson and my old friend Bill Pristanski, who knew Boddington's father, George Boddington. Andrew had been the deputy campaign manager under Tim Hudak, a disastrous campaign to say the least, but many vouched for Andrew and said that he was one of the "good ones."

Richmond drafted the confidentiality agreements for all my staff to sign. These agreements were put in place to protect me, so that my staff could not do to me what Mark Towhey, former chief of staff to Ford, did to the mayor of Toronto, namely, write a book about Ford's time in office. Richmond's position was that people working for you should not be able to do a tell-all about the premier, once they or the leader are no longer in office.

Unfortunately, the confidentiality agreements were between the employees and the Leader's Office, rather than between the staff and me personally. That would come back to haunt me. As Richmond reasoned, at the time we drafted those agreements, I was the Leader and controlled the Leader's Office. After all, who would have guessed how this would all turn out: that my personal information would be used against me by my own chief of staff, Velshi? But I'm getting ahead of myself here. That's all to come.

Despite the many people around me, I referred to my inner circle as the "Seven Horsemen." They were: Walied Soliman, Mike Richmond, Alykhan Velshi, Dan Robertson, Logan Bugeja, Rick Dykstra and Andrew Boddington.

I added someone else to the mix. Rebecca Thompson had worked in Ottawa for the Conservative government and later for Sun News. She was seasoned, and I trusted her. Many years earlier, we had had a relationship, but we both moved on from that. Becky has since settled down with her partner and son. We sat down together, and she gave me a great deal of advice, which I appreciated. I figured, rather than advise from a distance, she should join my team officially as my director of communications. I felt pretty good about my team as it was evolving.

My first obvious task was to get a seat in the Legislature. I couldn't do my job as leader and face off against Premier Wynne without a seat. It was up to her as premier to call the by-election.

Prior to being leader and even during my leadership campaign, I had little interaction with Wynne. I met her in 2007, when I was still a federal MP, and I took note of her because we were both doing outreach in the Indo-Canadian community.

I thought Wynne had run a very strong campaign for the leadership of the Ontario Liberals, and that her speech was the best. I got a sense that she was a hard worker. It was when she beat Hudak in the 2014 election that I saw she was also a real hustler and had made great strategic decisions. She just outplayed Hudak — her victory was impressive.

After I won, I waited for the premier to call a by-election. I waited and waited. Wynne pointed out that it was her prerogative to call a by-election anytime within six months. So the PC caucus began to goad her on social media and in press releases in the hopes of shaming her into calling the by-election expeditiously. "When will the premier call a by-election, so that Mr. Brown can take his place as the Leader of Her Majesty's Official Opposition?" they goaded.

By the end of July 2015, Wynne promised that a by-election would be held as soon as the Legislature returned in September. I would run in Simcoe North, the riding that had been held by PC MPP Garfield Dunlop. Dunlop decided to retire and make way for my candidacy in that riding. He had not supported me during the leadership race. But he came to appreciate my work as he watched me sign up 40,000 members. He told the media it was his granddaughter, a page at Queen's Park, who asked him to step aside, so that I could have a seat in the Legislature. It's a great story. And however it happened that Dunlop decided to move aside for me, I was incredibly grateful. This riding was next door to Barrie and an area that I felt very connected to.

The Simcoe North by-election was held on September 3, 2015. I won 53.7 per cent of the vote with a commanding margin of nearly 12,000 more votes than my second-place rival, Liberal candidate Fred Larsen.

Once I had a seat, we needed to fill the vacant seat caused by Elliott's departure from the party. Another by-election in Whitby-Oshawa was called for February 11, 2016.

Elliott and her husband, the late Jim Flaherty, had both been MPPs for that riding. They were loved by their constituents. And the Liberals thought they could be competitive here because they assumed there would be much ill will toward me, having beaten their own front-runner candidate for leadership. I thought to myself that the best way to send an "F-U" to the Liberals would be to win *big*.

While the nomination for selecting the PC Party candidate wouldn't take place until November 2015, I was already deploying teams of supporters to door-knock full time in September. We had managed to door-knock through the riding twice before the actual nomination race, which ultimately selected municipal councillor Lorne Coe. Our internal party tracking had us consistently 30 points up over the Liberals.

As usual, I deployed resources that the party wasn't used to. I had all my cultural supporters in Whitby-Oshawa reaching out to groups that voted Liberal. We had a Muslim campaign, a Tamil campaign and a Filipino campaign. We noticed that on the "walk sheets," used to identify voter preference, many who had originally been identified as Liberals were now with us. I knew we were going to do better than people thought.

The Liberals lost that riding, and many told me after that they were surprised by how badly. They had brought in Justin Trudeau for a big rally in Whitby-Oshawa. Trudeau had just been elected prime minister in October 2015, and the by-election was January 2016. At that point, he was at the peak of popularity. His approval rating was at around 55 per cent. In politics, that's high.

At the time Trudeau appeared at the rally, the Liberals and the NDP were neck and neck. The rally caused a two-point bounce for the Liberals and a two-point slide for the NDP, essentially bumping them to third place from second. Big deal. We still won the riding by 30 points. The Liberals had essentially mobilized the popular Trudeau to avoid a third-place finish.

Meanwhile, in January 2016, a few months before the Whitby-Oshawa by-election, GG and I began dating. Genevieve had been working as an intern at Queen's Park when I became party leader. However, contrary to the allegations that would later appear in the Toronto Star, she never worked for me. GG left Queen's Park soon after my arrival and got a job working for Karen Miller, a well-established fundraiser who handled the True Patriot Love event, John Tory's campaign, and also did some fundraising for the PC Party. After that, Genevieve went on to work for SickKids Foundation.

From the start of our relationship, I kept GG away from my Queen's Park team. There were those around me who felt that my relationship with her was a political liability because of the 16-year age difference. Rebecca Thompson was among those who felt it was absolutely despicable that I would be involved with someone so much younger. She believed that every guy would give me a high-five, but that women would think it was absolutely unacceptable.

My mother was worried about the age difference, too. She felt that GG was great. In fact, it was my mother who had urged my friend Walied Soliman to set us up when she met GG for the first time at an event. However, she was not aware of how old GG was at the time, and now she worried that our relationship would be used to build a comparison between me and Donald Trump, who has a young wife. For the record, my mother hates Trump.

On the other side of the coin, Robertson thought the whole thing was ridiculous. Mind you, Robertson's wife is 15 years his junior, so his opinion didn't count for much. But there were also others whom I respected, like Caroline Mulroney, the former prime minister's daughter and a candidate I recruited to run in York-Simcoe. She told me that I really shouldn't worry about it: "Look at the age difference between my parents. Genevieve is a wonderful lady. You should put it out there."

Brian and Mila Mulroney have about the same age difference as GG and I do. Pierre and Margaret Trudeau were about 30 years apart. For those who say we live in different times, I would point out that Peter MacKay and his wife have the same age difference and GG and I — and he's a contemporary of mine.

I didn't know what to think. While it all seemed pretty trite to me, it clearly raised eyebrows among some.

As a result, no one knew we were together, except for family, friends and close political staff. Looking back, GG was treated very poorly by many of the people around me. The stories and accusations that would make their way back to me I knew were untrue. I chalked these up to veiled attempts by some to drive a wedge between us. But I didn't fire anyone over it.

I now realize just how resentful Genevieve must have felt. And she was right to feel that way. I am not big on confrontation of an emotional and personal nature. I was of the view that once the election was behind us, I would then be in a position to dedicate more to the relationship, if we were, in fact, still together. Then I would move ahead without regard to what anyone said or thought, or what the media wrote.

The secrecy and fear of public scrutiny gave way to tremendous stress. Thankfully, there was one friend of mine with whom GG could speak — Kaydee Richmond, Mike's wife, who understood how difficult our hidden relationship was for GG. She offered herself up as someone who GG could talk to when she felt the need.

Genevieve didn't want scrutiny and frankly I didn't want her or our relationship being subjected to the nasty, public fishbowl that is part of the political circus. Finally, in an attempt to alleviate unnecessary stress, Walied decided that he would have some focus groups done to determine whether or not people would really care about the age difference. Walied didn't think it would matter, but because some were so against my relationship, he, too, wondered whether or not we were possibly missing something.

By July 2017, Walied had completed the research and wanted to share the results. I told him that it really didn't matter anymore. The week before, Genevieve and I had called it quits. The stress finally caused issues that eventually led to the decision to pack it in. Walied pressed me, anyway: "OK, Patrick, but do you want to know the results?"

He sent me the results that indicated that the people didn't care at all. In fact, to my surprise, people liked me more. It made me more human because I was capable of loving someone. Had I to do it over again, I would have just come out in the open with my relationship.

On March 5, 2016, shortly after the Whitby-Oshawa by-election, we held our first party policy convention and AGM to elect a new executive. The convention also kick-started the formulation of a year-and-a-half-long policy process that would culminate in a party platform, the People's Guarantee.

At the AGM, Richard Ciano was removed as party president and replaced by my good friend Rick Dykstra. Both Dykstra and Jag Badwal, also a friend and supporter, were running for party president. I really had no preference between them. I had known Dykstra from my days in Ottawa, and I knew Badwal from the Indian community for over 10 years. I urged them to get together and work it out, so there would be no contested election. Both were great assets to the party, and it was my hope that between them they could figure out who should be president and who should be vice-president. And they did. It wasn't acrimonious. They agreed that Dykstra would be the president, and Badwal would be vice-president.

TOP
Patrick Brown, at three years of age.

BOTTOM
With the Brown family.

TOP
At St. Mike's High School.

BOTTOM
With the "Great One."

TOP
With "Grapes," at Hockey Night in Barrie.

BOTTOM
With Mike Gartner.

TOP
My first day in the House
of Commons as Simcoe
North MP.

BOTTOM
With Doug Ford, Babu
Nagalingam, Raymond Cho
and Wallied Soliman

V

TOP
Meeting with my mentor,
Bill Davis.

BOTTOM
Launching my leadership bid
for the PC Party, 2014.

TOP
Building my friendship with
former Mississauga Mayor,
Hazel McCallion.

BOTTOM
With, Narendra Modi, now
the prime Minister of India,
at one of my leadership
rallies in Toronto.

TOP
Walking out of Queen's Park over Liberal scandals, 2016.

BOTTOM
Playing tennis with Andrzej Kepinski and rising Canadian tennis star, Denis Shapovalov, on January 23, 2018.

TOP
Patrick at Ford family home in 2015 helping to alleviate campaign debt for now Premier Doug Ford.

BOTTOM
Doug would be infuriated when I met with John, but I tried to maintain a big tent conservative party which could welcome both John Tory supporters and Doug Ford supporters into it.

At the convention, I was keen to unveil a new PC Party and not the same old, white, hard right party of the past decade. I wanted to show that we were beginning an evolution into a Davis-type of conservatism. William Grenville Davis was Ontario's 18th premier from 1971 to 1985 and part of a dynasty that lasted for 42 years. He was known for his ability to hold all the factions within the PC Party, both progressives and social conservatives, together.

I loved the fact that at our convention the delegates were about 50 per cent visible minorities, and I realized that the speakers also needed to represent the diversity of the province. Michael "Pinball" Clemons, an incredible motivational speaker and an icon of the Canadian Football League's Toronto Argonauts, also happened to be a personal friend of mine. I reached out to him because I really wanted him to run as a candidate in Oakville-North Burlington. At the time, I felt that we could win that riding, and I believed Pinball could have made the difference for us.

We came pretty close to bringing Pinball on board. He was about 90 per cent of the way to being a candidate. At one point, Pinball was even considering announcing his intention to run at the convention. In the end, he lost interest because being an MPP would put him in conflict with the work of his own foundation, the Pinball Clemons Foundation, dedicated to improving youth development. Instead, he decided to give the keynote speech. It was a tremendous speech, and the audience went wild.

It was also at that first convention when we unveiled our new party logo. We wanted a fresh, new look. Designed by Dan Robertson, the new logo featured a green bud to represent environmentalism, a red "P" to represent the progressive side of the party and a blue "C," reflecting the more conservative elements of the party. It really encapsulated my belief that no one had a monopoly on a good idea, that we were stronger together and that we would be a diverse and inclusive party under a big tent.

When it came to policy at the convention, Robertson felt that one of the big issues we were going to have to confront was climate change. He wanted to know where I stood on the matter. Did I believe in it? Of course, I did.

"Well then, we're going to need the party to buy in to the idea of carbon pricing," Robertson announced matter-of-factly. He wanted me to draw a line in the sand at that first policy convention and to announce to the delegates and the world that I would support carbon pricing.

He explained that Trudeau had already said carbon pricing was going to be a national mandate, meaning that every province was going to have to put a tax on carbon. I wasn't convinced that was the route I wanted to take. I felt we had to get the party on side first before making any grand announcements at the convention. Robertson disagreed and explained that while it would be more convenient to do it that way, he didn't want the media to pre-empt my image as a different kind of conservative.

"I want there to be a gasp at the convention. I want people to be shocked. Because if the media starts to write about it beforehand or after, it won't be a big story," he said. Robertson wanted a splash — a real reaction — someone at the convention who would get upset by the announcement. "That's a story! And you'll be the first conservative leader in the country to endorse carbon pricing."

Robertson went on: "Preston Manning and Stockwell Day have both endorsed carbon pricing, but they are older, retired politicians. You need to do it at the convention as a newly elected leader of the Ontario Progressive Conservative Party."

I compromised with Robertson. I told him that at the very least, I would need to get caucus onside first, before any convention took place. Robertson didn't like disagreement, but I was adamant on this point. For me, this was like hockey. You may want to surprise the fans, but you don't want to surprise the team.

In preparation for the March convention, I called a caucus retreat during the Whitby-Oshawa by-election. That's when I told members of caucus that we were going to have to take a position on climate change. I have always believed that being a conservative is also about conserving and conservation. And as conservatives, we should not be threatened by the idea of supporting conservation. I presented the options. I told them that while this policy may be a divisive debate today in our own party, increasingly, Canadians are of the view that we have to do our part to help clean up the environment. Why would we as a party want to be on the wrong side of history?

Finally, I told them that while I would typically hear everyone's opinion, then make the final decision, this time I wanted a vote. It was the only time I used this process with caucus.

Jim Wilson really helped turn caucus. He stood up and told caucus that during the federal election, he went to a class in his riding, and some students yelled at him and accused the conservatives of not caring about the environment.

Wilson said, "I'm sick and tired of the Conservatives always looking like we don't care about the environment. I don't want to be yelled at by students anymore. We're on the wrong side of this issue, and it's high time we get on the right side of it." Now, Jim Wilson had been in provincial politics for a long time, so hearing this message from him was important. Caucus members started piping up that they were hearing from young people, too, and that there was no longer a debate about man-made climate change.

We took the vote. Every single caucus member but two (the two were Michael Harris, the MPP for Kitchener-Conestoga and Toby Barrett, MPP for Haldimand Norfolk) voted for carbon pricing. All the others voted in favour, including Jack MacLaren, Steve Clark and Vic Fedeli, who not only voted in favour, but also did so enthusiastically. I have kept emails in which Vic Fedeli reiterated that this was a great idea. Lisa MacLeod was absent from the meeting; a fact I was getting used to. MacLeod had a terrible record of attendance at caucus meetings. She'd often call in sick, but most of us thought she just didn't want to attend. She was not a team player.

I understand these same individuals have since changed their position, but that doesn't change the fact that the March 2016 caucus was overwhelmingly in favour of supporting carbon pricing. Armed with caucus support, I felt more confident going into the convention.

The support lasted for some time. But in 2017, after the federal Conservatives were defeated in Ottawa, people started waking up to the reality of Justin Trudeau's carbon pricing — and it wasn't popular with everyone. Lisa Thompson, the MPP for Huron-Bruce who had supported carbon pricing in that caucus meeting, was getting so beaten up in her riding that I had to switch her from being environment critic to indigenous affairs critic to take the heat off her. I put Ted Arnott, MPP from Wellington-

Halton Hills, into that role. Arnott was a real Red Tory, and like me believed 100 per cent in climate change. He would be completely in lockstep with me on this issue.

At the convention, when I announced in front of the delegates my belief that polluters must pay, Dan Robertson got the reaction he wanted. There was a gasp from the crowd. One person wailed "NOOOOOO!" Jason Kenney, who attended the convention, walked out of the room.

Looking back, it was a mistake to pre-empt that position until after the policy consultation process. I think I should have brought the party membership along with me. It had been a media stunt to shock the party and garner attention. But I believe it backfired. If, instead, I had travelled the province and engaged in consultations with groups, I am convinced that I would have succeeded in bringing people onside.

Dan Robertson eventually joined Caroline Mulroney's leadership campaign to replace me as party leader after my takedown, but he would also quit a day later, when she walked away from her position on carbon pricing. She had been a big believer in climate change and carbon pricing. In fact, her father had called me about a week after the convention and said, "Patrick, Conservatives have allowed the left to own the environment as an issue, but Brian Mulroney did not. For voters who cared about the environment, they were more likely to vote for the Right Honourable Brian Mulroney than for [Liberal leader] John Turner!" (I always found it funny that Mulroney often talked about himself in the third person. But he was so good, he could get away with it).

He also pointed out to me that he was the greenest prime minister in Canadian history, and that he had Elizabeth May (now the leader of the federal Green Party) working for him. "So good on you, Patrick, for taking this issue back!"

Good on me? Perhaps. It's a fact that leadership takes courage. It's also a fact that courage makes enemies. Now it was time to sit down with Kathleen Wynne, someone who was hopefully not an enemy, but an adversary.

I had sent a letter to Wynne soon after I became an MPP. In it, I told her that one of my key campaign ideas was that there was no monopoly on a good idea. And if a good idea came from another party, we should embrace it. I wanted us to focus on what we had in common and not what divided us. So I proposed regular meetings in which we could find and focus on those commonalities.

Wynne didn't respond immediately, but eventually she agreed to meet with me at her Queen's Park office. Both of us had our chiefs of staff present. I began the meeting by reiterating that it was my hope that we could focus on what we might advance together.

Wynne responded swiftly. "I know what this is about, Patrick. You just want to 'get' me."

This was not the way I thought the meeting was going to go, and it was my hope that we could move some things ahead collaboratively. She continued, "Patrick, it's your prerogative to ask to work together. It's politics. But you just want to 'get' me."

I tried to push the reset button by explaining, "Let me give you an example. I've studied your speeches. You want to move ahead with financial literacy in the classroom. And I agree. So what can we do together to promote this?"

Her response was, "We're already doing it. NEXT."

I then offered up another example. "You guys made a statement about reducing inter-provincial trade barriers. And I put out a press release praising you because I'm not blindly partisan. What can we do to make it easier to push goods?"

"We've already attended to that. NEXT," was her very terse response. She then asked me if I had any ideas to offer. "Where's your platform? All you do is criticize. Why don't you come here with ideas?"

It was the most hostile meeting I could ever have anticipated. I believe that she wanted to send me the message not to waste her precious time. There would be no meetings, no collaboration and no, we aren't going to work together. That was the first and last meeting in private. We had public meetings at which we would shake each other's hands. But that private meeting was horrific.

In fall 2016, my then chief of staff, Pina Martino, decided to run for the nomination in Etobicoke Centre and was the odds-on favourite to win, having been the candidate in the 2014 election. But late in the race, my policy adviser, Kinga Surma, who had supported Christine Elliott for leader in 2015, decided that she, too, would run for the nomination in that same riding. Surma was not well-known and her victory seemed unlikely. But she won.

The allegations reported in the media were that Doug Ford bought PC memberships, intimidated Martino and helped Surma win the race. Surma and Ford were close. Surma's former boyfriend had been the executive assistant to then-councillor Ford five years earlier, and during her time in my office, Ford would visit her at Queen's Park. This created a media distraction each time he showed up. Martino tried to bring order to the office and asked Ford to stop dropping by, which angered him. Martino and Ford butted heads. While Ford has denied allegations that he in any way influenced the nomination victory for Surma, it strained the relationship between my office and Ford.

Things in the PC Party were not great, either. Yes, we were on the heels of two strongly won by-elections. But, the party's debt was suffocating. This was a reality that confronted me from the day I took office in May 2015. The debt was a staggering $7 million. The interest payments alone were tough to maintain.

Not being the most popular party, the Ontario PCs had developed a rhythm of going into debt during an election campaign, then spending the rest of the time in opposition trying to raise money to pay it off, just in time for the next election.

Once an election was called, it would go into debt again — the cycle was one of never-ending red ink. Apart from the debilitating payments, the party was never really able to do anything significant to ready itself for a general election because between elections, the PCs were always in debt-repayment mode. The Liberals and the NDP had small debts in comparison to the PCs.

This was something I needed to tackle if we were going to be able to fight the kind of campaign we needed to fight during a general election. While this was always the plan, I got very serious about it in spring 2016.

Kathleen Wynne and the Liberals were being raked over the coals by the media as a result of a Toronto Star exposé on questionable fundraising practices. It had been discovered that the premier's office had put fundraising quotas on key ministers, with the expectation that they would deliver on their respective quotas. Why ministers? Because access to ministers was in high demand by corporate stakeholders, who could pay big dollars. Access to ministers was a commodity that could be sold. The Toronto Star started reporting on a number of high-priced fundraising events that were being marketed to stakeholders as opportunities for face time with the respective minister.

I went hard on Wynne in the House over these flagrant cash-for-access fundraising events. We tried to prove that some of these payments were resulting in special deals or contracts for the donor companies. In any event, the optics were terrible.

The newspapers continued to hammer away, until finally Wynne was forced to deal with fundraising reform. She argued that during her previous minority government, she had tried to curtail corporate donations, but the PC opposition led by Hudak would not support the reforms proposed. This is true.

The Liberals enjoyed corporate contributions, which included massive spends by a coalition of unions branded under the banner "Working Families." The group spent millions putting out impressive ads, demonizing conservatives. Many believe these were instrumental in gutting support for the PCs. Of course, the PCs were also dependent on corporate Ontario for fundraising and doubly dependent given that the party was, and had been for a long time, in a perpetual state of slaying debt.

Wynne was shamed into reforming the fundraising rules and eliminating corporate donations. I'm convinced that Wynne assumed we would not support any proposal that eliminated corporate donations, which wouldn't really have mattered since the Liberals had a majority government. While the legislation would hurt the Liberals, Wynne was likely convinced it would destroy us. They had raised a good amount with the cash for access schemes, and we were drowning in debt.

Instead, I shocked everyone, including my own caucus and the media, by declaring that I would strongly support the proposed restrictions. Many were furious. How would we ever be able to borrow money if we hadn't paid back the debt?

A series of amended acts were passed in 2016 that banned corporate and union political donations, lowered the amount that individuals could contribute by 90 per cent and prohibited candidates from attending fundraisers, including their own. I found that provision to be ridiculous, but I believe it was included because the Liberals were worried about the PCs' star candidates and the amounts that could be raised if they attended fundraisers.

None of these provisions would kick in until January 1, 2017. That gave me some time to clear our massive debt. If we were going to win a general election and any by-elections in between, we needed to be solvent by January 1, 2017, before the rules changed.

I considered how many people or corporations it would take to tackle the debt of $7 million if each was responsible for raising $25,000. That number was 234, and so Project 234 was born. We identified 234 individuals to be our fundraisers, each with the target of raising $25,000 over the course of the next six months.

From the spring to December 31, 2016, at midnight, when the new fundraising rules kicked in, I would spend every single day at fundraising events. This meant that every lunch and dinner on my calendar was fully booked. On some evenings, I attended four different events. I was exhausted. I had even scheduled three fundraisers on New Year's Eve, something that everyone believed would be impossible to do. These were held at the world junior hockey tournament. That night we raised $65,000. We even had a Toronto-Dominion banker come to the events, to register the money into our account before the clock struck midnight. When I think back, it was an unbelievably exhausting exercise. But it worked.

In November 2016, just before the December deadline, Tony Miele, chair of the Ontario PC Fund, called me up and asked for an urgent in-person meeting. We met at a Tim Hortons on Mapleview Drive in Barrie. When he entered, he walked straight over to me and gave me a big bear hug. "Patrick," he said, "We're out of debt!" He was shocked. We managed to clear $7 million of debt in just over four months, something that took years to accomplish in the past.

"Tony," I said, "Don't tell a soul that we are out of debt. We're going to keep on fundraising until December 31st at midnight. I want a war chest."

Miele never mentioned a word, and we kept on fundraising. On January 1, 2017, we ended up with a surplus of $4 million. I received a three-minute standing ovation at the first caucus meeting in January 2017. We had accomplished something that had never been done in the history of any political party in Ontario and certainly not by an opposition party.

When I left office, we maintained that surplus, which meant we had more money in the bank than the Liberals and the NDP combined. On top of it all, we had prepaid many campaign expenses, finished a flashy policy launch, had conducted a province-wide bus tour and had completed a $3-million ad buy. Project 234 was the most remarkable project Ontario fundraising had ever seen.

As I mentioned earlier, strong leadership can also produce strong enemies. Despite the victories that were stacking up, there were a number of individuals and groups who were not happy with me. Let's begin.

As I wrote earlier, Lisa MacLeod hated me because I ran against her in the PC Party leadership race and beat her badly in her own riding. Her own staff defected to me during the race, and she couldn't hold the riding for Christine Elliott, whom she backed after she dropped out of the race. I took the riding 80–20. She was bitter. She had promised everyone that I was going to get wiped out.

When I became leader, I put MacLeod on the front bench, despite the fact that every organizer in eastern Ontario hated her and resented me for backing her. As far as I could tell, MacLeod was not a people person. She was mean to people; she went through more staff than anyone else. Pierre Poilievre and John Baird — both Ottawa-area MPs — hated her and have told me so. They both warned me when I took over that she was "bat-shit crazy."

Still, in MacLeod's mind, I was out to get her, regardless of what I was doing to protect her. She hated me, she hated Jack MacLaren, she hated all the regional organizers, she hated people in Ottawa and so on.

There was a candidate, Goldie Ghamari, who was running against MacLeod in Ottawa for the nomination. So what did I do? I called Ghamari and told her that she could run in any other riding, but not against MacLeod. Period. I thought she'd beat MacLeod handily, so I intervened to protect her. Six months later, another candidate, Ottawa businessman Riven Zhang, decided to run for the nomination against MacLeod. He had a very big Chinese community behind him. Again, I went to MacLeod and told her not to worry about the nomination because I was protecting her.

Eastern Ontario organizers, including Terrance Oakey, Brian Storseth and Debbie Jodoin and some of her own staff, believed that MacLeod made up the mental health issues she claimed to have suffered during the nomination races in order to endear the public to her and to make it difficult for her to be defeated in the nomination. I told them that whether or not these claims were true, I could not let anyone push her out because, as I insisted, we needed to give her the benefit of the doubt. This did not go over well with the eastern Ontario organizers.

None of what I did for MacLeod ever registered. I finally said to her, "Lisa, I don't hold grudges. But you need to stop having these episodes where you believe I'm screwing you. I am protecting you. We are on one team. You're on the front bench for a reason."

When I think about Lisa MacLeod, I think about a person who is always angry. She was just angry with everything, with everyone and with her situation in life.

Members of caucus hated her. If anyone else in caucus went off script the way MacLeod did, they'd be kicked out. In fact, caucus was less than impressed that I gave MacLeod far more latitude. But I was living under the illusion that I needed to show the defeated leadership candidates some love, like Matt Damon in the film *Invictus*, when he says to Nelson Mandela's supporters, "Let's get rid of the Springboks [Rugby team]. That's the white folks' favourite sport. We'll teach them a lesson after what they did." And Mandela responds, "No. We have to show them love to bring in unity." I now think this concept works out better in the movies.

And then there was Tanya Granic Allen, a prudish activist-turned-celebrity during the 2018 leadership race, where she announced in a live TVO debate that students would do better in math if they weren't learning about anal sex. Since then, she has forever been crowned as the "Anal Sex Lady" amongst PC Party members— not the way I'd want to be remembered, but different strokes for different folks, I suppose.

Granic Allen was running an organization called PAFE (Parents as First Educators), an anti-sex education group. They had been supporters of

Monte McNaughton and wanted to be players in the party. During the 2015 leadership race, I had agreed to providing parents with more consultation on the sex education curriculum.

The Anal Sex Lady and her followers were pissed, so that when I became leader they'd push me on this point of revoking sex education. All I would say is that we needed to do a better job of consulting next time. But they were after a stark commitment that there would be no sex education in the school. They wanted it in writing.

In summer 2016, Granic Allen called and booked a meeting with me at my Queen's Park office. At the meeting I reiterated my promise that next time we would consult parents, educators and experts. I explained that the curriculum got updated every five years, which provided for an opportunity to do so.

Not good enough for Granic Allen, who kept pressing for a written commitment that I would ban sex education in the classroom. If I didn't agree to that, her group would begin running anti-sex education candidates against me. *Great*, I thought.

I asked her, "How can you possibly say you want no sex education in the classroom? Tell me what it is that you want out. Are you saying you don't think we need to teach kids that homophobia is bad?

She answered, "Absolutely. My organization won't stand for that. Patrick, it's immoral."

She was also bitter and twisted that conversion therapy couldn't be billed on OHIP. I had heard that Granic Allen was very involved in promoting conversion therapy, but to be honest, I had no idea what it was. So before the meeting, I had to look it up. I discovered that it's a controversial therapy predicated on the belief that being homosexual is something that needs to be cured, and this therapy is about curing gay people. Whoa! I found this offensive.

So the meeting began with the two of us taking a photo together, all smiles. And, it ended after about 20 minutes, with Tanya Granic Allen leaving absolutely livid because I said I didn't agree with her. To say it didn't go well would be a bit of an understatement.

It was singularly the worst, most-negative meeting I ever had at Queen's Park. Granic Allen left in a huff and a puff. And I was thrilled to see her go in a huff and a puff. I told my staff that I want nothing more to do with Tanya Granic Allen.

I understood that we had played "footsie" with the religious right when I was in Ottawa, and when I was part of the conservative coalition. And, I had come to the view that I really didn't like these people because in my view they were intolerant. So when I became leader of the party, I decided I wasn't playing this game anymore. I wasn't going to accept support based on hating others.

During my leadership campaign, I had told my people that I was going to march in the Pride Parade. John Tory had marched in the parade, but as he assured the PC Party, he was only going to show up as a private citizen and not in his official capacity as the leader of the PCs. There would be no delegation and no party banner.

In fact, before me, never before had a PC leader marched with a PC banner in the parade. I decided I was going to have a delegation. My leadership team freaked out because they were afraid we'd lose McNaughton supporters. So we agreed on a response that if asked in a radio interview or in a debate whether or not I would march in the Pride Parade, this would be my answer: I'd attend every event and I'd consider that invitation when I received it, though I knew full well that I was going to march.

In summer 2015, I marched with a full PC delegation. And I pissed off a lot of people. Charles McVety, an evangelical leader and conservative activist, was royally pissed. So was Frank Klees, former PC cabinet minister. And you know what? I felt great about it because for the first time I was leader of the party, and I didn't have to worry about appeasing anyone. I could do what I felt was right.

My sisters were pleased. They used to hate it when, during the leadership, people would call me a SoCon. Stephanie actually sent me a video of my nephew, her son, Colton, saying "Paddy, BE NORMAL" during my 2015 leadership bid. She translated Colton's sentiment as meaning that I didn't have to hang out with these people because it wasn't me. I was not hanging out with them. I was trying not to alienate them. I needed to get through the leadership process to be able to be who I was — a Progressive Conservative.

My sisters marched with me at the 2015 Pride Parade, and it shocked everyone because the Liberals had me pegged as a SoCon. The fact that literally a few months after winning leadership of the party I was marching in the parade threw everyone. Once again, no one should have been surprised, but still no one had done any research on what I stood for as MP in Barrie, that I had attended the Pride flag-raising.

Of course, I pissed off all the social conservatives, like Jim Karahalios. He was furious that I had marched in the 2015 Pride Parade with a PC delegation. I had been warned that he had given Rona Ambrose a really rough time on the pro-life issue and that he was a crazy social conservative. The next time I heard from him was after the convention over the carbon price declaration.

I had been told by many that his new mission was payback. I am not going to say that the federally mandated carbon tax was not an issue for him, but in my view, he leveraged the opposition to that tax to punish me for not supporting the social conservative movement and for marching in the Pride Parade.

While working on McNaughton's leadership campaign, Karahalios had access to the membership list, which he simply took. He was also working on the federal leadership campaign of Brad Trost, a pro-life candidate, so likely would have had that membership list as well.

I believe he used these lists to mount a campaign against me. We took him to court. Karahalios won under the new law brought in by Wynne, Anti-SLAPP (Strategic Lawsuits Against Public Participation) laws that had been designed to protect free expression and fair comment on issues of public interest. This law was brought in to end the practice of northern resource companies that were launching lawsuits to silence Greenpeace. I found it tough then, as I do now, to accept that this law should have applied to someone who I believe had taken without permission the party membership list to undermine the party leader or the direction of the party under that leader. I also don't believe that the intent of that law was to be used for these purposes. We lost that one and we appealed.

Actually, the person who was most behind the decision to appeal was Vic Fedeli. He was furious that his constituents were complaining about being solicited by Karahalios' group. Fedeli felt that it was wrong for Karahalios to use lists that had been meant for a very different purpose, and he didn't agree with the judgment. On this point, Fedeli was right. And frankly, the lawyers felt that we would win on appeal. But that appeal never happened. Soon after I left office, rumour had it that Fedeli settled with Karahalios and paid him six digits to compensate his legal bills. I was shocked. We may well have won on appeal, and Fedeli and I were on the same page, that the legislation used did not apply in spirit to what Karahalios had done. What shocked me more was listening to Fedeli talk about the legal battles that had taken place on my watch and the money spent. He was a major supporter of this battle and did not have to settle.

Since then, Karahalios worked on Granic Allen's campaign. I understand that he helped broker the deal with her. His wife became a candidate in Cambridge and won during the 2018 general election.

Interestingly, Karahalios had been arguing that I couldn't appoint or disqualify candidates. All of a sudden, he became silent when Ford did what he accused me of doing. Ford appointed 11 more candidates and was poised to appoint all 33 had it not been for the vocal opposition of 1 MPP, Mike Harris. He disqualified more than any leader I have seen. Frankly, the leader *is* allowed to appoint and disqualify. I just find it odd that Ford and his supporters criticized me for doing exactly what he did.

Another group that turned on me was the Good Ole Boys. These are the folks who blame the ethnic communities for everything because they believe that they are not to be trusted. The old PC Party was very comfortable being a right wing, rural, white party of 10,000 members. It was their country club. Under my leadership, we had 50 per cent minorities.

And then, of course, there were the Climate Dinosaurs. These are the folks who cling to the notion that climate change is either not real or it isn't man-made. I needn't go into the reasons for their opposition to me.

Of course, all of my enemies were emboldened by the fact I was rising in the polls, and Wynne was tanking. This time, the party had 236,000 members, which was confirmed to me in an email (that I still have) from a party official. We were debt free. We had a war chest. For the first time in a long time, the party was poised to win an election. And they were furious that I'd be the one leading the party to victory.

Yup, there's nothing like the prospect of winning to cause headaches and garner enemies. Everyone wants a piece of success. And that is what led to what I refer to as my nomination frustrations.

On September 1, 2016, a by-election was held in the riding of Scarborough-Rouge River. It had been called by Wynne to replace Liberal MPP Bas Balkissoon, who resigned suddenly, saying only that he wanted to spend more time with his family. Balkissoon had had held this seat for the Liberals since 2005. But the seat itself had been in Liberal hands since the riding was created in 1999.

In that nomination race, Ford announced that he was considering running. The leadership team that had to vet Ford was dead set against him running. Dan Robertson, Brett McFarquhar, members of the party executive and some high-profile potential candidates had problems with Ford running.

Bob Stanley and I were of the view that we should give him a chance. We took a vote, and I was the tiebreaker to give Ford a chance to run. In the end, Ford decided against it. As he told me: "I'm making too much money with my company and I'm not going to run." Instead, together, Ford and I pursued Raymond Cho.

Cho was an 80-year-old Korean-Canadian who had run in the 1988 federal election for the NDP. He later dropped his NDP affiliation and took out a membership in the Liberal Party, but he ran in the 2004 federal election as an independent candidate in Scarborough-Rouge River. In 2005, Cho sought to be the Liberal Party candidate in the provincial election, but the Liberal riding association chose to go with Bas Balkissoon, instead, without any nomination process.

Cho had then become our candidate in that riding in 2012. He didn't fare well in the 2014 provincial election, placing third. That was the election in which the Liberals won a majority government.

It was clear to me that this guy was not an ideologue, having belonged to all three parties at one point or another. He was a pragmatist, well-liked in his community and his polling numbers were great.

Cho agreed to run and became the candidate for the PC Party. There were 11 candidates running to win the seat in Scarborough Rouge-River. Of course, there was a Liberal candidate, Piragal Thiru; an NDP candidate,

Neethan Shan; and another nine candidates who had thrown their hats in the ring. These came from a number of smaller interest groups, including one being supported by Granic Allen. This candidate was against sex education. What a surprise.

Granic Allen was delivering on the threat she made in my office of running SoCons against my candidates. These moves were intended to break up party unity by the social conservative elements. This riding was made up largely of Chinese, Muslims, Catholics, Hindi, cultural and religious groups that had misgivings about the sex education curriculum.

My team was concerned, expecting that unless something was done, we'd bleed support to them. If we ended up losing by one per cent, it would have been these people who had cost us the victory. By late summer to early autumn, the polls had us tied with the Liberals. The team decided that we should put out a letter that said I agreed to scrap sex education.

I said no. The only thing we were going to say is that we would consult more. That was it.

I left to go up north, and somehow a letter was sent out from my office. Ford and Cho were involved, pushing the letter out. Walied thought I had approved it and so he OK'd the letter. Unbeknownst to him or anyone else, I had sent Tamara Macgregor, my Communications Director, a message saying that such a letter was not to go out. But Macgregor was also not at the office at that time. We were both on a northern tour. By the time she relayed the message that I would not approve the letter, a thousand letters had already gone out. It was a massive screw-up.

When I found out the letter had gone, I was furious. I made the decision that we were going to walk it back. We were not scrapping sex education, and that had to be clarified before, not after the election. I told my team, "You have 24 hours to give me a plan on how we're walking this back, or I am going to tell the media that this letter was not authorized."

While before I was prepared to use the language of consultation, now I wanted to be crystal clear with exactly how I felt. That is when I wrote that famous post to Facebook in which I was emphatic. I said that having had time to think about it, I had come to the view that we need sex education in the schools, and that in retrospect, I think Wynne was right.

I also say in my post that all the myths that I heard out there during the leadership campaign were just that, myths. People said it was being taught in Grade 1, and it wasn't. People said that parents couldn't pull their kid out if they didn't want their kid to attend, and that was also false. It was said that a parent couldn't view the lesson plan that showed a detail of what would be taught, and that was not true. It actually stated clearly in the curriculum that parents could actually view the lesson plan.

I wrote this Facebook post myself, then I sent it to Mike Richmond and Walied, and they fixed a bit of the grammar and it was posted. Charles McVety, already upset with me about marching in the Pride Parade, sent out an email to everyone saying, "I want $10 back." This referred to the cost of purchasing a PC membership. I got scrummed at Queen's Park, and the media was hammering me that, "Charles McVety wants his ten dollars back!" I responded that if he wanted his 10 bucks back, he could have it. I wasn't prepared to win support by hating one group. It got a great deal of media attention. I was seen as a flip-flopper.

Neither Ford nor Cho agreed with me. My team, and in particular Ford, pleaded with me not to walk this back until after the by-election was over, which would have been in one short week. But I just couldn't do that. If I had, it would have clearly misled the voters. I needed to come clean, that I was not against sex education, and that, in fact, I supported it.

One week before the election, we corrected the record. I remember being at Cho's office, and he was in tears. He said, "I can't believe this! How could you do this?"

I responded, "Raymond, you know we can't tell voters that I'm going to get rid of sex education, when you know I'm not going to."

Apart from my Facebook post, I had also written a letter that was posted online in which I said that I don't want anyone voting for me under the pretense that I am going to get rid of sex education. And the online responses I received from that letter were fantastic, much along the lines of "finally an honest politician." And the polls that reflected we were tied with the Liberals, 35 per cent to 35 per cent prior to my declaration, increased. Now we were at 38 per cent, and the Liberals fell back to 31 per cent.

On Thursday, September 1, 2016, Cho won the riding with 38 per cent of the votes. The Liberals came in second, 2,429 votes behind, with about 29 per cent of the vote. I believe that Cho was the first Korean-Canadian ever elected to the Ontario Legislature.

Following the win, PC Party senior adviser Babu Nagalingam joked, "We will now be called Scarborough-Blue River," pointing to the signature blue colour of the party.

CBC reported:

"Tonight there is a blue wave that has crossed the Rouge River in Raymond Cho," PC leader Patrick Brown said. "Tonight we made history. Thanks to your hard work we won a riding that had been Liberal since 1999." Ahead of the by-election, Brown acknowledged that his changing position on the Liberal government's sex-ed. curriculum could cost the party the seat but it clearly didn't hurt the PCs Thursday night. After promising last week to get rid of controversial changes to the curriculum, which encompasses topics such as same-sex relationships, gender identity and masturbation, Brown did an about-face on the topic on Monday, calling it a "mistake" to pledge to scrap it.

Wynne called the result disappointing and said that it gave her cause for reflection: "The good people of that riding have elected Liberals for many years. I'll be talking with our Scarborough members in the coming days, as well as our outstanding candidate, Piragal Thiru."

This showed me two things. First, that I was on the right side of the issue, and that following your gut is right. The second thing I learned was that I really had developed a better ground game than what the party had been accustomed to. My ground game in Scarborough-Rouge River was miles ahead of that of the Liberals' and the NDP's. We won Tamil polls in heavily concentrated Tamil communities, even though our candidate was Korean and running against two Tamil candidates. Where we used to get maybe one per cent or two per cent in Muslim polls, we were now getting 35 per cent or 40 per cent. We weren't winning these polls, but we were placing a close second.

That, too, was crazy. People were saying not to bother canvassing in those polls, they were Liberal polls. And I thought, *No, we're going after all those polls. Let them know the type of conservative I am.*

Caucus was not really a problem during this sex education dust-up. Generally speaking, they agreed with me and they didn't want to make this an issue. Obviously, Jack MacLaren, Monte McNaughton, Rick Nicholls, Randy Hillier and Bob Bailey had issues because they represented socially conservative ridings, but everyone else just wanted to put this issue to bed.

The by-election in Sault Ste. Marie was called for May 31, 2017, the last day of the Legislature. I believed that the Liberals were nervous about their chances of winning this riding, so they called the by-election on the same day the Legislature rose. My law school buddy, Ross Romano, had become a city councillor up in the "Soo," as it is called. I felt that I was really strong in northern Ontario. I had built a solid ground game during the leadership and had visited northern Ontario numerous times, maybe 15 times by that point.

Under Tim Hudak, the North was dead for the PC Party. The North had seats they never targeted, and in fact, Hudak skipped the northern leaders' debate. Everyone viewed the North as a write-off — a Liberal/ NDP stronghold.

I always felt the North shared our economic values. I was the guy going up there all the time, talking about economic development, saying we shared their values. I would tour every single small town. In fact, my first trip as leader of the party was to the area known as the "Ring of Fire."

When Romano ran, I told him that we were going to create a coalition of powerful groups. We'd get the firefighters and the police to help us. We were going to reach out to Laborers' International Union of North America, a strong union that had supported me in the past. We were gonna win here, and no one would see it coming!

In the previous 2014 election, the PC Party finished a distant third, behind the Liberals and the NDP. We got only 12 per cent. In this by-election, we won it handily, and the Liberals fell to third, thanks to labour and first-responder community support.

Next, I set my sights on Sudbury, traditionally NDP stomping ground; although, the Liberals had taken the riding in 2011 and 2014. Troy Crowder lived in Barrie for a while, and we played hockey together. Crowder was a former NHLer and is loved in his home town of Sudbury. His mom runs the Santa Claus parade, and she was helpful in my leadership campaign, signing up a whack of people in Sudbury to vote for me. I think I had about 80 per cent of the party vote in the Sudbury riding. I knew that Crowder was 90 per cent ready to run, so I told him to spend election day with me in Sault Ste. Marie because he would see what it would be like to win.

Romano's victory convinced him. He was ready. I told him that the numbers in the Soo were worse than they were in the Sudbury last election. If we could bring it home in the Soo, we could do so in Sudbury.

The tracking polls in Sudbury, before I stepped down as leader of the party in January 2018, showed that we were neck and neck with the NDP. I was hoping to put resources there, and that was going to be one of our surprise wins.

The Niagara West-Glanbrook by-election was held in June 2017. This was Hudak's riding, and it was now up for grabs. I wanted Rick Dykstra to win the PC nomination, and so did the party. However, Ken Zeise, Snover Dhillon and PC Party First Vice President Jag Badwal were all rivals of Dykstra. They worked hard to ensure that he failed. They supported Sam Oosterhoff, a 19-year-old, pro-life, home-schooled, fresh-off-the-farm teenager. And not because they liked him or because he would be the best candidate, but because he could beat Dykstra. And he did. Oosterhoff won, I was really upset. I had no idea then that Dykstra had lost in part because of the efforts of these people.

I called Sam that night, before his victory was announced. Because of his SoCon views, I had Mike Richmond draft up a pledge for the young Oosterhoff to sign. Failure to do so would result in me not announcing the victory. My call with him was brief. I said, "Look. I have to sign your forms. You're going to sign a pledge that you will *not* bring up gay rights or abortion in the Legislature. And if you sign that, I'll sign your forms, and we will announce the results." I told him that my job in the Legislature was to hold Wynne accountable for things like the hydro mess. These were the issues I was concerned about. Oosterhoff did sign the pledge. And thank goodness that he did because, quite honestly, I really don't know what I would have done had he not. I mean, he did win the nomination, and I suppose that I could have cut him loose if he won the riding. I could have forced him to sit as an independent.

Oosterhoff went on to win the riding against Liberal Vicky Ringuette and NDPer Mike Thomas. In the end, he won more than 53 per cent of the vote. Ringuette came third. Oosterhoff became the youngest MPP in Ontario history, at 19 years of age.

We ensured that he wasn't sworn in as MPP before the vote on Bill 28, which gave same-sex couples and those using reproductive technology legal recognition as parents. He would not have supported it, as he told the Toronto Star, because he felt it was disrespectful of mothers and fathers. He pleaded with the media that he was not a homophobe, but many in the media were somewhat suspicious.

Actually, Oosterhoff turned out to be a really good MPP and did very well in some very tough scrums, as soon as he showed up to Queen's Park. He also turned out to be a really decent team player. Oosterhoff's nomination was a big issue for me at the time. But I had no idea that it would turn out to be relatively mild, given the issues I was about to face in other nominations races.

I had received some advice earlier from Stephen Harper. That advice was that it was best to spend more time and resources on background checks during the nomination process than it would be to spend valuable time dealing with a crisis during an election campaign. Harper would know. In 2015, some of his candidates put him on the front page of the papers. One candidate, Jerry Bance, was caught on video in 2012 peeing in a cup in someone's kitchen and dumping the urine down their sink, while he had been hired to do some home improvements in their house. I believe the CBC referred to it as "urinating," and Wendy Mesley called it "surprising behavior.". To this day, you can google that story by typing in "Conservative Candidate Pees in Cup."

In an attempt to manage these media stories, Harper lost valuable days on the campaign trail. In the end, he had to fire three candidates. His advice to me? "Do your vetting, Patrick. It'll save you valuable time later."

I decided to raise the candidates' fees to $2,500 from $1,000 in order to enable us to cover the costs of two vettings per candidate by two separate companies. I wanted to know if anyone had skeletons in his or her closet. If that meant we'd have to disqualify them, so be it. I didn't care. I didn't want to have any candidate I couldn't defend during the campaign. I kept focused on one thought: "Conservative Candidate Pees in Cup."

As it turned out, the candidates were at times the least of my worries. The campaigns were something different.

As we began winning by-elections and rising in the polls, interest in running for the PC Party was climbing to insane levels. More interest in nominations meant more candidates and more vetting. Nomination races were getting out of control. We never had so many people wanting to be PC candidates.

Before the new fundraising rules kicked in, we started to assess which riding associations were ready to go, meaning that they had robust membership sales and candidates. We found 30 ridings where we could have quick nominations. We offered them the right to have early nominations; the riding presidents had to agree, as did the candidates. Twenty ridings agreed to move forward with nominations.

One of these ridings was Brampton North, where Jass Johal, a paralegal and strong community activist, was nominated by acclamation in November 2016.

There were originally a few candidates vying for the job in that riding, and one was disqualified for immigration fraud. But Johal, through his large network, signed up a record 6,600 memberships in this riding. That was the most in the province. Just to put that in context, the PC Party under Hudak only had 10,000 memberships throughout the entire province. Walking into headquarters with 6,600 memberships in one riding made you a gorilla! Johal set a new record for the party. After he delivered these memberships, the other two candidates dropped out of the race.

Johal was acclaimed as the candidate. The PC Party would make allegations after my takedown that his nomination was wrapped up in a business deal between us that never actually took place. This will be dealt with later on.

The Scarborough-Rouge River by-election was really a game changer. It showed we could take down a Liberal stronghold. It showed we could win anywhere. And it signaled a real shift in momentum. After that by-election, we had more than 900 people vying for nominations; compare that to about

150 to 200 candidates who were running for nominations when Hudak was leader of the party.

I had heard stories before of people stealing the envelope box at weddings, but now I was starting to hear that in Brampton West, a guy had just taken off with the ballot box. I mean, who does that? I held a midnight conference call to discuss the situation. We determined that as bad as the stolen box was, the number of missing ballots was not enough to bridge the gap required to change the result. So we let the results stand.

But that was the tip of the iceberg. I had no idea just how crazy things were getting. I was hearing stories of fake IDs in a race in Hamilton; of people in other ridings producing counterfeit ballots, forcing the party to reprint different ballots that would be impossible to replicate; and reports from people I trusted that some campaigns were essentially paying operatives to stuff ballot boxes.

These allegations involved people working at party headquarters. Though not proven, some allegations became subject to police and media investigations. I couldn't get over the lengths that people would go to in order to win a nomination. We clearly had a problem.

We were trying to stay one step ahead of those trying to cheat the process, but it wasn't easy. I finally lost it and held a conference call with the Seven Horsemen. I said, "For fuck's sake! This is becoming a shit show! I trusted you guys to run these nominations. And then I keep getting hit with media stories immediately after the nominations, talking about problems. I want a recommendation on how this will be fixed moving forward."

That was big for me. I am not known to drop the F-bomb frequently.

Part of the problem, in a nutshell, was that there was a hunger, a hysteria actually, to win these PC nominations and win government. And the nomination process in these ridings was largely being run by volunteers who were ill-equipped to deal with the huge efforts being made by various campaigns to win.

What people should know is that nomination meetings are largely run by maybe 10 or 20 volunteers. They have to oversee the conduct of campaigns that have spent around $100,000 to win that nomination.

That's when I realized that we needed to hire some professional help —
some independent, third-party company to oversee the nominations
process. Rick Dykstra and Bob Stanley didn't want to hire oversight. They
argued that it would be too expensive. A professional audit firm would
charge $10,000 for every meeting. Volunteers cost nothing but a slice of
pizza and some pop.

I put my foot down on this one, and we hired the well-known firm PwC. I
took some nasty comments on social media from those who remembered
that this was the same audit firm that managed to mess up at the Oscars.
The presenters had mistakenly been given the wrong category envelope for
Best Picture. Hopefully, its Ontario branch would prove to be better.

So we hired PwC. But even with PwC on board and watching over, I
continued to hear stories that made me want to pull my hair out. A good
example was the Scarborough Centre PC nomination race of June 2017.

In that riding, a young Tamil candidate, Thenusha Parani, was running for
the nomination against Antonio Villarin and Christina Mitas. The riding
was largely behind Mitas, and Ford was also supporting her. But Parani
came in and blew everyone out of the water. She won the nomination by a
large margin, having signed up many more members and getting her vote
out.

I believe that the riding was upset that a Tamil candidate, who had been
with the party for only a few years, signed up a such a significant number
of members and won by such a large margin. Many wanted Parani
disqualified because they claimed she was too recent a member of the PC
Party. But I said that she had been involved with the party since the 2015
leadership campaign. And there was no rule against someone running who
had been with the party for a few years. She met all of the requirements.

I believe that if they had called a new nomination race, Parani would have
won by even more votes than the 600 or so that she had managed to take.
She was beloved in the Tamil community.

Typically, nomination meetings are held in a location selected by the riding
association. In this case, they picked a voting location that could fit about
150 people. The complaint afterwards by the riding association (that

supported the losing candidate) was that the place (selected by them) wasn't big enough.

Their arguments didn't make sense to me. The location was certainly not big enough to accommodate thousands. But it didn't have to. It simply had to accommodate voters coming in to vote over the course of a few hours. The fact that there were long lineups is because the riding association did not expect so many to show up to vote. They were clearly unprepared to process so many.

In addition, the riding association had booked the venue only until 9:30 p.m., after which time there was apparently another booking. At one point, the venue staff shut off the lights off— I suppose to signify closing time — leaving people in line. As I recall, the number of voters left waiting in line was about 15.

The poll closed. The ballot boxes were all taken to party headquarters. The scrutineers were there to certify the vote, and those who didn't get to vote were visited at their homes the next day, with scrutineers in tow, and given the chance to cast their ballot. After all was said and done, Parani won by about 600 votes

Some of Mitas's supporters called the police. Here we had let the riding association pick the location and we were still in trouble. This was a messy nomination race, despite the fact that PwC had provided oversight. And no, I don't think it's because PwC messed up at the Oscars.

But the Mother's Day weekend of May 2017 proved to be the height of my nomination frustrations.

The Hamilton West-Ancaster-Dundas nomination of May 2017 was a mess. We had four candidates running: Ben Levitt, Vikram Singh, Jeff Peller and Jobson Easow. All candidates were vetted, but the results came in late, just days before the nomination.

They showed that two of the candidates had serious problems. Peller, it turns out, had run an escort agency and apparently had struggled with a crack cocaine problem, issues he acknowledged in a letter he wrote, where he explained that this was a difficult period in his life, but that he had overcome it. We had what we needed to disqualify Peller, and we should have done so. But, Peller's family was friends with Wayne Gretzky, who had supported me. And I allowed friendship to interfere with good judgment — big mistake that I regret. But Peller was not a front runner, and it was unlikely that he had any chance at all.

Singh's dad had been allegedly involved with some extreme groups in the 80s. Because of this, the team responsible for vetting candidates suggested he was a non-starter. Singh's supporters came to us and we told them that Singh was going to be disqualified. Supporters sent from the Sikh leadership, advised us not to disqualify him but rather to approve him, so as not to offend the community. Singh, we were promised, would not show up to the nomination, nor would his supporters. If we disqualified him, there would be a stain over him and the community.

I thought that seemed reasonable. He would save face, as would the community. If he didn't show up, he wouldn't win. Problem solved. But it was very stupid, actually, in retrospect. Another big mistake.

I was not present at that nomination, but I was getting reports that things were turning into a real mess. First, Singh *did* show up. He and Peller were allegedly involved in fake memberships. In fact, three of the four candidates had allegations of some sort against them. The only one who didn't was Easow, who ironically, also didn't have a hope in hell of winning.

Easow was actually my friend and my preferred candidate, even though I didn't share that at the time. He was from the Malayali community. We had gone to India together, and after I finished with the formal delegation, he and his good friend Thomas and I went to the backwaters in a boat in Kerala. It was there that he told me he wanted to run, and I made it clear that I couldn't interfere with his race for the nomination. I had to remain impartial. He said he understood and respected that. If people were to look up me and Easow on the Internet, there would be many photos of us together. He finished fourth, despite the fact that he was my closest friend in the race by far, something that many knew.

The race was really between Singh and Levitt. The result came in, and Levitt won. What a mess, but at least he didn't have any vetting issues.

Velshi, my chief of staff, who was very good friends with Levitt, told me not to worry, that everything would work out. My staff kept me sheltered from this kind of stuff. And that is why leaders have staff: to ensure things are going according to process without getting caught up in the mud.

When I would ask, "How are things looking for Hamilton?" the response was basically, "You don't need to know." Just to be clear, any leader or minister who says that they are fully briefed on all the sordid details of everything that goes down is lying. If staff feels it can be resolved without implicating the politician, they do so. That is another hard truth about politics. I was intentionally kept out of the details.

So Levitt won, and Singh, who was not supposed to show up because he hadn't actually passed vetting, lost. He decided to take the party to court over fraud charges. Meanwhile, Bugeja, my personal assistant, was running the contentious credential's box. If people's ID didn't match up, they would go to the credential's desk, where their information would be checked and verified. The ballot box at the credentials desk ended up with more ballots than voters checked off.

Velshi and Bugeja were, at the time, close. Bugeja was also loyal to me. She had access to all my personal files and all the passwords to my accounts. She would keep track of them. I was told after January 24, 2018, she provided them to Velshi after I stepped down as party leader. These personal documents were apparently used against me by the party after my takedown. More on that later.

But what I had been told by people at Queen's Park is that Velshi used the Hamilton nomination and other things to pressure Bugeja into handing over access to my personal documents at a time in which I no longer had access to the Queen's Park office. I have no proof of this, but it is what I had been told. All I knew at the time of the Hamilton nominations was that Velshi wanted Levitt to win, and Bugeja was in charge of the credentials desk ballot box.

Later I got a call from one of Singh's top guys, who said that it didn't make any sense that Levitt had so many votes. I lost it. This was a bit rich, given that we were in essence fighting over a nomination race in which his candidate was not supposed to even participate.

I was clear: "Normally, if I hear these rumours, I'd be tempted to quash the nomination, but not when you told me your guy wasn't going to show up for the nomination."

Ultimately, they knew I was right. They went hard after Dykstra, Bugeja, Stanley and me as party leader. In the media I was blamed for the fraudulent behaviour during this nomination race. Interestingly, the aggrieved group that was taking the PC Party to court over this, supported me when I ran the second time for the leadership. This led me to view that they mustn't have really believed that I had been involved. Why would they want to get out the vote for a prospective leader of the party who they felt was responsible for stacking votes to defeat their candidate?

If I had completed my run for leader the second time around, I would have won those Hamilton ridings, largely due to Singh's organization. Instead, as I will get to, I withdrew from the race.

The police were called in to deal with the fraud allegations over the Hamilton nomination and the credentials box. The party retained a lawyer to represent me just in case, but when my lawyer called the police to ask if they needed to speak to me, he was told that based on their investigation, I was not a person of interest. They said that if they were going to lay charges, it would likely be by mid-March. I was never called. I understand that they interviewed a number of people, including Velshi, Bugeja, Dykstra and his assistant.

When Ford became leader, he overturned the nomination, and they had a new race. Ford disqualified Singh, which I should have done and not bothered with the bullshit that he wouldn't show up. Hindsight is always 20/20.

The Richmond Hill nomination meeting of May 2017 that was held at the Toronto Montessori School on Bayview Avenue at Highway 407 was another mess. Four candidates presented: Lara Coombs, whose campaign was being run by John Mykytyshyn; Ted Leider; Scott Sun; and Daisy Wai.

The vote resulted in a tie. In these situations, the tie is broken by the Chair of Elections, who in this case was Bob Stanley. On the recommendation of the local riding association president, Stanley cast his vote for Wai. Coombs had signed up the most members, but she just didn't get them out.

Brian McLean, a 58-year old supporter of Coombs, later came forward, alleging that he showed up to the meeting but was not able to access the speeches that preceded the voting. McLean needed to use a wheelchair to get around, having suffered a spinal cord injury diving three decades earlier, and there was no wheelchair access to the auditorium in which the speeches were taking place. So he went home and did not vote for his candidate, Coombs. That was his story.

The party nomination committee heard the appeal and it found that Coombs never identified to the voting organizers that there was an issue with Mr. McLean. Had that happened, they would have helped McLean by providing him with a ballot or helping him access the auditorium to hear the speeches and vote. There were four hours allocated for voting. Surely, in that amount of time this might have been raised with the organizers. But it wasn't.

The problem was that Wai, who won by one vote on a tiebreaker, argued that she, too, had supporters who were physically impaired and didn't vote. So now the thinking was if they had to let one supporter vote based on his allegations, could they reasonably deny the other supporter or supporters?

It appeared to the party lawyer's interpretation that both candidates could be inventing these issues to alter the vote using supporters who may not have actually shown up, but were being mobilized after the fact. Photos were not helpful because they could be taken after the fact.

Mykytyshyn was adamant that Coombs was telling the truth, but he was not an impartial voice because he was being paid by Coombs's campaign. What was the truth? Did McLean show up and was unable to vote? Why wasn't anyone running the nomination meeting notified? Was he the only one? What about these other registered supporters? Should all those who had been physically impaired and had registered but didn't cast a ballot be allowed to vote as though they had intended to be there? Had they all shown up? Where do you draw the line?

Ultimately, I don't have any answers to these questions, but I think now, as I thought at the time, they were all relevant. A registered voter should come forward at the time to an organizer and put their complaint on the record when it can be resolved. Even if a suitable accommodation could not be found, at least there would have been a legitimate record of that voter's issue. Instead, no one could prove who had or hadn't been there at the time before the vote, nor that others also were or were not in the same boat.

Riding officials do not run the nominations, the party officials do. So any bias of the riding officials would be irrelevant. If anything, the party officials were closer to Coombs. But she lost. I didn't interfere. I knew Coombs because she had worked as Executive Assistant to Jim Jones, a PC MP under Jean Charest. There were some religious issues in her background that sparked a debate on whether or not to disqualify her. I didn't know Wai at all, other than I had heard she was beloved in the Chinese community. Interestingly, in my second bid for the leadership, Coombs supported me, and Wai didn't. Much as I liked Coombs, I felt they were grasping at straws.

On that same Mother's Day weekend, and in the riding of Ottawa West-Nepean, Jeremy Roberts and Karma Macgregor were both seeking the nomination. Tremendous pressure was put on me to disqualify Roberts. People were telling me that he was the "pawn" of Lisa MacLeod. (Did I mention that MacLeod was not well liked amongst eastern Ontario organizers?) They were saying that MacLeod wanted to have a loyalist in that riding, and he, like MacLeod, would be a thorn in my side.

Initially, Roberts told me that he knew I was friends with Macgregor and her daughter Tamara but that he "wouldn't hold that against me." The media published that I had dated Tamara, but this is not accurate. I had some minor romantic history with Tamara many years earlier when we were younger. Nothing came of it other than a good friendship. We never were an item. We never dated. Even her mother wasn't aware of that one encounter.

Macgregor was quite involved with the conservatives and had worked in Scarborough. She was the mother hen of the Senate, which she ran. She was a lovely lady, would have made a great MPP and, frankly, a good minister. She understood the legislative process upside down and she has been a real seasoned asset on Parliament Hill in Ottawa.

The allegation in this race was that people were buying up PC Party memberships, and that there were more members per house than actual residents. For example, there were 20 names of PC Party members all registered to one apartment. I understood that people buy up memberships for their supporters. Everyone knows it, every party does it and no one really clamps down on it — sort of like jaywalking. These sorts of tactics happen in all parties. It would take a surprising amount of naiveté to be shocked over this practice, even though many in the media claimed to be.

As far as I was concerned, all registered voters had to show up with ID. So if they didn't show up or they showed up without appropriate ID, they couldn't vote. If there were questions about a voter's legitimacy, then that voter had to present themselves to the credentials desk for further verification.

In this nomination meeting, Roberts's campaign challenged a number of voters. All of these voters had one thing in common: they were minorities, largely Indian and Somalian, to be precise.

At the end of the nomination meeting, there were around 15 more ballots in the credentials box than there were people's names crossed off the registry. In short, there were more votes cast than there were voters crossed off the list at the credentials desk.

We had an emergency conference call, and the way it was explained to me by those at the credentials desk handling the ballot box with the extra ballots was that in the flurry of people being sent to the credentials desk, on occasion, some may not have been checked off the voter list as they cast ballots.

This is not unheard of. During busy moments, sometimes voters cast their ballot, but their name is not crossed off the list. In fact, Stanley confirmed for me that in many nomination races in the province, the number of actual ballots cast and the number of names stroked off don't completely match and may be off by a few.

What was suspicious was that while there were around 15 more ballots in the box than there were people who were checked off the registered voter list, 15 ballots in the box were all stuck together. How can 15 ballots make it into the box all stuck together? A red flag, for sure, which was exactly why Roberts wanted a new nomination.

So we have Roberts saying this was fishy, and frankly, it was. Meanwhile, we received complaints from the Macgregor campaign that people of colour were being challenged or being told by Roberts's people to go home. In one case, I heard that one of Roberts's scrutineers told a Sikh voter to "go back home; we don't need any Muslims here." This reflected total ignorance — a Sikh is *not* Muslim.

I had party officials telling me that they could not believe how racist Roberts's people were. So while Roberts argued that something was fishy, we had Karma saying there had been human rights violations, and that this was a case of utter racism.

Karma's argument was that the credentials desk was overloaded because Roberts's group had challenged every Sikh and Somalian voter. Karma raised the possibility of a human rights challenge. The PC Party lawyers were concerned that we would be liable if we didn't take this seriously. But we knew that this was going to be a mess either way: if we turned down Roberts's appeal, then we were in trouble, and if we moved forward, we were in trouble with Karma.

In my view, the anomalies in this nomination race *were* about race. The old Ottawa West-Nepean riding association was comprised of about a hundred white people, and now we had more than 300 Somalians, more than 300 Sikhs and 200 Filipinos — it started to reflect Ontario. The Ole Boys Club did not like that at all.

That being said, both Jeremy Roberts and Karma Macgregor launched what I thought were legitimate complaints. In the end, we upheld Karma's nomination, and we quashed Roberts's appeal. Why? Because we determined that the behaviour of Roberts's team was repulsive and offensive. Had it not been for his behaviour challenging the legitimacy of *only* ethnic voters of colour, we would have likely approved his appeal, and we would have had a new nomination. We also were very concerned about a legitimate human rights complaint from Karma.

What were we going to do about these nominations that were under a cloud? Velshi wanted to overturn Ottawa, but not Hamilton. Robertson and Boddington wanted to overturn both of them. Dykstra, Bugeja and Stanley didn't want to do anything, arguing that it would create a precedent. If we overturned two races, then what about all the other races with losing candidates who wanted to have nominations overturned? In the end, three wanted new nominations, three did not.

I was frustrated. Here we were with recommendations that were all over the map. So I told the team that I was going to leave, and they were going to fight it out and give me one recommendation. They came back the next day and said they agreed on one recommendation: to do nothing. And that was it. Something was put in the papers that various nomination meetings were recommended to be overturned. But the final recommendation that they all signed on to was actually to do nothing.

Were there times when I put my hand on the scale? Yes. I had a goal of having the most female candidates in our party's history; the record was about 21. I didn't want us to be the party of old white men. I wanted a plan to get 50 female candidates on board. When I left, Queen's Park had about 45, so we were well on the way. We identified talented women. There was Gillian Smith in University-Rosedale. I thought she was a star. She was from the Toronto Region Board of Trade. Martin Abel had run and lost in that riding before, and I respected him greatly. I encouraged party officials to sit down with Abel and ask him to help support Smith as a candidate in this riding. But in the end, he said, "No." He wanted to run, so we let him. We didn't disqualify him. But here's what we did do. I made sure that people at party headquarters were signing up members for Smith. So she would win.

Then there was Flamborough-Glanbrook. I had had a breakfast with councillor Donna Skelly, and she had impressed me with her belief that we had to go back to the Bill Davis era, to our party's roots. We needed to get beyond the people who held positions against climate change and gay rights and so on. We were of the same mind. We did a few events together, trying to build relationships with unions and city council in Hamilton. I really wanted her to run, but she told me she wouldn't because she felt the PC Party was out of touch.

Finally, we convinced Skelly to run, but there was another individual who was also running. He was a pro-life activist, very involved in his church and he would have killed her at the polls. I believed his positions were out of sync with a modern Ontario. That being said, he was a very nice man. He had signed up 3,000 members, and Skelly might have signed up a few hundred.

I sent someone to talk to him, to ask him to step aside. His response was simple: "No. If Patrick wants me to step aside, let him ask me directly." I invited him to Queen's Park, where I told him that I thought he was a star. I told him there were lots of opportunities for him in the party. But I needed more female candidates. I also told him that he probably heard rumours that I would not approve his candidacy. And much as I liked him and was grateful for everything he had done for the party, I was asking him as a favour to step aside. He said, "OK." His supporters were upset, but he did step aside. I had tipped the scales.

Another example of my tipping the scales was with Caroline Mulroney. I wanted her to run and had pursued her for about a year. She believed in gay rights, climate change, sex education and all the things that represented a modern Progressive Conservative party. I was friends with her father, Brian. We belonged to the same tennis club. I played tennis with her husband. But she didn't want to run in the city of Toronto. I presented her with Etobicoke-Lakeshore, as her kids played hockey there. She didn't want to run there, either. We showed her polling in Burlington, Ont., but her dad felt that this was a swing seat. He wanted a safe seat.

When Julia Munro, the MPP for York-Simcoe, decided to retire as the longest-serving female MPP ever, I called Brian and told him that this was the safest seat I could offer — and perhaps the safest seat in the province. Peter Van Loan, the MP in the same riding, discouraged her initially because he thought she faced opposition from the very right wing Trillium Party. This was a riding, he argued, that had done well with the Reform Party, another very right wing conservative party. He felt she would not be in sync with a rural riding that might favour a harder right wing candidate than what she represented.

We had a bad conference call, where Van Loan almost talked her out of it. I thought the train had gone off the rail, and Mulroney was really upset. Frankly, I didn't agree that this riding was so hard right. Many people from Toronto have moved there in the retirement years. The riding in my view is more moderate. But Mulroney was concerned with what she had heard on the call.

I asked Soliman to call Van Loan. He said, "What are you doing, Peter? We want her to run. You are supposed to be encouraging her. Can you help us, instead of talking her out of it?" Van Loan was actually quite helpful.

In that riding, there were seven people interested in the nomination. I told Van Loan that I needed a favour from him. Could he please talk these people out of running for the nomination because I needed a star candidate, and I needed Caroline?

Van Loan met with each prospective candidate, including the mayor of Bradford and the local riding association president who had also announced her intention to run for the nomination. We managed to get an acclamation. I said to everyone that Caroline Mulroney was going to be a sure-fire minister. She'd serve the riding with distinction. Her nomination was to the betterment of the PC Party. And there is another example of where I tipped the scales.

The fact is that when you are doing well in the polls, people do crazy things. Every political party experiences that. Take a look at Carolyn Parrish's nomination for a federal Liberal seat in 1993, when Jean Chrétien won his majority government, crushing the federal PCs. She was on TV, trashing the party for not running a proper nomination and alleging there was cheating. There were an overwhelming 10,000 people voting. That's what happens when numbers are good, and the stakes are higher. Never in my wildest dreams had I expected people to go to the lengths they did to win.

But I did act. If there was a problem with people falsifying ballots, I got new ballots made up. If people were stealing or stuffing ballot boxes, I said to "hire security." When people complained the volunteers were not running the nomination meetings well, I hired PwC. Each time I heard about an issue, we came up with a solution. We banned organizers who we heard were causing problems from being on-site during a nomination meeting. A great example of that would be Dhillon.

Dhillon had been heavily involved in the PC Party for a long time and well before I was leader. He got involved in provincial politics when he placed his assistant in PC MPP Todd Smith's office. I think he got really excited about politics. He started to hang out at Queen's Park around 2010 or 2011 with Smith and was generally helping the provincial party with outreach. I met Dhillon for the first time in 2007 on a trip to India. He loved being involved in nomination and leadership races. He ended up supporting my leadership, as well as that of Andrew Scheer when he ran for the federal Conservative leader in 2017.

Dykstra and I discussed Dhillon and the nomination meetings that Dykstra was in charge of overseeing. Dhillon and Patrick Tuns had both been accused by party insiders of some shady nomination activities. Dykstra and I agreed that neither should be allowed in the building during the votes. The problem was that Badwal, the party's first vice-president who handled the other nominations, happened to be best friends with Dhillon. Badwal wouldn't take the same approach that Dykstra did. And frankly, while I love Mykytyshyn, people would complain about Mykytyshyn harassing them as well. It wasn't just one person; there were many who were allegedly berating party officials. And every complaint was met with the justification that "they're only volunteers, Patrick."

As a result of the problems with the volunteers, my office and party staff were *voluntold* by me to get down to these nomination meetings, to ensure that these anomalies, harassments, etc., were stopped. Now the complaint was, "Why are leader's office staff and party officials intervening?"

You couldn't win. But it really didn't stop the media from reporting on these anomalies as though they only existed in one party. Many of these reports did not include all the facts.

For example, The Globe and Mail reported that a candidate's application was being held up in Burlington. I had not been involved in vetting or anything else. I let the party officials do their job and I got briefed after the fact. In this case, the reason for the hold-up was because the candidate, Jane Michaels, had claimed on her candidate application not to have had any bankruptcies. When two officials who conducted the party investigations reported back, they found court documents that indicated that she did have at least one bankruptcy. The candidate responded that she had forgotten about that one. Further checks were conducted with a nearby courthouse, and in the end, the investigators found she had been involved in multiple bankruptcies. That is what held up her candidate application.

The Globe and Mail reported another issue in the riding of Carleton, where a guy claimed to have been disqualified as a candidate to run for the party. Did anybody ask why he was disqualified? Well, as it turned out, we found a Facebook page where his position was that those not born in Canada should not be allowed to run for public office at any level. He was asked in his candidate interview by the panel of interviewers, "How do you reconcile this view with Patrick Brown's new modern inclusive PC Party?"

His response was to restate that he felt that those not born in Canada should not be allowed to run for public office. There were five people conducting the interview. After that response, the candidate asked if the committee had any further questions. Soliman apparently said, "Nope! No more questions!"

It was a short interview, and the committee thanked him for his time. He was disqualified because his views were bigoted. Of course, in The Globe and Mail article, no background was provided, and the full story was never told.

To be clear, the party constitution allows the party executive to make up the rules of nominations, and the executive branch made rules to allow the leader to influence the outcome of a nomination. Those rules existed when I was leader, and they still do now.

Retrospectively, I really should have just appointed candidates where there were preferred candidates and be done with it. I should have appointed Karma because I believed she could have been a potential minister.

But I am of two minds on this. On the one hand, I do think a leader needs to have loyal team around him or her. As evidenced by what would happen to me on January 24, which I refer to as my "Night of the Long Knives," having a caucus that you were involved in shaping is important to being able to weather the storms and disagreements that are bound to happen. A leader should not always be worried about some coup that may be brewing.

However, on the other hand, maybe there's too much power for the leader. When I was in Ottawa, a good friend of mine, MP Michael Chong from Wellington-Halton Hills, put forth a motion on an act designed to make the process more impartial. I seconded that motion. I think there was a lot of merit in what he was putting forward. It might have served provincial politics well.

The motion essentially said that it's not the parties who should run nominations, but in the case of Ontario it would be Elections Ontario to run the nominations. The fact that you can just pick your friend and appoint that person anywhere is perhaps too much power. And even when you don't, there is the perception that you did. It would certainly stop many of the complaints.

It would also mean that the leader would lose the ability to pick people he or she trusts, can work with or would necessarily be a good choice for cabinet. And it could potentially give way to mob rule. The bottom line is that I continue to be of two minds on this. There is really no easy answer.

Did I make mistakes? Sure, and I have pointed some of them out along the way.

But, for those who are of the opinion that nominations are clean processes when a party is in a striking position of winning a general election, that is utter *bull*. And, for those who believe that there is a way to control every aspect to ensure total integrity of process, that's utter bull as well. Finally, there is no party that has not had nomination issues, whether or not the media has covered the story.

Politics is about power. It is also about wanting to do good things. But to do those things you need power, and that means having to win to get your chance. Politics attracts many people for many reasons. Thankfully, not all of them are successful in taking office. But the motivation of power can and does often lead to some pretty bad behaviour. With 900 candidates vying for 124 MPP spots, and with the polls showing the PCs ahead and Wynne's popularity in the absolute basement, these matches were often vicious.

I did my best to handle crazy situations that I could not have predicted.

Apart from my nomination frustration, the year ended on a high note. On Saturday, November 25, 2017, we unveiled the PC platform that would take us into the June 2018 election. It was called The People's Guarantee because it was a covenant with Ontarians that if I broke any promises I made, I would resign. In front of a packed Toronto Congress Centre hall, I signed my name to the pledged commitments that I had just unveiled. I was serious. Too many people believe that politicians break their word. I wasn't going to do that, and I wanted to show that I was putting skin in the game — my skin.

For months leading up to November 25, I had been called "The Man with No Plan" by Liberal cabinet ministers. It was a catchy sound bite, which certain writers at the Toronto Star picked up on and quoted frequently.

"Where's your plan, Mr. Brown?" Liberal MPPs would goad me from across the aisle. Brad Duguid, Liberal MPP actually recited the words to a well-known Beatles' song during Question Period on September 20, 2017:

"To quote the Beatles, Mr. Speaker—I've wanted to do this for a long time:

He's a real nowhere man,

Sitting in his nowhere land,

Making all his nowhere plans for nobody."

Oh brother. It got a great laugh from the other side of the House. But just like that old proverb says, "He who laughs last, laughs best." And that is exactly what was about to happen.

While the Liberals and the media laughed at us, and more specifically at me, for having no plan, we had been active over an 18-month period constructing a tremendous plan. I had called upon a few key experts in their fields to become co-chairs of each portfolio in government. They would each work, on a volunteer basis, with the PC critic of that portfolio to consult riding associations, stakeholders and the public. They'd also provide their own expertise in parsing out the most important concepts for the eventual platform. The work involved was gargantuan, and some co-chairs clocked ridiculous amounts of time trying to ensure that they captured the concerns and issues in the consultations, as well as policy and platform promises that could be made.

The resolutions that resulted from this work were then voted on by the party members through an online process which would provide me with the platform direction and create a platform.

There were some major promises that included the largest middle- class tax cut in a generation, lowering it by a staggering 22 per cent. This would be paid for entirely using revenues from a carbon tax that the federal government under Justin Trudeau had mandated. These sorts of commitments were expected of the PC Party. But there were others that were not, such as our health-care commitments, which included the largest provincial investment in mental health to signal to the world that the PCs did have a social conscience and an understanding of human issues. For too long, we as a party had been silent on issues like health care and mental health. The Liberals had dropped the ball on mental health, and the health-care system was a mess. We had a promise for a dental plan for low-income seniors and another to reduce the costs of child care by providing a 75 per cent refund to parents. We promised to upload the Toronto Transit Commission's subways in order to bankroll more expansion and create a more regional transportation service beyond the city's borders.

These were the big commitments, but there were many more, smaller promises designed to make life more convenient and affordable. These included promises such as free Wi-Fi on GO Transit trains and a new $500 tax credit for motorists to buy snow tires.

We promised to scrap some Liberal programs, too. First, we would toss out a Liberal slush fund known as the Climate Change Action Plan; we'd dismantle the $2-billion-a year cap-and-trade program with Quebec and California because it wasn't benefiting Ontario; and we'd withdraw from the Western Climate Initiative. Instead, we would abide by the federal carbon tax, a measure that would put a price on carbon and encourage green solutions. Finally, we promised to introduce a trust, integrity and accountability act to put an end to the political corruption that had become a hallmark of the Liberal government.

In a stroke of genius, it was suggested that we ask Kevin Page, a well-known Canadian economist and Canada's first-ever parliamentary budget officer, to review the costing assumptions behind the platform. Page was known to be tough, rigorous and highly non-partisan, and his stamp of approval was significant and would silence critics.

The visual presentation of The People's Guarantee was fresh and modern. It was laid out to look like a magazine, with a snappy cover that highlighted a big, smiling picture of me. My image was surrounded by key platform promises written in sound-bite fashion using different and interesting fonts. It was meant to be punchy and accessible to the reader. There were pictures throughout and short, catchy pieces that described the promises and why they were important. At the end of the magazine was a section called "The fine print," where the details, including the cost commitments, were provided.

There was tremendous excitement when we handed out the embargoed copies of the magazine platform in the PC caucus room on the third floor of Queen's Park. It was clear that Robertson, who designed the look, had really hit a home run. It reflected my belief that platforms are too often boring, same old-style documents, and we needed something that was splashy. I thought back to the Jean Charest rock concert–style speech I organized at St. Mike's high school. This time, I would be at the centre of the show.

Practising speeches was not typical for me, but I did practise my platform speech more than any other because I knew it would be one of the most important of my life. The teleprompter would only be used to provide some bullet points to ensure that I covered off everything, instead of the verbatim script that is often used. This allowed the address to have a relaxed and conversational approach.

That morning, the Toronto Star had printed a massive front-page exclusive on our platform with full coverage. It was all positive. Most of the delegates were making their way to the Toronto Congress Centre and hadn't yet seen the impressive Toronto Star media coverage, but the rest of the province did. Unbeknownst to me or anyone else on the campaign team, Velshi, my chief of staff, had negotiated an exclusive with the Toronto Star. It was spectacular and dominated the entire front page of the paper. Inside there were more articles.

Many on my campaign team were pissed because they felt that these decisions needed to be vetted by the whole team to ensure that we understood the implications of having one media outlet over another get an exclusive. In fact, in brokering the coverage with the Star, we had upset our long-time media friendly, the Toronto Sun. The Sun had covered a number of issues of importance to us, when other papers wouldn't. Now Adrienne Batra, editor-in-chief of the Toronto Sun, was livid. After all the nasty things written about the PC Party and me, how was it that we were rewarding that paper with an exclusive?

Obviously, from my viewpoint, it was precisely because the Toronto Star was so critical of me and the PC Party that having them positively cover our platform was huge. It was a victory because Wynne and her Liberals believed that for the most part, they had the ears of the Toronto Star, which played heavily in Toronto, an area dominated by Liberal-held ridings. By brokering this deal, Velshi shifted the playing field. Their favoured paper was now giving us great coverage. The image alone of certain arrogant Liberal cabinet ministers waking up to their morning coffee and seeing the front page of the Toronto Star on November 26, 2018, was worth the *mea culpa* I owed to the Toronto Sun. Later that day, I called Paul Godfrey, president and CEO of Postmedia, which owned the Toronto Sun, and I apologized. I knew it wasn't fair to the Sun and I felt very bad. Godfrey, Batra and the Toronto Sun were kind to put it all behind them, and for that I was very grateful.

The turnout for the convention was amazing. The fluorescent lighting in the large hall provided an institutional feel and a stark comparison to the show that was to come. The first part of the day featured the introduction of all the candidates and addressed the business of the party. During lunch, the media attended embargoed briefings from technical staff. The number of media present that morning was significant. It seemed like everyone knew they were witnessing the platform for the next government of Ontario.

After lunch, the delegates waited impatiently to re-enter the main hall for the unveiling of the platform. After a long wait, they were herded back into the main hall. Over lunchtime, it had been transformed into a dark auditorium with a show-like stage that suddenly lit up while music blared from large speakers all around the great space. My sisters took to the stage to introduce me. Then it was my turn. I walked out with my sleeves rolled up, ready to deliver the future.

I spoke to the crowd as though I was in their living rooms. I told them how hard things had been in Ontario. And I prefaced each major platform piece with a succinct story that illustrated the challenges people were facing. When the promise was finally announced, big cheers would go up.

 Everyone felt the emotion as I talked about the kids who had attempted harming themselves and who had waited silently on lists for help. I believe that most people have known someone with mental illness, so this hit a nerve. And, when I announced the largest provincial investment to date in mental health, the room exploded. Everyone jumped to their feet in protracted applause. Just as I thought, no one was expecting it. After I announced the last major policy plank, I walked over to a mammoth-sized contract on which I signed my name. If I didn't deliver on these key commitments during the term, I would resign. Balloons cascaded from the ceiling, and the audience roared.

***

The year 2017 ended on a high note. I was poised to lead the PC Party to victory in the election on June 7, 2018. We were winning by-elections in safer seats by wide margins. We were winning seats in ridings such as Sault Ste. Marie that we hadn't held since 1981. Even CTV referred to me as "an ascending star in the Canadian political universe (who) now threatens to topple Liberal leader Kathleen Wynne and become Ontario's next premier in the June provincial election". Our coffers were full of cash, party debt was all paid off, our memberships were through the roof and we had star candidates running for us. And, even the Toronto Star was praising us for the platform we had just unveiled.

By January 2018, my personal life was also looking up. GG and I had rekindled our relationship before the end of 2017 and were spending time together again. We were taking it slowly, but it really felt great. I was a happy, lucky guy.

Tomorrow would be January 24, 2018. I'd be playing tennis. Something I loved to do. The stars were aligned — all was right in the universe.

What could possibly go wrong?

CHAPTER 5

NIGHT OF KNIVES

I listened to my caucus, my team, my colleagues. I remember that early into the call, someone said, "Oh, that fucking Lisa has already gone out with a statement."

As I listened in, what I heard horrified me. Some of my colleagues had transformed into hyenas.

Late in summer 2016, I took a trip to Ontario's Georgian Bay, to the cottage of William Grenville Davis, the province's 18th premier. Davis had been my model for governing. At the time, we were about one week away from the Scarborough-Rouge River by-election.

On a very sunny day, we sat for about four hours on the beautiful, spacious deck on Davis's stunning property, a property he referred to back in the day as "Queen's Park North." I wondered how many political dignitaries visited, and how many deals had been brokered at this place during his time in public office. If only those smooth granite rocks could speak, I was sure they'd have plenty of great stories.

Davis's son Neil and Neil's wife, Ruth, were also there, as were some of his other children and their spouses. Davis designated the person who brokered the meeting as the "boss" of the session and the person who would determine who would sit where in the circle of chairs on the large deck. It made me smile that, after so many years, Davis still understood the art of politics.

Being at the cottage of such an icon in Ontario's political history was pretty cool. I wanted to use the time to explain what I was all about, answer any questions he had and ask for advice. We spoke of specific issues, political stances, of the great and ugly realities of managing a big blue tent and, of course, of my riding- by-riding prospects. The details of these conversations will remain forever at that cottage, guarded by the granite below.

There is, however, one thing about that meeting that I'll share. It's a piece of advice Bill Davis gave me before I headed back to the large boat that would return me to Honey Harbour. The advice was simple, almost too simple:

"The most important thing, Mr. Brown, is that you have around you good, smart people whom you respect and trust. That is essential. Not just people who tell you what you want to hear. Mr. Brown, whom do you have around you that you really trust? Who gives you honest and good advice?"

At the time, I didn't realize just how important that one, simple piece of advice actually was, nor how it would come back to bite me in the ass. On January 24, 2018, I would find out.

In the introduction of this book, I set out what took place on the worst day of my life: the CTV emails; the complete shock; the rushed statement I made at Queen's Park; and the walk back to the black sedan in which Shan Gill, my driver, would take me back to my temporary home, the apartment on St. Mary's Street.

I entered the apartment. It looked the same as when I left. Yet, everything was different. I had now officially averted the world to the fact that something big was going to break at 10 p.m. If anyone out there wasn't paying attention, they would be now.

A small group had gathered at the apartment: John Sinclair, executive director of PC caucus services; Goldy Hyder, my debate coach and CEO of Hill +Knowlton Strategies; lawyer Mike Richmond, my long-time friend; Walied Soliman, my campaign chair and friend; Rebecca Thompson, my director of communications; Rob Godfrey, son of former Blue Jays' President and CEO Paul Godfrey and a supporter; and my sisters, Fiona and Stephanie. Dimitri Soudas made an appearance, then left soon after.

It had been 9:55 p.m., as I was standing dazed in front of the media in the caucus room, that Alykhan Velshi, my chief of staff; Andrew Boddington, my campaign manager; and Dan Robertson, my chief strategist, had all resigned via Twitter, in a cafeteria in the basement of Queen's Park. While I made that walk down the marble stairs of Queen's Park's west wing, my only knowledge at the time was that not one of these guys was with me, as had been promised. I was alone.

Richmond had seen them leave 15 minutes before we all left for Queen's Park. "Where are you going?" he asked.

Apparently, they were going to the Legislature building early to ensure that everything was "set up" properly for my hasty press conference. They clearly did make it to the Legislature, and I think that set up is an excellent description of what they did next. While I stood at that podium upstairs, trying to get out the message that they had instructed was my best course of action, they got out their smartphones and tweeted out their resignations.

I found out about all this when I got back to the apartment. There were more rats jumping ship: Josh Workman, who had been hired by Andrew Boddington and who had been helping organize southwestern Ontario, quit; and Nick Bergamini, my press secretary, quit. Bergamini had worked in Harper's office and had been hired by Velshi. I suspected late in the game that Bergamini might not be acting in my best interests. He wasn't working with Becky, which was a little absurd, since she was the director of communications. Bergamini presented himself the next day, January 25, to the office and got his old job back under the new interim leader, Fedeli. Ken Boessenkool, who had been brought in by Velshi to work on the campaign, also quit.

That one I couldn't believe. Boessenkool resigned because of these allegations against me? Gimme a break!

In 2012, Boessenkool resigned as chief of staff to British Columbia premier Christy Clark. It was widely reported that he was dismissed for allegedly making an unwanted advance in a bar toward a young female political staffer in the B.C. government. In his letter of resignation, Boessenkool admitted to acting "inappropriately" and said he regretted his behaviour. He apologized to his wife and four young daughters.

When Velshi implored me to hire him as part of my campaign team, I didn't want to because of those allegations. But Velshi pushed hard and vouched for him, saying he was very sharp. And now Boessenkool was resigning? Unreal.

In my view, none of these men behaved at all professionally. Worse still, not one had the courage or decency to resign in person or to provide me directly with any communication on their intentions while they crafted my next moves. Had I known that they intended to bail, I would not have taken their advice on the press conference or anything else, for that matter. I would have had the opportunity to release them from their duties and attend to my crisis with people who I felt would be there for me.

Think about it. When a senior-level person decides to resign from a company, they aren't asked to participate in sensitive strategy sessions. They are thanked for their service and often they are walked out the door. I should have had that same option. Instead, I operationalized a plan constructed by three assholes who knew that it really didn't matter what happened because they were all about to jump ship, like the rats they are.

The fact that they did what they did, and the way in which they did it, speaks volumes about their character, or in this case, lack thereof.

I will always believe that each would have been regarded with respect had he acted professionally and discharged his duties to me as leader in a professional manner. While in my employ, they should have done everything possible to protect me, and they did not. They were aware that something was going to break, but they did nothing. I'll address that in the next chapter.

At 10 p.m., CTV aired its broadcast live with Lisa LaFlamme, who introduced the piece as a CTV National News exclusive: "Disturbing allegations of sexual misconduct against the man who wants to be the next premier of Ontario."

The newscast featured images of me walking to the ill-advised press conference, and the shadow of a woman (her identity was withheld) talking about her alleged experience. CTV also provided audio tapes of the second self-described victim. Now it was all out there.

I had been receiving text messages from my girlfriend, GG, throughout the evening. She was still at her workplace, SickKids Foundation, because she knew some on the team did not approve and didn't know we had rekindled our relationship. GG was growing progressively more frantic. She'd take little breaks from her work to respond to the influx of calls she was getting on her cellphone, and she was reading all the media reports that started flooding in.

Her messages to me were consistent: "DO NOT RESIGN."

Finally, well into the night, GG figured her best bet was to head back to Mississauga to get her car and show up at the apartment to support me.

Meanwhile, CTV continued to run with hourly repeats of its news broadcast. Social media had exploded with the story. My phone was ringing off the hook.

Hyder was very honest with me. He was clear, that in his opinion, it was doubtful that I could survive the CTV story and the domino effect it caused. "Your team, Alykhan and Andrew and Dan... they fucked you, Patrick. And in light of the story and because of them resigning, I really see no way that you can survive the weekend." I knew I needed to survive the night and the weekend before making any rash decisions, but I trusted Hyder, and I was taken aback that he was so defeatist.

The staff's resignation was, in Hyder's view, an insurmountable optics problem, even though it had been a result of the domino effect caused by the CTV story.

Walied Soliman and those who remained at the apartment were there to support me, no matter what I wanted to do. We debated whom to make my chief of staff, now that Velshi had decided to move on. The group agreed on Becky or Richmond. In the end, we agreed on Becky.

I huddled with those who were still part of my team. Walied believed we needed more time to think, and if I were to survive we needed to win the weekend. First and foremost, we needed to keep as many caucus and candidates onside. He suggested that we start calling caucus members to shore up my supporters. Most were not picking up our calls.

Monte McNaughton, MPP for Lambton-Kent-Middlesex, did answer. He warned me that other caucus members were already mobilizing against me. Ross Romano, MPP for Sault St. Marie and my old law school buddy, told me the same thing. I called MPP Rick Nicholls, who was in the Caribbean. I think he may have had a few beverages in him at the resort when I called, but he immediately offered his full support.

I talked to Toby Barrett, who was also the caucus chair. He told me that in his part of the province, people were telling him that the whole thing smelled like a takedown, and that many felt the allegations were BS. He also gave me his support. I felt a glimmer of hope.

I was told that Fedeli, my finance critic, was already campaigning to be party leader. I tried to reach him, but he wasn't picking up. *Odd*, I thought. Fedeli spent the last three years sucking up to me and jumping every time I called.

It was then that Rebecca Thompson noticed the invite that was sent out by email, requesting an urgent conference call with caucus. My phone had been ringing off the hook all night, and I had stopped looking at it, so I missed it. Becky came into my room and told me that caucus had organized its own conference call. She asked if we should call in and just listen. My guess was that they were not expecting me to call in.

The call was set up by Michael Harris, MPP for Kitchener-Conestoga. Harris sold the meeting on the grounds that this was pretty bad stuff, and caucus needed to get together to discuss it all. I find this somewhat ironic, given that a few months later, the party's nomination committee would turf Harris after reviewing some flirty text messages that he exchanged with an intern back in 2012. Apparently, he was not married at the time, and no complaint was ever filed by the intern who didn't work for him. There was a great deal of chatter that the real reason for his removal was actually because he wasn't "in" with Ford's team after Ford won leadership of the PC Party. I can't imagine he sees the world the same way now as he did when he booked that caucus call, but who knows?

At 10:52 p.m., and before any statement was issued by either Premier Wynne or NDP leader Andrea Horwath, our very own Lisa MacLeod sent out the following tweet:

> Every citizen of Ontario deserves respect. Everyone has the right to be free from unwelcome behaviour or advances. I do not and will not tolerate abuse or harassment, and I will do everything in my power to fight against it. My heart goes out to the women who have been impacted by this behaviour. It takes courage to come forward and make these claims. These women deserve our support and thanks.

Maclean's magazine got hold of a secretly taped recording of that conference call, which it had transcribed and published a month later. "Sources" identified the speakers though some of the speakers were not identified. As far as I can recall, the transcript of the recording as printed by Maclean's on February 24, 2018, is authentic. I have included much of that transcript below and have put in front the names of the people speaking when identified. My comments are in italics:

The conference call began at around 10:30 p.m. Rebecca Thompson called in, but we stayed silent for 20 minutes or so, and I listened to my caucus, my team, my colleagues. I remember that early into the call, someone said, "Oh, that fucking Lisa has already gone out with a statement."

As I listened in, what I heard horrified me. Some of my colleagues had transformed into hyenas.

> John Yakabuski, party whip: "I can sit here and say, in my 15 years, nobody has been any more loyal to their leaders than me. I feel for Patrick, but my honest view in the climate we live in today and what we saw with Glen McGregor's press [report] there…we would be facing 1993 for the federal Conservatives if Patrick leads us in this

campaign. And I don't think he could have handled the press conference any worse. I mean, I thought his statements were fine, but then the way he, it's just, he talked about the court of public opinion. That's where we're living, folks. Every one of us depends on that public opinion in our own ridings, too. And we're not impervious to what's going on with our leader. I think that jointly, we should, in a very kind and compassionate way, request as a unified caucus that Patrick step down."

The recording chirps with beeps and rings as more caucus members enter the call. One agrees. Another says a roll call must be held. Caucus members are still dialing in.

Some are careful to avoid assuming the allegations made against Brown are true.

"It's Gila [Martow] here. I think we have to be very careful that we're not saying we believe one side or the other side. We don't know the facts. But just that we have to ask that he step aside because this matter has to be settled while he is not the leader and then if it gets settled to everybody's satisfaction, we would welcome him back to the team in some capacity. Whatever was available. But I think that we have to be careful with the language that we're not accusing anybody."

The roll call continues. The conference is chaotic and beeps throughout, indicating someone has joined or dropped the call.

"It's [Jeff] Yurek speaking. We need a statement tonight. We can do one as a group tomorrow, but we need something tonight because I'm getting hammered already."

A female MPP says: "Well, we all are getting hammered. We've got to take a breath here."

Yakabuski begins to draft a statement on behalf of caucus on the fly: "Dear Patrick: On behalf of the members of Progressive Conservative caucus, I am writing to inform you that it has been decided that it is in the best interest of the party and ultimately the people of Ontario that you resign your role as leader of the PC Party of Ontario and leader of the opposition effective immediately."

"Asking him to resign? That's weak," a male voice responds.

"That you *must* resign," Sylvia Jones corrects.

Other members weigh in. "Good enough for me." "I second it."

Next: the matter of whether Brown will be able to remain in caucus.

"I hadn't considered that yet, but I would suggest if he resigns as leader, that's not likely going to be an issue because we're not going to see him at caucus. But having said that, he is still the sitting MPP," Yakabuski says.

He's still an elected member, one notes.

Finally, MPP Ted Arnott asks caucus about the allegations themselves. The CTV report was still so fresh that some members had not heard the claims in full.

"What, exactly, do we know for sure?" Arnott asks.

"Two women accused him and so far, four — two of his top staff and two of his top campaign team — have urged him to resign," Jones responds.

Actually, these "top staff" members had not urged me to resign. They told me that they we would fight these allegations and win. They called a press conference for me, which they sold as the way to get out ahead and start the fight. They crafted my address — never mind that it was the worst possible thing for me to do under the circumstances. They did all this while they were planning to resign.

"Who are the women? Do we know who they are, and what exactly are they alleging?" Arnott continues.

"I've read the allegations, Ted. They're two young women, and there's — I'm not going to reiterate," [Randy] Hillier says.

Figures. Randy hated me so much because we launched an internal investigation into his alleged physical intimidation of a PC candidate. We were contemplating sensitivity training or kicking him out of caucus entirely.

"Next question," a male voice continues, "has anybody reached out to Patrick to try to talk some sense into him?"

"Don't you think it makes sense to approach him and tell him this is about to happen before we do it, and allow him the opportunity to resign on his own?" Arnott asks. "He has to resign after we do this, and it's worse for (us) if it plays out that way."

Yakabuski: "Well it's not like we're going to publicize it, but he's made it clear. He's allowed. Ted, we're in the midst almost, you could say we're in the campaign. He put his self-interest ahead of us and the party by basically saying you guys can all quit, but I'm not. I really want you to think about that."

Martow says she is texting with Walied Soliman — one of the senior campaign staffers who has chosen to stand by Brown. "I said: 'It's Gila here. He will be asked to resign by caucus. Unanimous. It would be far better if he steps down while he clears his name. I'm on the conference call with caucus right now.' So at least we, you know, we tried to make it more pleasant."

Laurie Scott asks what the party constitution says, and Sylvia Jones concedes that it doesn't grant caucus the right to fire the leader.

Arnott: "If we call for his resignation unanimously, it doesn't matter what is in the constitution. He will have to resign."

The roll call continues, as the caucus tries to figure out who is on the line, who the caucus spokesman will be and who is writing the letter.

Ernie Hardeman: "I totally agree with the unanimous position, but I don't agree with the at midnight in the night," he says, "when there is no news cycle, a unanimous decision on a caucus call when not everybody is there. We should meet tomorrow morning and we should settle this all in a proper way. Tomorrow morning is still considered acting immediately."

But others quickly note this is simply not a political climate that will tolerate stalling.

Yakabuski: "Today, we had the doctor from United States gymnasts, 175 years in jail. We had the Leader of PCs in Nova Scotia resign — same issue. We had the RCMP going on about numerous multiple recruits and candidates for recruitment being sexually assaulted by a doctor. The climate is such that any delay only gives more time for negative response from people that feel that we're not ready to be the government."

The caucus debates whether to issue a statement saying they will meet in the morning, which would give caucus time to review the allegations more thoroughly, and to ensure the decision is truly unanimous. But as the conference continues, messages about the allegations against Brown and his dismal press conference continue to proliferate on Twitter.

Yurek: "We live in an age of social media; we can't wait for the next news cycle. This is happening now. Lisa [MacLeod] is getting multiple tweets and comments about issuing a statement. So we need to do something now. I can't wait until the morning on this. I am not going to let my reputation dwindle and be questioned because of an allegation on our leader, and we're just mollycoddling around trying to make the right decision. We need to act now. We need to make a statement. Otherwise, I'm going to make my own statement, because we all know at the end of the day he needs to step aside, show accountability and leadership until this is cleared up."

Caucus unity is quickly dissolving, with the risk that individual members will strike out alone and denounce Brown should the group refuse to issue a collective statement demanding his resignation.

Suddenly, a non-caucus member chimes into the call.

"Hey everybody, it's Rebecca Thompson."

"So I'm sitting here with the leader, with Patrick," she says. "We've listened to your entire call."

The conference goes silent for several beats.
There is muttering in the background.

"Are you listening?" Thompson asks.

Thompson: "What we'd like to do is to have a discussion with you about this. Tomorrow morning. Patrick wants to listen to everything that you have to say. And then Patrick is going to step down."

What? Who gave Becky the authority to say that? I didn't agree to that. Rob Godfrey muted the call and quickly bellowed: "Rebecca, you've got no fucking authority to say that! Shut the fuck up!" He said that in front of everybody, and my sisters chimed in.

The call was unmuted. I spoke into the line:

Me: "You guys, it's Patrick. You guys, I'm always going to do what's right for the party so please don't pre-empt this. I just want to talk to you guys tomorrow to tell you why I feel this is an unmitigated falsehood. But we even have a female who was with me that night who has signed a statement to that effect who was in photos with me that night, saying that this is completely false. But ultimately, I realize this is an age of social media. I am always going to do what's right for the party, just give me the chance to meet with caucus tomorrow, rather than rush into any decisions at midnight."

At this point, I was trying to walk back what Rebecca had said. Above all, I needed time — time to think and time to respond.

Hillier: "Patrick, you don't have a campaign team and you don't have the confidence of caucus. And we're a few short months away from an election."

"There is no other decision to be made."

Me: "Randy, I'm always going to do what's right for the party, but let's go over all this tomorrow. I'm not going to make a decision at midnight."

Hillier: "What's right for the party, Patrick, is for you to step down."

Me: "Randy, first of all you're asking me to accept allegations that are categorically wrong, false, lies. Having said that, even though they are false and lies, I'm a team player, so let's meet tomorrow and find out what the best course of action is."

What was right for the party was to be modern and inclusive. What was right for the party was to have a significant membership, which I had built up. What was right for the party was a solvent party that had the means to launch a proper election campaign. What was right for the party was to attract a great slate of candidates that was more reflective of Ontario. These were MY accomplishments. Patrick Brown was what was right for the party! And I'd be damned to let these bullshit allegations remove me. Regardless of an election win, would the PC Party be so much better off under the stewardship of someone else? I didn't think so.

Hillier: "Your team has vacated you, Patrick."

My team of backstabbers.

Me: "Randy, I've got Bob Stanley here, Walied Soliman here. I've had the caucus chair Toby Barrett call me and tell me I have his full support. Having said that, despite the fact that we have the caucus chair, the campaign manager Bob Stanley, my interim staff, Rebecca Thompson all here offering their support, what I will say is I'm not going to do anything that hurts the party."

Sam Oosterhoff: "This is hurting the party, Patrick. Patrick, this is hurting the party. This is really hurting the party."

Me: "Listen, it's like being hit by a truck with these statements. Imagine this happened to any of you. Imagine people are making up bullshit about you, and you've got no time to respond. So what I'm asking is, let's meet tomorrow and we will find an orderly way to go about this. I'll be party-first."

Hillier: "What would you consider 'in orderly fashion,' Patrick?"

Me: "Well, let's figure that out tomorrow."

Hillier: "I think there is strong motivation and requirement that we deal with this tonight and understand what possibly could be your orderly departure."

Me: "Randy, if it's necessary for me to resign in the best interests of the party I will. But what I want to do is I want to meet with caucus tomorrow. We'll bring Walied and Bob and Mike and everyone, and we will make a decision together. What I'm saying is, let's not rush to a judgement at midnight. And you know we'll talk about everything tomorrow. You guys take your time to [inaudible] folks and we'll deal with this tomorrow."

Hillier: "I think if I could put any stock in your statement, Patrick, it would have required a conference call ahead of your press conference this afternoon."

Here, I felt sick. Hillier was partially right. The press conference was a terrible decision dreamed up by the key people I trusted, who, while selling this idea to me, had one foot out the door already. I should have called a caucus meeting, instead, and not for the purpose of resigning, but to have let everyone know that I was leader, and that anyone who didn't support me could have walked. There'd have been many candidates lined up waiting to run in their place.

Me: "I said if it's the will of the team then I'm prepared to resign. But can we please allow me to do this with some dignity to meet with you guys tomorrow. We have half a caucus on this call. I'm saying that I'm going to be a team player. I've been a Conservative all my life. I'm never going to put the party in a difficult position so we will decide what to do tomorrow. You've got my commitment that if I need to fall on my sword, even though and I stress this, they're complete bullshit lies. Even though they are, I will always do what's right for the party. Let's meet tomorrow, pick a time that works for everyone and I will be there and I'm willing to fall on the sword."

At this point, I simply wanted to buy myself time to think. Too much had happened since I walked off that tennis court only five hours before.

Jones: "I think the number I have is 21 who are on the call, I can't justify to the media that travel schedules did not allow us to meet until 3 o'clock. I just can't."

I had no idea how many were on the call. All I know at this point is that not one of my supporters was on the call.

Oosterhoff: "We need to make this decision tonight."

They wanted me dead now. They didn't care about truth or innocent until proven guilty. They didn't believe in due process or any process, really. They wanted me dead.

Me: "Why don't we pick a time as early as it's possible tomorrow that works for caucus. If 10 a.m. is too early, make it 11 a.m. I think it signals I'm going to meet with caucus to go over this shows that we're taking this seriously."

MacLeod: "I think the time for taking it seriously went when John Sinclair [executive director of PC caucus services] called me this evening and the fact that we lost our senior campaign team. Most members on this call have been elected as long as me — some maybe a little bit longer or a little bit less.

We're going into a campaign and we've just lost it now. I think Patrick, with all due respect, you don't have the confidence of your campaign team. You don't have the confidence of our caucus. You actually have to give those on this call and those candidates you recruited a fighting chance on June 7. And the only way you're going to be able to do that is to reverse your decision that you made this evening on your press conference. And I know many members of this caucus are antsy, but the reality is that we're in a day and age that we need to be very clear about who we are, and we need to be very clear on where we stand. And I think for the good of the party, the best thing you could do is to let us run this Progressive Conservative (party) in the next election without 20 more minutes of this conversation."

OK, if things weren't so awful, I must say that Lisa MacLeod's remarks would have presented some comic relief. Are we kidding? Which Lisa was this talking about doing right for the team? Would it be the Lisa, of the "I Can't Keep Staff Cause I'm So Nasty" Lisa? Or perhaps the "I Can't Work Well with Anybody" Lisa? I couldn't believe my ears.

And of course, speaking of doing what is right for the team, collaboratively, and with a unified voice, wasn't it Lisa who put out her own tweet in support of my accusers at 10:52 p.m.? I wonder if she bothered to clear it with the "team" first, or if this was her way of bullying the outcome she hoped to achieve.

Me: "Lisa, I believe passionately that we need change. I believe passionately in our message. I would never want to stop us from getting to the finish line. One day is not going to make a difference, and you have my commitment that I will do what is right. Another press conference at midnight would be ridiculous."

MacLeod: "Actually, it wouldn't. It would give us a fighting chance tomorrow morning to start off the day fresh."

Yes, well, no point arguing with someone who has now found religion on team spirit, albeit in the context of throwing me under the bus.

Hillier: "Patrick, you are at the finish line. Tonight is the time to make the decision. I think it's clear and overwhelming that caucus wants you to step down and I think you should now consider how best you can do that to save what is left of your reputation, and possibly live to fight another day."

Me: "Randy, I will do what is needed, but I'm not going to do it at midnight. Please allow me to do this with some dignity."

"And I will not be waiting, Patrick," Hillier says.

Good ole Randy, clearly another advocate for "the team approach." If he didn't get what he wanted, he'd do it his way. My political enemies from caucus like MacLeod and Hillier were going for the jugular.

Yakabuski: "We can't have every member going on their own, doing things singularly which doesn't speak in a unified voice with every member trying to save their own ass, which is not what we need to do, we need to save our collective ass. Patrick, I think you can see what's happening here. The longer this goes on, the more chance there is of further damage, of people doing things and people will feel under a great deal of pressure. And (if) people are approached by a women's group or something? Or somebody like Laurie, our women's critic. What is she going to say? If I'm approached by the sexual assault centre in Renfrew County? How am I going to answer this?"

Me: "You guys, I'm not going to make a decision at 11:20. I've got the team here. I've got Bob and Walied and everyone let me talk to them. I'm not doing this at 11:20. I will do what's right for the party."

Hillier: "It will be better for you, Patrick, if you do it. Rather than caucus. We're giving you the option to exit on your own terms tonight before caucus sends a statement out tonight."

(The premier has just posted on Twitter. NDP leader Andrea Horwath is also weighing in, calling for Brown's resignation.) "She beat us to the punch."

Me: "You guys, I'm not going to do this tonight. I'm willing to fall on my sword tomorrow, if that's what caucus wants. But I have been getting conflicting messages. I spoke to [MPPs] Toby. I spoke to Ross. I spoke to others. Having said that, you guys are making it pretty clear to me. I will always do what is best for the party. [Inaudible] give me the dignity to do this properly tomorrow. Here's Mike; you want to say something too."

Richmond: "It's pretty clear listening to this where caucus is, and we all see what is going on here. I know you all, I know you are all great people I know you all put yourself in (Patrick's) shoes to some extent and recognize that after politics a young guy has to make a living and find something else to do — whenever that after-politics is. I'm asking you a favour as what I consider friends, let him do this his way so he still has a chance of doing something with his future. Please. Just out of pure decency."

Jones: "He could have a good future when he beats the allegations in court but we've gone past the public opinion, that's the problem, Mike."

Yakabuski: "Mike, when you say on his terms, what do you mean on his terms? Like 10 o'clock tomorrow morning? Like, like, this can't go on. Like, it can't be after tomorrow."

Richmond: "Give him some time to write a statement or a speech and do it in the light of day not in the cloak of darkness which is embarrassing, itself."

MacLeod: "We didn't embarrass ourselves, okay? We were all just at work and coming home for supper when all this broke, Mike."

Vic Fedeli says that if Brown going to resign, then caucus needs to show it is decisive.

Vic's remarks came as a surprise to me. His was the biggest betrayal because I always thought I treated him well. I recall Fedeli sucked up to me non-stop with compliments like, "You're the best leader we ever had," and, "So proud of the work you're doing in northern Ontario, you inspire me..." He'd lay it on thick; it was over the top at times.

Most of these people I thought were with me, my colleagues. And suddenly, to hear them viciously attack me was devastating.

Smith: "And listen, as far as Patrick having the opportunity to defend himself and tell his side of the story, trust me, the media is going to want to cover that. But we have to rip that Band-Aid off tonight if that's the decision that's going to be made. Patrick will have every opportunity tomorrow with the biggest media throng that he has ever seen to tell his side of the story and to defend his own reputation. It's not as if we are taking that away from him. That is going to happen. But as far as we're concerned, for the good of the party, I think we have to put out a statement at midnight tonight after a thoughtful and heartfelt conversation with caucus, the leader came to the decision that this is the right thing to do he will be holding his own press conference at 10 o'clock tomorrow morning."

Rebecca Thompson begins to argue about the news cycle, saying it begins at 6:00 a.m. Caucus doesn't need to put out a statement before 6:00 a.m.

(Jones asks Rebecca to confirm that the resignation statement will go out at 5:45 am the next morning.)

Hillier: "Caucus should put out a statement now, saying that Patrick Brown will be announcing his resignation tomorrow morning."

Thompson: "No, no. Again, again, again, for the sake of..." Rebecca Thompson tapers off. "He's been your leader for the past three years for the sake of ensuring that..."

Hillier: "For the sake of the party, it needs to be done tonight."

Thompson: "Randy, for the sake of the fact that he can have a dignified release about this."

"He can still have that," a male MPP says.

Thompson: "He can still have that without caucus pushing down the pedal on this."

Hillier: "We're giving you the option to do it now."

Richmond: "…human being for five…let it be his decision, not yours. Don't execute him. You don't need to execute him. Please."

Thompson: "By the way, you'll make the story worse."

Hillier: "If you drag it out.

Caucus members finalize the details of the release; they want Brown to focus on his resignation, not to use the opportunity to defend the allegations of sexual impropriety.

I would let Rebecca draft something, but I would say no to any draft. That's what I would do. I wanted to talk to caucus face to face. I needed to buy some time; I needed time to think. At this point, things were moving quickly, and all I felt was shell-shock. Everything was a blur. I was not about to make big decisions on the spur of the moment.

By now I was exhausted — emotionally, physically, mentally and in every other possible way. I just wanted to get off the line and have some time to think and plan my next move in light of the fact that these allegations were lies.

Walied Soliman gets on the line and asks for a thirty-minute break. The caucus will reconvene at midnight.

Wynne's Tweet 11:12 p.m. January 24, 2018:

> It's a difficult and brave thing to do to come forward in the way these young women have done tonight. My government and I have been clear on the issue of sexual harassment and assault. In fact, our policy and our ad were called "It's Never Okay."

I went back to my room with my sisters. So much to process. That call was a punch to the gut.

I shouldn't have been surprised and I wasn't by the reaction of a number of caucus members. I knew that Lisa MacLeod was humiliated three years ago when I beat her in the leadership and by a country mile in own riding. She was always a difficult person who had issues with everyone. Her reaction was no surprise.

Randy Hillier was a hard-right caucus member who detested the moves I had made on the party on inclusion, on the environment, on gay rights and on Islamophobia. He was the definition of the angry white man. I had warned him on numerous occasions not to be drunk at party functions. He hated me, and he was jumping at this opportunity to take me down. I had also muzzled Hillier on a bunch of issues. His position now was also no surprise.

We were also investigating allegations that Randy Hillier had physically accosted another candidate, Goldie Ghamari, now the MPP for Carlton. This was reported by multiple news sources when Ghamari took her complaints public. There was a good chance the way the investigation was going, that Hillier would be taking sensitivity training or have been booted from caucus. Not surprisingly, after I was no longer leader the investigation disappeared.

I believed that Hillier and MacLeod had been the ring leaders that night.

But there were surprises for me. As I mentioned, the biggest surprise for me was Fedeli. *Fedele* is the Italian word for "faithful" or "loyal." In this case, Fedeli was anything but. In my view, his interest in forcing my resignation had less to do with the allegations against me and more to do with personal ambition. Why else would he be actively campaigning for party leader when the television set was still warm from the CTV 10 p.m. national newscast? I saw it as opportunism and betrayal.

In retrospect, I believe that Fedeli was pissed at me for recruiting two high-profile candidates who could rival him for the position of finance minister: Peter Bethlenfalvy and Rod Phillips. Bethlenfalvy served as the chief investment officer at C.S.T. Consultants Inc., which offers a registered education savings plan. He has also held various other senior financial roles: senior vice-president of financial regulations at Manulife Financial; co-president of DBRS Ltd., the bond-rating agency that downgraded Ontario's long- and short-term debt ratings in 2009; and he had been the senior vice-president of Toronto-Dominion Bank in New York. He was a big catch.

So was Phillips. He had served as chief of staff to Toronto mayor Mel Lastman. He had been Jean Charest's federal chair in 1997, and president and CEO of the Ontario Lottery and Gaming Corporation, Postmedia and of a Toronto organization promoting the city's urban agenda called CivicAction.

Fedeli had always expressed that finance was his dream posting. He also lobbied some of my friends for that position. But, despite having made him finance critic, a mutual friend Cam Milani told me that Fedeli was petrified that I had recruited Bethlenfalvy and Phillips, each of whom could also have been finance minister. The fact is that I hadn't made any decisions about whom I would put in the role of finance minister if we had won the election. And I suppose that would have angered Fedeli, who believed he should be the heir apparent. But my philosophy is that you don't measure the drapes before you get the office.

At the same time, I always believed that Fedeli was a very competent guy. I felt he could have handled the cabinet position very well. But I really wasn't settled on who would be finance minister. I believe he knew that, and that it petrified him.

I was also very hurt by Yurek's comments. I always thought I had treated him very well, too; however, as I played back the discussions in my mind, I realized that his concerns were not personal. His constituents had not accepted the 2014 decision by the then-leader of the PC Party, Hudak, to announce the 100,000 job cuts. He was likely worried that if caucus didn't step in immediately, it would trigger a similar reaction from his constituents. However hurtful, Yurek's remarks were more about fear than they were about betrayal.

And I was really hurt that my deputy leaders, Sylvia Jones and Steve Clark, were calling for my resignation on the phone. I thought we worked well together, and that they might have at least sought to hold a separate call with me first.

Becky and Richmond became more despondent with time and began sharing their concerns with my sisters. Becky was now convinced that I couldn't survive. And, both Richmond and Becky were concerned that there was a movement afloat to remove me that went far beyond these allegations. In fact, the allegations were the result of this movement. CTV had given them wind. These accusers had been part of a bigger scheme. And if I didn't step down as leader, whoever was behind all of this would bring out more ammunition. They threw out the possibility that the next concocted story about me may be criminal. What if their brother ended up in jail? My sisters were horrified at these scenarios, yet they were still adamant that I should ignore all advice to resign.

Walied called my mother and asked her to convince me to resign. She was pissed and refused to do so.

Becky went into the side room to work on my draft resignation. I told everyone remaining that I didn't want to resign at 6 a.m. I didn't want to cave to a lie. Everyone left the room, and I was alone with my sisters.

A second call with caucus took place at about midnight. It was short, but I wasn't on it. I only discovered after the fact what had occurred. I was with my sisters in my bedroom and hopeful that a draft resignation letter might distract caucus sufficiently to buy me some time. I had no interest in approving its release.

I later found out that on that call, Walied read the resignation letter that Thompson and he had drafted. Hillier apparently had concerns that it was not clear enough.

I was told that Walied erupted at that point. "Is there anyone else besides Randy who doesn't understand what I just read out?"

No one else came forward, and the short call ended.

After the call, I walked into the side room. It was then that the bottom fell out of my world. Becky told me that the statement of resignation, the one that had been read to the caucus, "was gone."

It had been sent out to the world over Twitter, *my* Twitter account, to be precise. And the resignation statement was also posted on the PC Party website.

Becky had gone ahead, without my approval, and sent out the resignation. I freaked: "What do you mean, it's gone?"

She told me she was doing this to protect me. She told me that someone had to protect me. Walied appeared utterly defeated — shell-shocked. He was out of it. He confided that when Becky sent out the statement, he had assumed she had my go-ahead. He told me that he was surprised when I looked surprised.

Wow. Again, something very big was sent out without my approval. The first time it was the famous sex education letter, promising to abolish the curriculum during the Scarborough-Rouge River by-election. But this one was fatal.

Feeling sick and light-headed with shock, I went back into my bedroom and collapsed onto my bed. With my sisters by my side, I burst into tears. What had just happened? In just seven hours, I had been gutted like a fish.

RESIGNATION

Published on January 25, 2018:

These allegations are false and have been difficult to hear.
However, defeating Kathleen Wynne in 2018 is more important than one individual.

For this reason, after consulting with caucus, friends and family I have decided to step down as Leader of the Ontario PC Party. I will remain on as an MPP while I definitively clear my name from these false allegations.

Over the past three years I have led a major transformation of our party taking it from 12,000 to 200,000 members, fundraised more money than any provincial party in Canadian history, and recruited some of the most qualified and diverse candidates in the history of our party. I have developed a pragmatic and winning campaign platform after a historically comprehensive policy process.

These important building blocks are essential for defeating Kathleen Wynne this year and her tired government that has repeatedly made reckless decisions and put insiders ahead of the people.
I'm confident the president of our party and caucus will convene an expedited process to elect my successor who I look forward to working with.

Did I think of revoking the resignation? Yes, I did. But I also thought: *What a shitshow this already had become. How ridiculous would the party have looked once it had been put out on Twitter that I was revoking it? Rebecca Thompson controlled my Twitter account. So how would it look that I put out a statement on Twitter and five minutes later, I am revoking it? How could I possibly survive this, now that a resignation has been put out in my name?*

To this day, I believe that Becky believed she was trying to protect me, but she didn't. She was convinced that more women would be coming forward. None did, even a few weeks later, after I threw my hat in the ring to get my old job back. To this day, as I write, not one other woman has come forward.

After my resignation had been sent out, it hit me: *What do we do as a party, if I am not the leader? Who was going to pick up the torch for a moderate, inclusive PC Party with me gone?* At about 2 a.m., Walied announced that Caroline Mulroney was on the phone and wanted to talk to me.

She was almost in tears and told me that the sole reason for her involvement in politics had been because of me. I recruited her, and she believed in what I was trying to achieve. She told me she was devastated at what had happened, and that she knew this was not something I would do. Caroline couldn't believe what had been done to me. Finally, she also told me that she was being advised by her staff to put out some "vanilla" statement on the matter, but that she was conflicted and didn't know what to do.

I told Caroline that she really needed to take the torch and lead the party, and that I would help her through it.

GG had arrived outside the apartment at midnight and had waited until she saw Bob Stanley, Rebecca Thompson and Walied Soliman getting into a cab. She then knew it was safe to come up to the apartment. When she arrived upstairs, the only people there were me and my sisters, Fiona and Stephanie. Everyone else who had been there was gone.

GG didn't leave my side for the next three weeks. She took a leave of absence from work, as she didn't want me to be alone.

There had been many women who came on to me during the course of my political career. I always wondered whether they were interested in me for who I was as a person or because they thought I was about to be premier or MP, or councillor, and because I was getting a lot of media attention. I never knew what their real intentions were.

It's hard for people to understand that power and media attention are tremendous aphrodisiacs. You expect to see that sort of attention with hockey players or millionaires, not with politicians. But guess what? It does happen, especially when you are a young politician who has ambition.
It's tough to explain until you actually see it. My sisters found the attention I got quite abnormal. They thought it was ridiculous that people would just line up to talk to me. But politics is not a normal world.

Anyway, I was always skeptical about women. They would be there on the good days, but would they be there on the bad? Now here I was, ruined — at least that was what I felt at the time.

Bam! And then it hit me. The people I treated very well, people who traded on my name and power as party leader and who made a living off me, had ruthlessly abandoned me, and worse, they had hung me out to dry.

But here was this wonderful person who had been hidden away from the world, from the media, shunned by my political team and taken for granted by me. In my worst possible hour, and despite my not going to bat for her throughout the relationship, there she was waiting for me outside my apartment until 2 a.m., when it seemed like it was all over for me. GG would be there for me for the next three weeks — perhaps the worst three weeks of my life.

She showed a level of maturity during the course of these events I didn't expect, but I really appreciated. I saw in her everything I could possibly want to see in a life partner. I loved her deeply, and I knew that she loved me. Funny how clearly I was seeing this now, even though everything else seemed blurred.

I opened the door, and GG walked through. Sobbing and exhausted, I collapsed at the apartment that night with her. My sisters set up beds on the floor in the kitchen. The next day, I left Toronto and went back to my home in Barrie. *Screw them all.*

> "My thoughts turn immediately to the women who came forward, knowing how difficult it is, it can be … uh … to salute them for their courage and their leadership."
> — TV statement from Prime Minister Justin Trudeau

Five months later, Trudeau would face his own #MeToo allegations. Interestingly, he reflected somewhat differently on these. As Kelly McParland of the National Post explained: "Trudeau is giving himself a #MeToo exemption from his own standards…. zero tolerance, it appears, only applies to others."

CHAPTER 6

PUTTING IT ALL TOGETHER

"I believe the women...I will not sign Patrick Brown's nomination papers."

He believed the women? I was surprised at Fedeli's cavalier, holier-than-thou attitude, given that he knew full well that he may have dodged a bullet himself.

It was not until the next day, January 25, 2018, that I began to fully realize what had happened to me, and that what CTV had started was now escalating into an insurrection. I read with disappointment the statement put out by Caroline Mulroney via twitter:

> We are living in a powerful moment where women and girls across Ontario, across Canada and around the world are ending their silence—and their stories of sexual harassment are being heard.

> We must always listen in hopes that the future will be different for women like us, and for young women like my daughters. When we hear allegations, we must listen. We must make sure these injustices are never tolerated, and that we respect and honour the brave women we are hearing.

> This is a sad day. Women are facing yet another story of harassment. We have heard too many of them. But women across Ontario will continue fighting together. We are working to build a world where no woman has to say "me too" ever again.
> Caroline Mulroney

Wow. That was certainly more than the "vanilla" statement that Caroline spoke of in the wee hours of the morning. At this point, nothing should have surprised or disappointed me. But after the conversation of the night before, this really did. And it hurt. When I spoke to her, I pointed out that this statement didn't reflect at all what she told me on the phone. Caroline answered me that her staff sent it out, and she didn't even know what was in it. I had no idea at the time that her "staff" was now made up of two of the three Horsemen who bolted from my barn the night before: Boddington and Robertson.

I then found out that my former chief of staff, Velshi, who had also resigned the night before, showed up the next day at the office of the leader of the official opposition in a suit. What was he doing back at the office?

Velshi was reporting to work. As I was told, he ran around the office declaring that "this [my resignation as leader of the party] is the best thing for the PC Party." He was heard saying, "Don't be sad. This is a great day for conservatism."

Also on the day after, hundreds of people changed their Facebook profile pictures, deleting any that showed me. While many of them believed me and not the allegations, the general gist was that the truth didn't matter. Survival was the issue, and they felt that they couldn't be connected to someone with those allegations against him. I felt like I was living in a scary movie, when your life is being erased before your eyes. Some people who wanted to see me said they wouldn't meet with me in public. It was humiliating. I felt abandoned.

On January 26, Fedeli, who was named interim party leader, made the following press release:

"I am asking Mr. Brown to take a leave of absence from the Ontario PC caucus while he has a chance to defend himself…I believe the women… I will not sign Patrick Brown's nomination papers." [If I tried to run in a Barrie riding in the spring vote.]

He believed the women? I was surprised at Fedeli's cavalier, holier-than-thou attitude, given that he knew full well that he may have dodged a bullet himself. A little-known fact is that in December 2017, I received a handwritten note from an individual who worked for the party. In that note, she accused Fedeli of inappropriate behaviour. The letter had been left on my Queen's Park office desk. While, frankly, the accusations were not anything I could picture being consistent with Fedeli's character, my personal assessment of him was obviously irrelevant and not enough to disregard the allegations.

Fedeli was informed that I intended to look into this matter. I also sent a strong message to him that he was not to contact or be around that individual. I decided to speak directly to the staffer since the note had been sent to me personally. She was more than willing to talk to me. She was adamant that she didn't want any action or any investigation done, period. She wanted it to go no further. I respected her wishes, and certainly without her involvement an investigation would be less than productive. I understand that soon after Fedeli became the interim party leader, the woman was let go, but kept on the Legislative payroll.

I was told by that individual that she was furious to see Fedeli's sanctimonious statement, in light of her own accusations against him. The day after my takedown, when she heard Fedeli say, "I believe the women," she called me up and said, "That son of a bitch; I'm going to crucify him, nail him to the wall!" She asked me, "Do you want me to do this?"

I responded, "I don't want you to do anything you don't want to do. That *last* thing I want is anyone saying you are coming forward because of me." I told her my advice was crystal clear: "Do whatever you think is right, but this cannot be about getting back on my behalf."

After that, the woman's lawyer at the Wilcox Law Office contacted the media, and on January 30, 2018, the allegations were made public. Some say it is the reason why he never did run for leader of the party. Of course, none of what she alleged in her note was proven in a court of law or ever went to court.

There's nothing like defeat to understand who your real friends are, and who was just along for the ride. As I watched everyone pile on, I will say that there were quite a few decent people who actually cared about me and reached out, including Laureen Harper, wife of former Prime Minister, Stephen Harper; Peter MacKay, former federal minister; Prem Watsa, founder, chair and CEO of Fairfax Financial Holdings; and Carlo Fidani, philanthropist and chair of Orlando Corporation. There were caucus members who also reached out, including Norm Miller, Ross Romano and Gila Martow. To these people, I will be forever grateful.

One individual, in particular, stands out. Kim Kieller, a local Barrie lawyer who had been sexually assaulted years ago, came over with baked goods. She told me that all she could think of doing to help was baking, so she brought fresh, homemade butter tarts. She also confided to me that she had never shared her own story, but she wanted to now. She had known me for 20 years and she could not believe that the allegations made by these women were true. More importantly, in her view, these allegations diminished her story and other real stories of abuse.

Rob Ballagh, a local doctor, also wanted to come by with his wife. My friend Brian Storseth, who had been a federal MP with me, drove to Barrie to stay with me. Alex Nuttall was around a lot. Phil McColeman, an MP and friend, offered me his place in New York. Brian Jean, former Wildrose leader, had a place in Australia and invited me to stay there for a bit.

My hockey buddies would show up to pull me out to play hockey as a distraction. Obviously, GG and my family were around. From caucus, Todd Smith reached out, and Toby Barrett and Rick Nicholls, which I really appreciated. Many weeks later, when I went to the Legislature, there were many other MPPs from all political stripes who treated me very kindly.

I was inundated with emails and text messages from people who were supportive and just wanted me to know that. I didn't respond to any of these messages. It was all too raw, and I was overwhelmed.

I went underground for about a week after the Night of Knives. I stayed at my home in the township of Oro-Medonte, Ont. GG called SickKids Foundation, where she worked, and told them what happened and that she would require time off. She took three weeks off from work. Fiona, my youngest sister, took two months off from her legal practice to be there for me.

I think it was the late Sen. John McCain who said that after his defeat to Barack Obama in the 2000 presidential election, that he slept like a baby: he'd sleep for a few hours, then wake up and start crying. The days that followed my resignation were dark and numerous. I, too, slept like a baby in Sen. McCain's terms. I'd fall asleep for about four hours and wake up with that awful sinking feeling, when the reality of my situation returned to mind.   Mornings were awful. I'd pull myself out of bed with a gnawing feeling in the pit of my stomach.

Not all the messages I received were supportive. We would get nasty emails from reporters. My sister Stephanie had some weirdos following her around. As a result, Fiona installed an alarm system at her condo. I had my house swept for bugs and hired my long-time hockey buddy, Justin Heran, to provide some security. It was a weird time. We really didn't know who was out to get me.

Stephanie looked after Mom while Fiona and GG concentrated on looking after me. My mom, who had never struggled with depression, started getting anxiety attacks. She wouldn't leave the house for months. All the things she loved to do, such as babysitting her grandkids and playing tennis, were cancelled. A few times she'd book a walk with a friend or invite a friend over for a few minutes. But more often than not, she cancelled these appointments. It was hard for my parents to watch me get beat up by what seemed like everyone at the time.

My dad would call me from the Brampton courthouse or from his criminal law office where he worked. "Paddy, no one believes this." His calls were regular and encouraging.

What surprised me was the number of people who were worried that I might commit suicide. I can honestly say that despite the horror of my predicament, I never for a second thought of doing that. That doesn't mean that I didn't have a severe existential crisis: How could my entire life be defined by some lies told by two women anonymously? It was harrowing. The accusers had ruined me with their lies. I was convinced that my pursuit of public life was done.

I didn't want to leave home, but I had to. I was scheduled to have a cyst on my spleen removed at Barrie's Royal Victoria Hospital (RVH) and I felt that it was important that this procedure not be postponed. After all, it could have been something serious. Afraid and embarrassed to be seen in public, I wore a baseball cap and sunglasses. I didn't want to talk to anyone after my world had crashed down around me. As I sat in the waiting room, a man recognized me. He walked up to me and put his arm around me and said, "Hey, Patrick, everyone believes you. We know this isn't you." At that point, every single person in the waiting room realized who I was. And every single one of them started lining up to shake my hand and tell me that they believed in me. It was a very emotional experience for me.

Coming back from the hospital, I stopped at a gas station in Barrie, and a middle-aged woman came up to me and said, "Patrick, stand up for yourself. Everyone believes you." I broke down into tears.

Those experiences at RVH and at the gas station gave me my voice and my strength back. I realized then that people at home believed me and were on my side. It was then when it hit me that things weren't over for me, that there was an incredible sense of goodwill out there for me. I would survive, I would thrive and I would vindicate myself.

And it was after that, that I called my former campaign chair and asked to get the copy of the email sent from CTV the night of January 24. I now had the resolve and the stomach to go through that email line by line and read every single word. I was committed to doing what that lady told me to do: stand up for myself.

I had purchased plane tickets to travel to Costa Rica with GG and stay at the beach house of a hockey buddy, Shea Thurlow. He had invited me down, thinking that a change of scenery would do me good. But now I couldn't bring myself to get on the plane. I needed to stay in Ontario and fight these ridiculous allegations that I was able to review more clearly. I also needed to figure out who was involved in setting me up — who was *behind* the CTV story?

I had little doubt that there were people behind the scenes who shopped around these lies. I also had no doubt that there were many political enemies who stood to gain from my demise, and those who jumped on the bandwagon. CTV legitimized this pack of lies. And I blame CTV for my takedown.

I knew the name Glen McGregor. In the 1990s, he worked for *Frank* magazine, a tabloid rag that traded on rumours and making fun of current affairs personalities. I have no idea how many lawsuits were filed against them. But you get the idea. It wasn't considered ethical journalism, nor did it pretend to be.

McGregor had been associated with a controversial magazine ad featuring a contest that invited young Tories to "Deflower Caroline Mulroney." Women's groups were appalled and joined together to denounce the ad as an "incitement to rape." It was a very bad joke in extremely poor taste and quite insulting to women. If you ask me, CTV putting *that* McGregor on *this* story was a bit of a bad joke in poor taste as well.

In any case, CTV needed to be brought to justice. I asked Richmond to do some research for me on who would best represent me in a defamation case. With his help, I hired Howard Winkler and Julian Porter. Reading their respective profiles, I knew I was hiring the most respected lawyers in the field. Winkler only took on litigation cases which he felt were of public importance or personal interest. Porter, now in his eighties, is an icon in Canadian law and has decades of experience, including arguing cases before the Supreme Court of Canada. He's well-known for his ethical standards and his ability and has authored a number of books on law. Both lawyers had been consistently and formally recognized by their peers in the area of defamation law.

Over the next weeks, Winkler and Porter pored over the allegations of the two accusers. They also interviewed some key witnesses whose accounts had supported me. Some of these witnesses had been contacted by McGregor at CTV, but for some reason, their accounts ended up on the cutting-room floor.

I had also hired some private investigators about a week after the Night of Knives, which was a costly move and not something anyone in their right mind would do unless he or she were actually innocent. I wanted to know who was behind this set-up — information that would have been irrelevant to any lawsuit against CTV, but was important for me personally.

When it came to investigators, we heard that the best in the business was Tom Klatt, a retired Toronto homicide detective. Klatt was also hired by the Sherman family to investigate the deaths of Honey and Barry Sherman, two well-known Toronto residents who were found murdered in their mansion. I also hired a fellow in Barrie who was the head of the Canadian Association of Private Investigators. These two worked well together. Finally, I hired Felix Valdez at OBN Security and Investigative Consultants Inc.

Valdez was a known quantity to me. He had been introduced to members of my team in fall 2017, through Peter Proszanski, a well-known lawyer who also did some fundraising for the party. At that time, Proszanski called my office. His law firm dealt with private investigators on a routine basis for insurance claims and other issues. He said we needed to meet with his top private investigator, Valdez from OBN, as soon as possible.

Walied Soliman, Alykhan Velshi and Shiv Ray, my tour director, met with Valdez, who explained to the three that he had been visiting a PI firm that his agency subcontracted from time to time. While at their offices, he noticed that there were surveillance pictures of me on a computer screen. Using some sort of undercover camera, he took pictures and now shared them with my guys. The photos clearly showed me getting in and out of my car. They had been taken in 2015. It was old surveillance and because of this, we weren't too worried. Still, Ray told my driver, Gill, to be on the lookout and aware of anyone tailing me.

In December 2017, Gill noticed that we were being followed, and he took pictures of the licence plate. We sent the picture to Valdez and Proszanski to find out who the car belonged to. After that, we all went on the December break.

About a week after the Night of Knives, Valdez reported back to Proszanski and me by phone that the licence plate belonged to the same PI firm that had been tailing me in 2015, the one that was a subcontractor to OBN, where Valdez worked.

I went to see Valdez at his office. There he explained that not only was the surveillance company the same one, but the person paying the bills for the surveillance was also the same individual.

Then he dropped the bomb. The name of the person paying the bills for my surveillance in both 2015 and 2017 was Jeff Kroeker, a big supporter of Elliott, my 2015 leadership opponent. Kroeker had been Elliott's former chief of staff at Queen's Park and also her former law partner.

"No," I told Valdez. "I'm sorry but you have this wrong."

I could understand that in 2015, Kroeker might have had me tailed to see if I did something stupid that could have benefited Elliott's campaign. That was believable. But now, Elliott was no longer in politics. She had suffered a bad injury from a fall. There was absolutely no reason for a supporter of hers to have me tailed. Especially since in December 2017, I was still very much the leader, and she was the patient ombudsman.

"You don't believe me?" asked Valdez.

He then picked up the phone in front of me, and with it on speaker mode, he asked the question to the investigator on the other side of the call. "Look, I just want to verify: Who was the guy who paid $118,000 on the Brown operation?"

"Jeffrey Kroeker." Was the response from the other side.

I pulled Valdez over and whispered very low, so as not to be heard. "It can't be. Ask him to specify 2017, *not* 2015!"

Valdez repeated the question differently. "So who brought in the money, the $118,000 in 2017?"

Again the response, "Jeff Kroeker — same guy who paid in 2015."

I wanted Valdez to report these findings to the party president, Badwal, and I made a tape of that call, which I still have. The weird part about this is that the party executive had uncovered phone records that showed that throughout December 2017, someone at party headquarters regularly spoke to Kroeker. Since Kroeker was no longer involved with the party at the time, I found it very odd that he'd be getting calls from PC headquarters. After all, Elliott had left politics at that time.

The phone records also indicated that directly after a call to Kroeker, on December 5, 2017, PC Party headquarters called a guy from a religious group who was on the public record as despising me for taking the party in a more moderate direction. There was one other interesting fact that was contained in the phone records that might have potentially related to one of the accusers, Joanna Bloggs. I'll get into that later.

As a result of all this, the following note was forwarded to the police, along with the phone records themselves by then PC Party executive director:

> In January 2017, the Ontario PC Party conducted an investigation into the surveillance of the previous PC leader Patrick Brown. The leader's office and the tour office became aware of an active surveillance of the previous PC leader. The party engaged in an outside security company OBN Security at the time to identify the source of the surveillance. The assumption was this was an effort of another political party given the PC Party's high standing in the polls.
>
> However, the investigation reported the findings to the PC Party president, executive director and PC Fund chair, that the payment behind the surveillance was Jeffrey Kroeker, and active member of the Ontario PC Party and was involved in the 2015 PC Ontario leadership race.
>
> Prior to completing my duties as executive director of the party, I asked for an audit of the party phone system and any unusual phone activity. The audit showed highly irregular phone activity leading up to the January debacle. Please find attached the phone records. The irregularities identified are highlighted…
> The integrity of our provincial democracy and party democracy must be protected. The party executive does not have the abilities to investigate the highly irregular nature of these findings. I ask that

you investigate whether the shocking events of the past two weeks have any correlation.

Bob Stanley
Executive Director, PC Party of Ontario

So why was Kroeker having anyone tail me in December 2017, when I was party leader? Why was party headquarters in touch with him, and why were these calls followed up with calls to my enemies in the religious right? Could this be part of a coordinated effort to remove me? Did Kroeker know about this CTV story breaking? Was someone trying to dig up dirt or benefit from the CTV story that I was not yet aware of? I didn't have any answers. Just more questions.

By now I was desperate for answers. I then got a call from some guy who claimed to run a media company in San Diego. He told me that the Russians were doing surveillance, and he knew I was being followed. He claimed to know this hit on me was going to go down on January 24, 2018. He claimed to have more information for me. He told me that he had been doing a shoot in Russia, and someone from the Russian embassy told him that what had happened to me had been a set-up by my own party.

The Russians? Seriously? I smelled a scam. I think this guy figured how badly I wanted answers, and he wanted to provide them, whether or not they were actually real. But to me, it sounded ridiculous. I suppose in the United States with all the buzz about the Russian interference in their elections, maybe he thought I'd bite.

Still, after what I had been through, I was prepared to see what Valdez could come up with for the money I had already committed to paying. People in my situation can and are easy targets for this kind of racket.

"Show me some evidence," I told him.

During this time, I had been informed that Velshi, my former chief of staff, had been working against me quietly as early as June 2017. Was this true? Did he get offered something to get rid of me? I really don't know. But I do know that many came forward after the fact to say, "I wish I had warned you about him." Kaydee Richmond did warn me. She felt he was dangerous.

McKay had warned me. Kyle Seeback, Conservative MP from Brampton West, had warned me, telling me that he didn't want to say anything because he had concerns that his words would make their way back to Velshi. "But Patrick," he said, "I had a conversation with Alykhan in which he was trashing you back when you were an MP. He said he hated your guts, and I couldn't believe you hired him as your chief of staff." I wish I had listened to those who came forward when I was in a position to fire him. Why would my own chief of staff be working against me? He stood to be the chief of staff to the next premier. Was he a plant to get rid of me? Who knows?

In the end, other than a few tidbits, the private investigators really didn't provide much help, even though their work did uncover a few knives from within my own party.

I then wondered whether or not the Great Canadian Gaming (GCG) Corporation, a company that owns casinos, might have been involved. It certainly would have deep pockets, influence and motive to see me removed.

Since 2012 in the province of British Columbia, the police had been investigating allegations involving a money-service bureau, a casino and the proceeds of organized crime. But what that investigation uncovered was much more. The fact that money laundering had been occurring was old news. It was the scale of the operation that startled police. On July 22, 2015, the RCMP contacted an official with the British Columbia Lottery Corporation to inform them that "police officers had been looking for a 'minnow' and found a 'whale.'"

The whale was that since 2012, more than $100 million had been laundered through B.C.'s casinos by loan sharks and VIP gamblers, with direct ties to Chinese organized crime units. A Sam Cooper of Global News reported:

> Criminal syndicates that control chemical factories in China's booming Guangdong province are shipping

narcotics, including fentanyl, to Vancouver, washing the drug sales in British Columbia's casinos and high-priced real estate and transferring laundered funds back to Chinese factories.

As a result of those findings, B.C.'s Attorney General, David Eby, commissioned a report to get to the bottom of how this illegal activity was enabled and to provide recommendations on how to stop it. The report was written by Peter German, a distinguished lawyer who held a number of high-ranking positions and had retired as a member of the RCMP after serving for 31 years.

It was made public in March 2018, a few months after I stepped down as party leader.

The report confirmed the flow of dirty money through certain casinos run by GCG, Gateway Casinos & Entertainment, and Paragon Gaming. This money fuelled B.C.'s opioid crisis and inflated real estate prices. In the report, German confirmed that Chinese organized crime networks with roots in Guangdong, Macau and Hong Kong had laundered at least $100 million through loan sharks and VIP gamblers in B.C. Lottery casinos. He later told Global News that the $100 million figure was likely a low estimate.

The companies had claimed ignorance of these activities. Unfortunately, the report did little to counter those claims. It described these companies as having "unwittingly" permitted the casinos to be used as laundromats for the proceeds of organized crime.

In that one word, "unwittingly," German's report absolved the casinos of any deliberate wrongdoing. Instead, he put the blame squarely on the shoulders of weak regulations. Eby blamed the former Liberal government for using the province's casinos as these "unwitting laundromats."

I'm sorry, but how the hell does $100 million get laundered in B.C., and the corporations that own the casinos are characterized as innocent victims of weak regulations? This didn't sit well with me or members of the press, either.

An independent news outlet, PressProgress, looked into possible political connections and discovered that both GCG and Gateway had made sizable political contributions totalling more than $312,000 to the then-governing Liberals over the two years leading up to the 2017 provincial election. This raised serious questions about just how "unwitting" were the actions of these companies or the government of the day.

After that report was issued, many articles began to appear in print and on electronic media, questioning the ignorance of the corporations which presided over these money-laundering services. Stories were published alleging that GCG had been welcoming and assisting Chinese organized crime units for at least 18 years.

Then another story was posted, reporting that GCG operated the casino aboard a Chinese-owned gambling ship called the China Sea Discovery. The ship was closed down a year after it began its voyages due to reports of gangsters, armed junkets and so on. The man who had allegedly bankrolled the China Sea Discovery was the late Cheng Yu-tung, a Chinese businessman, and prior to his death in 2016, the third richest man in China. As it turned out, he had never registered to participate in a gambling business in B.C. The major infraction was confirmed by Eby.

Eventually, GCG pulled out of the casino cruise business following a number of lawsuits. But according to former GCG staff and witness accounts, the B.C. government essentially dismissed allegations in favour of supporting the company's expanding gambling industry. Remember that the provincial government stands to gain from the revenues of these gambling activities.

In August 2017, and well after all the RCMP allegations were being reported in the media, the Ontario Lottery and Gaming Corporation (OLG) awarded GCG with a very lucrative contract to run the casinos in the Greater Toronto Area.

I remember thinking to myself; *This is the company that Premier Wynne wants to have come to Ontario to run our casinos?* I just couldn't understand why they would be putting a welcome mat under the feet of an organization that was embroiled in an investigation involving organized crime, money laundering and drugs, something Ontario is struggling with.

God knows that Ontario was absolutely strapped for cash and desperately needed revenues to pay for the many costly projects, contracts and bigger government that the Liberals had concocted over the previous 15 years. I wondered: *Did they care at all about the origins of the revenues being promised by GCG? Could it be that jackpot of dollars that the B.C. Liberal government enjoyed as a result of "unwitting" laundromat activities was simply far too tempting to give up?*

At the time, we noticed that GCG hired powerful Liberals lobbyists Bob Lopinski and Philip Dewan, a former chief of staff for McGuinty. Lopinski had worked for Wynne when she took office and had run her Liberal war room during the election.

Political election war rooms, besides conducting other more straightforward tactical activities, are generally where all the dirt is dug up and the smear campaigns are concocted. Many in the political world refer to these activities as "ratfucking" — a very vulgar term that I have never used, even though I must confess, it does have a way of capturing some of the essence of the job. Lopinski, the lobbyist for GCG, was a top guy at Liberal Ratfucking Inc. I didn't think much of this at the time.

Our PC caucus made a group decision that we would go after the Liberals in the Legislature on this deal. There were some misgivings, particularly Velshi, who wasn't sure about it. The team debated what to do. Sen. Di Nino and Soliman were both favourable to going after them because they felt that they were dirty.

For one week, Fedeli went hard in the House, asking tough questions of Premier Wynne during Question Period. Then, all of a sudden, Velshi advised me to stop going against GCG altogether. He told me that Fedeli would do so outside of the Legislature. This made zero sense to me. In the Legislature, all MPPs are protected from being sued for the things they say and allege. It's referred to as "Legislative Privilege" and enables MPPs to hold the government to account without fearing legal reprisals because of statements made. Our bench suddenly went silent. But Velshi was absolutely categorical. "Stop it now. Do not go after Great Canadian Gaming."

It just got weird, and I wondered why the about-face? Were people in the PC caucus being threatened? Were they being bought off? I don't know.

In December 2018, Wynne announced again that the OLG had selected GCG for still more contracts. Now it would be the dominant gaming company in Ontario. Shortly after this, I was taken down as PC leader.

As I mentioned in a previous chapter, my friendship with Kepinski, a minority owner of the Fallsview Casino, had put me on a bit of a collision course with GCG. But now, as I reviewed things in my mind, I thought that there might be more here.

I reconsidered the facts: GCG's lobbyist was Lopinski. He was part of the Liberal war room. I would be in his cross hairs. After all, I had heard a few journalists confide to me that very senior Liberal operatives were shopping around sex scandal stories about me. It wasn't too hard to imagine that the Liberal war room had knowledge of this or were directing it.

Now, Lopinski's client was GCG. Certainly, that company would have had an interest in seeing me removed. There is no doubt in my mind that had I become premier — and polling numbers at the time indicated that that was likely to happen — I would not tolerate GCG operating in Ontario on my watch. I believe that they realized that, too. They had something absolutely massive to gain by my removal. Here is how I saw it. GCG controlled the majority of casino interests in the province of Ontario, and my being premier would have really negatively affected their book of business. Gaming companies are all about the books.

Was there a chance that GCG was paying Lopinski to get it the licences *and* take me down? GCG had money and links to China's rich and famous. Activities in at least one of their casinos had been linked to Chinese organized crime and money laundering. Maybe one or both of these accusers had been paid, or maybe the sting operation was paid for by them? I can't prove any of this; however, the coincidences were there, and to this day I wonder.

I picked up my cellphone and called Jennifer Innes, a Caledon, Ont., city councillor and Newstalk 1010 radio guest for the Jerry Agar Show.

Two months before the CTV news story against me broke, Innes had called me to tell me that one of the other panellists on the show had pulled her aside and said, "Promise me you will not tell Patrick, but you need to stay away from him. He's about to go down on a sex scandal." Innes and I had known each other since I was 15 years old. Of course, she would tell me what she heard might be going on. Innes was very upset, almost in tears, as she told me what had transpired. Honestly, I didn't take it too seriously.

"Jen, don't worry, there's no sex scandal. I'm fine. This is crazy talk. I'm *not* going down," I assured her at the time. Deep down, I couldn't think of any story that could possibly surface because none really existed, and I was on good terms with former girlfriends.

After the takedown I called Innes back. "For curiosity sake, Jen, who was the person who told you that I was going down and what company are they with?"

She gave me the name of the panellist and the company: Navigator, which is a well-known lobby and strategy firm. Jaime Watt heads up Navigator and is also a strong supporter of Elliott. However, that was not the angle I was pursuing here.

I followed up. "Jen, could you do me a favour and ask if Navigator has ever done work for a company called Great Canadian Gaming?"

Innes answered, "Patrick, When we talked about the gaming issue on the radio show in November, that panellist couldn't comment and had to declare a conflict because Navigator was doing some work for one of the big casino gaming companies."

Who knows if Navigator did or didn't have a connection to GCG? It never appeared in the Ontario lobbyist registry as a lobbyist for GCG. But was Navigator providing strategic advice to GCG or instead to one of its competitors? How I'd have loved to know.

Regardless, it was significant to me that someone at Navigator was aware of what was going to happen to me two months before it happened. In my view, all these dots seemed strangely interconnected in some weird way: Kroeker, Navigator, Elliott, Bob Lopinski, GCG.

Just for the record, to this day, I don't think that Elliott was ever involved at all in any of this. But I do believe that some around her were, especially Kroeker.

The unique money-laundering method seen in B.C. casinos has become known internationally as the "Vancouver Model." At the time I am writing this book, this company still has all its casino contracts in Ontario.

With all these possible accomplices and motives spinning in my head, I put together my own investigative team. It was made up of me, GG and my sisters. We started getting tips, calls and leads. By now, my sisters were getting calls from all kinds of unlikely sources who had information. It was a real rollercoaster.

In the early days, it was very difficult to get people to come out on the record. We'd get all excited that a specific piece of information would change everything and prove that this was all a set-up, and that I was innocent. Then the individual would get cold feet and would just shut down. Lucky for me, this wasn't always the case, and eventually some people actually changed their mind and put things on the record in affidavits and statements that will be used in my lawsuit against CTV.

In our attempt to clear my name, we started moving beyond the allegations and the accusers to determine who, if anyone, had been feeding CTV. Had anyone paid these women for their stories? Had anyone been paid after the stories went public in order to ensure that I would never return?

Early on, I eliminated the Toronto Star as being the architects of my demise, even though I considered it briefly. After my leadership victory in 2015, the Star had sent reporters to interview people in bars, in Barrie. It was a pretty non-stop search. Kevin Donovan, investigative reporter for the Star, later told Soliman that despite best efforts, they hadn't really found anything, and that they typically didn't miss stuff. There was nothing they could find prior to 2015.

There were some who were simply messing with me. One lady, whose Twitter handle was "Medgadewar97," wrote: "I'll destroy your career just for fun." This was a person who never met me, but I was told she got kicked out of the Conservative Christmas party in Ottawa for bad-mouthing me. So that might be why she posted that tweet. Who knows?

In our investigation, we started with the allegations themselves. Without CTV providing a last name, it was difficult at first to identify the accuser, who was referred to simply as "Joanna." However, we started to do more research. CTV had identified Joanna as having attended Innisdale Secondary School in Barrie "over ten years ago." CTV said that she was underage at the time of the incident. Armed with these bits and pieces, we located Innisdale high-school yearbooks and we were able to narrow our search.

From the voice recording that CTV played, we were able to identify the accuser. That voice was identified by mutual Facebook friends as being 100 per cent the voice of Joanna Bloggs. I personally didn't know Bloggs, except to recognize that she hung out at some of the bars in Barrie.

Now that we knew the accuser's name, I was able to come to some conclusions. It would have been impossible for this woman, while she was in high school, to have been in the house she described with an upstairs bedroom and a door. I didn't live in that house until after Bloggs had graduated from high school.

What relevance did this have? It established that at the time of the alleged incident, Bloggs had not been in high school and had not been underage. It established that a significant claim made by this accuser was not holding up, which speaks to the credibility of her story. The claim that I was hitting on an underage woman in a bar was a huge strike against me in the eyes of the public. The fact that this was not true meant a lot.

On February 1, 2018, I posted this to my Facebook page to begin sharing some of the things I was discovering:

Earlier this week, I said the truth will come out. I have been investigating the anonymous allegations against me and can prove they are false. I will clear my name.

The first accuser told a story about an incident that she claimed took place in my second floor, upstairs bedroom with the door closed. At the time of the alleged incident, I lived in a ground floor, open concept apartment and there was no second-floor bedroom nor a door to any bedroom. THIS STORY IS FALSE. Interestingly, I understand from the first accuser's Facebook and from people we both know that she was housemates with a CTV reporter.

The second accuser's story is also absurdly false. It was she who tried to kiss me, while the woman I was seeing was in another room. I stopped her immediately and offered to drive her home, which I did. There are at least three witnesses, one of whom even spoke to CTV, that refute the details of her allegations. CTV left that out of the story.

Since the alleged incident, the accuser regularly presented herself as being my supporter and friend, including attending my events (she sat at a supporter table at my speech at the Economic Club of Canada in November 2016), requesting I connect her with my colleagues to help her write certain articles as recently as last year, "liking" a significant number of my Facebook posts long after she left my office, and, in fact, she even helped out on my leadership campaign. It is now known that this accuser and one of the reporters had a prior relationship. They both worked and socialized together. At no time did she ever act as someone who was anything but a friend and supporter. THIS STORY IS FALSE.

The #metoo movement is important. I support it. I embrace it. My drive to public service includes creating a safer and more respectful world for women. The #metoo movement is too important to allow outrageous allegations like these to derail it.

These past weeks have been hard. The hardest of my life. The night of January 24 was like being hit by a truck! No words can describe the hurt and pain suffered by me and my family. Yet, I find myself overwhelmed by the support for me across this beautiful province of ours. Thank you for believing me and believing in me. Thank you for your outrage at what happened to me.

I am a fighter. For my family, for my constituents, and for the citizens of Ontario. I will now fight for my name and reputation.

With this posted, I went back to my investigation. Through online research, we were able to determine that one of the reporters who broke the story, Rachel Aiello, not only knew the second accuser, Jane Doe, but she had also been a co-worker and close friend of hers. As we researched more, we noticed that Aiello and Doe had co-authored Hill Times articles together. They appeared in photos together side-by-each smiling. This came as a total shock to me. How was it possible that CTV didn't disclose this link? How was it that Aiello was not immediately removed from the story? And how could anything Aiello reported in connection to this story be taken seriously? Here's a reporter who is covering her friend's story, a story for which the reporter stands to gain, a story that could advance that reporter's career. In my opinion, this is a huge conflict of interest.

Then, on February 13, 2018, at about 3:30 p.m., CTV's McGregor made a call to Josh Valler at his law firm. Valler is a civil litigation lawyer in Barrie. He had volunteered in my 2006 campaign and worked for me over a few summers. Though we had known each other since 2004, we drifted apart after 2010.

McGregor introduced himself and advised Valler that he, McGregor, was just following up on some stuff. He asked if Valler knew what was going on in the news about me and if he was surprised by the allegations. According to Valler's sworn statement, he had only become aware of CTV's allegations against me after they aired on January 24, 2018. Valler told McGregor that he was surprised and that he never had any indication that I would behave in that manner.

Then McGregor asked if Valler knew Bloggs, which he did — they had been pretty close friends in the past. He explained that they would go for coffee once in a while and would talk on the phone from time to time, and that their families had also known each other for some time. He told McGregor that throughout the years, he'd see Bloggs around town and would say "Hi" to her, but that eventually the interactions tapered off.

Then McGregor asked Valler if he knew a person by the name of Jessica Sparato. Valler didn't have any recollections of her. Afterwards, Valler went online and looked her up. It was then that he realized that Sparato was a server at Jack Astor's in Barrie, when he was a teenager.

It was on that call with McGregor when Valler found out for the first time that Bloggs had identified him as the mutual friend who drove both Bloggs and Sparato to my place after a night partying at The Bank or the Queen's. McGregor did not indicate the day, month or year that this allegedly occurred. To be clear, no one from CTV ever contacted him regarding this story prior to going public with it on January 24, 2018. Nor had anyone from CTV contacted him after that broadcast, until this phone call.

At that point, Valler told McGregor that he never drove Bloggs and Sparato to my place, period. Valler understood from his voice that McGregor seemed shocked by this answer.

He also told McGregor that at the time in question, there would have been no chance that he'd have run into the girls at the bar, because he would have been 18 and therefore underage and not in a bar. Based on CTV's media reports and without clarification by McGregor that Bloggs had not in fact been underage, Valler persisted in assuming that Bloggs must have been about 17 years old at the time, which would have made him about 18 years old.

Whatever the year, Valler told McGregor he never drove Bloggs or Sparato to my place at any time, whether he was of legal drinking age or not.

Then McGregor asked a very peculiar question: Did Valler know a woman by the name of Jordana Springgay? This was a name that was never mentioned in any of the allegations. It was not a name I knew. And why was McGregor asking about some woman who didn't seem to figure into the allegations at all?

Well actually, Springgay worked for CTV in Vancouver. I believe that it was Springgay who gave Bloggs's story to CTV since Bloggs lived in B.C. I can think of no other reason why McGregor would raise her name. And I believe that McGregor was expecting that Valler would have not been acquainted with the name of Springgay at all. Then CTV could breathe a sigh of relief that Springgay had no personal connections to that specific accuser, Bloggs (unlike with Aiello and the accuser, Doe). If my suspicions on this are correct, it would certainly explain why McGregor was so shocked at what he was about to hear from Valler.

Valler responded to McGregor that he did know Springgay and that he knew her through Bloggs. Valler was also aware that Springgay now worked for CTV in Vancouver, and that she and Bloggs were best friends in high school because they all hung out together. He also told McGregor that he had regular contact with Springgay over the years and even invited her to his 25th birthday party in Toronto. What Valler didn't mention is that Springgay and Bloggs had also been roommates.

According to Valler, McGregor seemed absolutely shocked at what he was being told — that the CTV colleague in Vancouver was actually part of a group of friends and very close to the accuser. This, together with the Aiello/Doe connection, seemed to me to indicate that both stories were now stained with conflict. In my mind the dots were converging.

As a result of all these findings, CTV had to issue a new report. In it, it had to recant the part of the story which claimed Bloggs had attended high school and that she was underage at the time. CTV should have also printed that Valler, who had been named by Bloggs as the mutual friend who drove her to my place, actually denied having driven Bloggs to my place. And, finally CTV should have disclosed the Springgay connection, whatever it entailed. Instead, the February 13 story that CTV put out after my Facebook post and after the interview with Valler was baffling.

ACCUSERS STAND BY THEIR STORY

She [Bloggs] now says that she was of legal drinking age and out of high school. Brown was a Conservative Member of Parliament at the time of the alleged incident.

191

It has been a painful ordeal, her lawyer David Butt said.

"Just the backlash, the misogyny, the hatred, the online trolling of false, demeaning, and very hurtful things has really taken a toll," he told CTV News in an interview.

In a statement addressing the first accuser's timeline, Butt said: "These are the sorts of collateral details that inevitably fade over time... These sorts of issues arise routinely in historical cases and cannot be blamed on survivors, because coming forward is such a difficult act for which it often takes years to gather the strength and courage."

On Sunday, Brown posted a Facebook message saying he'd been investigating the allegations and "can prove they are false."Alise Mills, a conservative communications advisor helping him, said "forensic analysts" are probing the claims.

"Patrick has hired someone to do the forensics, a P.I., he's got a very strong legal team," Mills said in an interview on an Ottawa radio station.

The first accuser maintains the incident happened during a visit to Brown's home with a mutual friend.

That friend told CTV News he has no recollection of the night.

The first accuser said Brown offered her a tour that ended in his upstairs bedroom.

Brown claims the incident was "factually impossible" because, at the time, he was living in a one floor apartment....

...In that same home, a second allegation, from a former employee of Brown's who was 19 and in first-year university. She alleged the then-35-year-old MP got on top of her and tried to kiss her when she was very drunk.

Brown said that she was the aggressor.

"It was she who tried to kiss me, while the woman I was seeing was in another room," Brown said in his Facebook post.

"I stopped immediately and offered to drive her home, which I did," Brown said.

In a further attempt to disprove the allegations, Brown claims one of the women had a personal relationship with a CTV reporter who worked on the story.

CTV News took steps before publication and broadcast to ensure there was no previous contact with any of the journalists that would influence the reporting.

"I continue to stand by the detailed account of these events that I have previously provided to CTV," the second accuser said in a statement to CTV News.

CTV News asked Brown today if he thinks the two women accusing him of sexual misconduct are lying. He has not responded.

> — *With files from CTV News' senior political correspondent Glen McGregor and online politics producer Rachel Aiello*

The piece made me sick. It was a weird mix of lies, of omission and spin. First, the headline buried the lede: the accuser, Bloggs, was now walking back a key allegation — she had not been underage at the time the alleged incident took place. That should have been the headline if the intent were to report the news and not simply to defend CTV's position.

And how could any responsible journalists publish a quote from the lawyer of the accuser that essentially characterized such a huge correction as a "collateral detail"? It surely was not. The very notion that the accuser was underage at the time the story broke had a profound impact on the way people viewed me. It had a profound impact on caucus members who were concerned they were dealing with much more than sexual misconduct, that they were dealing with some predatory pedophile, that I was preying on underage girls, plying them illegally with alcohol and sexually assaulting them. These were not "collateral details."

And what the hell did McGregor mean when he wrote that Valler had "no recollection of the night"? This was not a full and accurate account of their conversation. Valler had been clear: he had no recollection because he never drove her to my place. It never happened. A small omission in the story, but one of huge significance. The denial became part of a sworn affidavit by Valler, a lawyer with a great deal more to lose than just his reputation. Falsifying statements on an affidavit could cost him his licence to practise law.

Another point that infuriated me was the way in which they downplayed a relationship between the accusers and CTV journalists. They never actually denied these relationships existed. After all, these were facts. Instead, CTV claimed to have taken "steps before publication and broadcast to ensure there was no previous contact with any of the journalists that would influence the reporting."

What exactly does that even mean? Seriously? How do you do that? Do you ask the journalist, the buddy of the accuser, to swear that she promises not be influenced in her reporting? What steps did they take, exactly? In politics, if there is any conflict or *perception* of conflict, you declare it and remove yourself from the file. And what about CTV's Springgay? No one other than McGregor brought her name up, so she must have had some involvement with the story, as far as CTV was concerned. The notion that McGregor wasn't aware that she and Bloggs were friends showed just how many "steps" were taken.

The other thing that pissed me off about CTV's report was that my Facebook statement of February 1, 2018, had been significantly misquoted. They missed a word — one word — but an important word. In relationship to Doe's story, McGregor quoted me as writing, "I stopped immediately and offered to drive her home, which I did." That is not what I wrote. What I wrote was that "I stopped *her* immediately…" *Her*!

***

I was disgusted by CTV, even after that piece came out offering a formal retraction on the issue of Bloggs being underage. The stories stood for all to read without clarification.

Many journalists commented on the lack of credibility of the accusers' stories in light of the many things that were surfacing. I appreciated this Twitter post by Jonathan Kay, a well-known Canadian journalist who was the editor-in-chief of The Walrus magazine and also a columnist for the National Post:

> @jonkay
> Both of the two women's stories about @brownbarrie are falling apart simultaneously. Never seen anything like this in Cdn journalism. Even in the US only comparable example I can think of is Dan Rather's "memogate" in 2004 (also before an election.)

We went back to our research. Focusing on Bloggs now, we also discovered that on January 19, 2018, only a few days before the Night of Knives, she was posting on social media that she would be heading to Costa Rica for about a month. The timing of the trip was scheduled soon after the story broke. I didn't think much of it, until we discovered PC Party phone records — the same records that had been forwarded to the police by the party executive.

On January 24, at 2:28 p.m., the day the story broke, and before I had been informed of anything, PC Party headquarters placed a call to a travel agent in British Columbia. Now that, to me, was very curious. Why was someone at PC Party headquarters calling a travel agent in B.C., where Bloggs resided the actual day the story broke?

Was there any connection between the PC Party, the travel agent and Bloggs? In short, was there any possibility that the PC Party was involved in assisting Bloggs in her leaving the country after the dramatic "anonymous" appearance on national television?

With more questions than answers, we turned to Doe, who was a huge question mark for me. I read and reread her statements and I watched her blacked-out image as she described her version of events. This was perhaps the most troubling aspect of this whole mess. Doe had been a huge supporter of mine. She worked for me in Ottawa as a full-time intern during summer 2013, the same summer she claims I assaulted her.

She continued to work for me throughout her university year and she returned to work in summer 2014. Doe volunteered to work on my leadership bid in 2015 and she "liked" various pictures of me on Facebook. Most notably, Doe "liked" a Facebook post that described me as a great boss and friend, and that I would make a great premier. Why would someone I attacked do that? Why would someone who I attacked and who no longer works for me do that? Why would a person with such a grievance call me up in 2016 and ask me if she could attend my Ottawa speech at the Canadian Club? I sat her at a table of my personal supporters, and after my speech she lined up all smiles to shake my hand.

I understand that the #MeToo movement is about women who had been silent victims finding their voice. But Doe had not only *not* been silent, but she also actually sought me out when she was no longer in my employ.

I remembered that I had first heard her name in connection to some story about me that CP24 was working on from Soudas, who had joined my team in 2017. He had worked for Prime Minister Harper as his press secretary and eventually his director of communications. Soudas made headlines when he was accused of interfering in a federal Conservative nomination race for the newly created riding of Oakville North-Burlington. The candidate who was seeking the nomination for that riding was his then-fiancée, Conservative MP Eve Adams. The allegations were that they were buying Conservative memberships for people. Both denied the accusations. In the end, Adams crossed the floor to join Trudeau's caucus, and in 2015 Soudas followed and joined the Liberal party. But by 2017, he was back in the Tory fold, and Velshi vouched for him and told me Soudas would help me out as a volunteer.

Soudas came to me a few months before my takedown and told me that he had been asked strange questions by a CP24 reporter, who wondered if I had ever dated one of Ambrose's staffers and if there "had been any issues?" Ambrose had been a minister in the Harper government when I was an MP.

I responded that I had in fact dated one of Ambrose's staffers: Rebecca Thompson. I added sarcastically that I was pretty sure there were no issues there. I told him he could ask her directly. After all, Becky was my current director of communications at Queen's Park. She was someone I trusted. We went back a long way, and both of us had moved on in our personal lives. In Becky's case, she moved on to an important relationship that had resulted in a son. Soudas and I just laughed it off.

About two or three weeks before the January 24 takedown, Soudas came to me again. This time he told me, "Patrick, I'm hearing the name Doe. Maybe CP24 wasn't referring to Rebecca. I'm hearing the name Jane Doe."

Well, that seemed to me as ridiculous as Rebecca with the history I laid out above. Puzzled, I gave Soudas her name and number, and told him to call her himself.

Velshi had a different approach to the situation. "Get a newspaper to hire her, so if she becomes an issue, she'll be working for one of our friends."

Good Lord — what a stupid idea! I told Velshi that was not on. First of all, I was absolutely convinced that Doe wouldn't make up shit about me (whatever it was that the reporter believed the issue to be since the story hadn't broken by this time). But if I were wrong, and if Doe were concocting some story or other against me, why would I ever reward that behaviour with a new job?

Soudas had this theory that perhaps Doe had soured. I just didn't believe it. There was no way.

Apparently, I was wrong. As my family and I tried to reconstruct the events, we stumbled across Doe's biography, which was posted on social media. In it, she described herself in this way: "My research interests include the use/rejection of feminism as a political tool and stem from a 'WTF' moment after Donald Trump was elected as President of the United States."

This was my "WTF" moment. Was that what motivated Doe to do this to me? Her new-found interest in feminism as a political tool? Perhaps she wanted in on the #MeToo movement to make a statement. The movement was still

197

young and had just exploded as a result of the sleazy Hollywood producer, Harvey Weinstein, who used his clout to allegedly assault attractive female stars.

Now a lot of past conversations were popping into my head. I began to rethink those two calls that I received on the evening of January 23, 2018, before CTV broke the story: one from Flynn, a former staffer in my Ottawa office, and the other from King, my Red Bull buddy. As I mentioned in the introduction, they told me that they had received calls from CTV's McGregor about a week before my resignation. But neither was provided any details or allegations, so they had no idea what CTV was really talking about at that point.

I flagged these calls to my senior team. And I got promises that they would immediately pursue a meeting with CTV to clarify and to put them on notice that any allegations they were thinking of making required proper due diligence.

Now, after the fact, I asked myself, *Did my senior team do any of what it said it would?* Judging from the emails that McGregor sent to Velshi on January 24, 2018, it didn't seem like there had been any contact between CTV and my team. Why weren't they protecting me?

Flynn was one of the people who reached out to me after my takedown. Having now seen the CTV broadcast and the allegations, she had information that she believed was very important.

Flynn now told us that she was with Doe at work the next day after the alleged incident, that they were speaking and that she had asked Doe if she had a good time the evening before. Doe, according to Flynn, was "smiling and giggly," and responded that she had kissed me in my room, and that I drove her home right after. She asked Doe if anything else had happened the night before. According to Flynn, Doe was adamant that nothing else had, and she confided to Flynn that she felt guilty about being unfaithful to her boyfriend. Flynn was clear that Doe did not appear to be in any distress or upset as she recounted the events of the night before.

Flynn confirmed that she never saw me buy drinks for Doe. Jim Garland, who managed The Bank nightclub, (a sports bar that no longer exists) had also given a statement to Global that I never bought drinks for anyone. I was considered a cheapskate in this regard.

When we heard Flynn's account of events, we were over the moon. Had this information been made available on January 24, it could have changed everything for me that night because it, too, would have cast a doubt on these allegations. Unfortunately, in McGregor's call to Flynn back in January, he never asked her anything that would have enabled her to tell him what she had just told us.

Our relief and excitement, however, was short-lived. Flynn told us that she did not want to put any of this on the record. Her husband was a federal Conservative MP for Huron Bruce, and he was afraid that CTV would come after him the same way they pursued Nuttall, Conservative MP for Barrie, after he defended me in a scrum in Ottawa. That video, still available on YouTube at the time I am writing, showed Nuttall calling into question the validity of the stories and calling the whole situation "an inside job." Immediately after Nuttall's remarks, CTV began running negative stories about him. Not recent ones, mind you. CTV dug up two-year-old allegations of voting irregularities that took place during the 2015 federal election and without any real reason, it began airing them again.

We were relieved that with time, Flynn changed her mind and did provide my lawyers with a sworn statement. In it, she reiterated everything she told us above, including about the giggly Doe, who confided that she kissed me and was feeling guilty about cheating on her boyfriend. She also provided the following information, which is paraphrased below:

Flynn and Doe had worked together at my office in summer 2013, the summer of the alleged incident. They were also good friends at the time (in fact, their Facebook profiles showed many photos of them together). Doe had been to Flynn's home and met her family.

The night of the alleged incident, Flynn was with Doe, as they had both worked together on the Hockey Night in Barrie event. After that event, she and Doe went to The Bank.

Doe did not appear intoxicated. Flynn did not see me buy drinks for Doe. In fact, she had never seen me buy drinks for anyone.

Later that evening, they both came to my house in Barrie; although, Flynn only stayed about 15 minutes. Doe did not appear to be intoxicated at my home, according to Flynn. Flynn would never have left Doe had she believed Doe was drunk.

Doe did not describe any inappropriate or unwanted behaviour by me that night, as she discussed it with Flynn the next day. Flynn asked Doe if she felt it would be awkward working with me. Doe answered, "No," that it would be fine. After that, Doe never talked about the incident again to Flynn and continued to work in my office through to the next summer.

Flynn also recalled that Doe asked for a raise and received it in summer 2014. Doe felt it was unfair that she was earning the same amount as the new summer students, especially given that she had run the Hockey Night in Barrie the summer before.

Also providing a sworn statement was my girlfriend at the time, Mikaela Patterson, who had been with me on the night of August 15, 2013, and was also a witness. She had come to my apartment the night the CTV story broke, and I stepped down as leader. It was her intention to provide a statement to CTV. That never happened, and as I found out now, it was Soudas who decided not to let her make a statement that night.

Patterson had been told by Soudas, instead, to go home and that she needed to take care of herself. "Patrick is ruined. It's over for him." She had been specifically told by Soudas that he didn't want her coming forward with any statement.

This version was certainly different than what I had been told that night. In any case, Patterson was now ready and able to speak. She not only provided my lawyers with a statement confirming her recollections of the evening of August 15, 2013, but she also gave interviews to Global News and CBC. Paraphrased below are some of the facts she recalled:

Patterson remembered Doe being around me, clinging to me and following me around the house, which annoyed Patterson at the time. According to Patterson, it seemed that Doe was interested in me. I would come over and talk to Patterson, and Doe would follow. She just wanted to be around me, it seemed.

I went upstairs, and Doe followed me up. Patterson recalls that we weren't upstairs for very long, and almost immediately I came back down and said I was going to drive Doe home. According to Patterson, there didn't seem to be anything wrong, and Doe didn't seem upset, nor did I. Patterson added that I was not the kind of person to do the things that were being alleged because I was not forceful, nor inappropriate.

According to Patterson, she, too, didn't think Doe was drunk, and she didn't see me giving anyone drinks. So this whole business about her being drunk while I was sober was not at all corroborated by Patterson, nor by Flynn.

***

With these affidavits in hand, we now turned our attention to the Liberals. I had always heard that they were desperate to dig up dirt on me. I had my garbage stolen in Barrie a lot. When your garbage is stolen, you assume it's some political opponent. They likely didn't find much beyond too many Red Bull cans.

But now, I had several journalists tell me that they had been approached by high-ranking Liberal operatives, who were shopping around stories involving women. These journalists didn't bite.

But this demonstrated some level of coordinated effort by the Liberals. Now I started to think of the 2016 call I got from a buddy of mine, Wyatt Turner, a bouncer at the Queens Bar in Barrie. "Patrick, I'm really shook up about this, but a guy I considered to be really decent, Steve Sparling, came in to the Queens today, asking for dirt on you." Turner told me that Sparling seemed extremely intent, which made him very uncomfortable. Sparling is a big developer. He is also a Liberal bagman and among the richest Liberals in Barrie.

Turner said that he told him, "Patrick drinks Diet Coke. There is no dirt. He's squeaky clean. The squeakiest clean guy I know."

I had also received a call from the owner of Mom's Restaurant in Barrie, where I used to have breakfast meetings once a month on Fridays with my riding association: "Patrick, we want to let you know that Ann Hoggarth, the Liberal MPP, and her staff were in here after you left. They were asking the staff if they heard any dirt on you." They'd come in about an hour after our breakfast meeting.

OK, so journalists are enticed to pursue stories. Liberal operatives are going around asking about dirt on me in various Barrie establishments. This was starting to look like a full-blown campaign.

That's when my sister Fiona got a call from a very unlikely source. I have in my possession a recording of a call placed to Fiona from Laura Miller after my takedown.

Miller is known as one of the Liberal defendants in the gas plant trial that sent Premier McGuinty's chief of staff, David Livingston, to jail for erasing emails. Miller, the deputy chief of staff for McGuinty, was found not guilty. During the trial it, was disclosed that her boyfriend had been hired to wipe clean the political staff's computer hard drives.

In her call, Miller said that she wanted me to know that the Liberals had set me up. She provided a name: Jorge Gomez. He ran Liberal caucus research at the time and also worked for Liberal MPP and Minister Steven Del Duca. I have this on tape. Miller also told us that Gomez had wined and dined women in Barrie to discuss a #MeToo story against me. The Liberals, in her view, had tried to take me down. But now Miller believed that the movement had been taken over by others.

The original plan, apparently, was to have girls come forward with their stories just before the election. It was apparently not the "game plan" that CTV would jump the gun almost five months before the election. My lawyers were provided with this tape. This was sensational, as far as I could tell.

While the tape was not too helpful in my case against CTV, it helped me understand where this whole movement originated.

After the Miller call, I got another shocking piece of information. I started hearing from people that political staff in the Liberal offices was starting to send out signals before my takedown that I would not survive. This would have been in January 2018, and these stories were coming from credible stakeholders. The messages provided at these Queen's Park meetings was that something was going to happen — stay tuned.

Would CTV leak a story to the Liberals? I didn't think so. So how is it that many staffers of the Liberal government knew that something big was going to go down, unless the Liberals had some involvement? That would certainly explain how they knew that a story was breaking that could be ruinous for me. I really could not come up with any other explanation.

In my mind, it was clear that the takedown had been engineered by the Liberals. They may have had help from stakeholders who stood to lose from my being premier. But either alone or with these other stakeholders, they teed everything up. My party, just finished the job.

***

So that was the Liberals. Now, on to the Conservatives.

On January 26, 2018, Soudas sent out a tweet, which read:

> "Ms. MacLeod informed me of rumours and allegations in regard to her then leader, Mr. Brown. She did not have specific details. Just rumors. I strongly urged her to raise these issues directly with Mr. Brown as I was a volunteer and she was a caucus member. ... I also urged her to raise this issue with caucus. She clearly did not."

Oh boy. I recall the rest of caucus being a little thrown by MacLeod's comments that she had heard rumours in December 2017. I knew that MacLeod knew Doe. They moved around in the same circles. They were photographed at events together, and many of these were posted on social media. Though I cannot prove they were friends, I believe that Doe and MacLeod had a very good relationship. Was it a big stretch to think that

MacLeod had a front-row seat? MacLeod and Fedeli appeared to be the first to immediately benefit from my takedown, he by becoming interim party leader, and she by being named to be the finance critic, the top job after being leader. That all happened very quickly after I stepped down. Was it possible that MacLeod had more than a front-row seat? Might it be that she was involved?

Perhaps when MacLeod said to the media after the January 24 takedown that she had "heard rumours" in December, had she been privy to more than rumours? I wondered.

Why did MacLeod not contact me or caucus with whatever she was hearing? I was leader at the time. It certainly would have given me and the party more time to mount a defence against these allegations. Was it because she hated me so much that she wanted this to go public with no chance for a defence? Who told her what?

Soudas had also mentioned to me that a source of his spoke of MacLeod. I had heard that MacLeod had been conspiring against me for some time. In fact, I was told directly by her former staffer that she had been ordered by MacLeod to drop off "brown envelopes" (no pun intended) to discredit me to the CBC in Ottawa. The brown envelope refers to anonymous information usually sent in a package with nothing to identify the sender. Often, these are used by political operatives or interest groups to leak information to the media without anyone knowing that they are the source. I still have the emails between me and this staffer confirming this to be the case.

I think that once the story broke, Fedeli, MacLeod and Velshi picked it up and ran with it. My theory is that they believed it would be a seamless transition to power for Fedeli. MacLeod would become the finance minister in an eventual PC win. In fact, MacLeod championed Fedeli for interim leader, which he became.

So, who dunnit? What do I believe?

Let's start with what I don't believe.

I do not believe that these two accusers independently approached CTV on their own. One accuser's allegations were from 11 years ago, and the other accuser's allegations were five years old. One accuser lived in Ontario, while the other lived in British Columbia. Yet within the few months before the election, they both decided independently to come forward around the same time? Both had strong relationships with CTV.

I had been through a great deal of scrutiny with people following me, sniffing around my garbage, trying to dig up dirt from local bars and people who knew me. Even the provincial and federal parties had vetted me. Yet in spite of all this scrutiny, six months before an election CTV finds these two women, when none had come forward before. This was a coordinated campaign, where lies and fabrications had been designed to bring me down.

I also don't believe that these accusers' actions had anything to do with the #MeToo movement, and both should be ashamed of hijacking what was supposed to help real victims of real predators. When allegations are real, a story breaks, and other victims also begin coming forward. A predator has a pattern of behaviour. It's typically not a one-off. Yet in my case, it was exactly the opposite. These two women both came forward at around the same time, both using the same technique of an anonymous interview with the news outlet. And yet, despite the fact that I became a villain and a household name overnight, despite the fact that have I interacted with hundreds of thousands of people over the course of my adult life, many of them women, no other woman has since come forward. Hmm.

Here's what I do believe. I believe these girls were either paid, coaxed, convinced or, in the case of Doe, maybe her WTF moment around Donald Trump and her new-found interest in "using feminism as a political tool" might have gotten the better of her. It just might be a case where taking up the #MeToo cause became more important for Doe than the facts. Perhaps she was fulfilling some higher sense of duty, and I was simply a convenient instrument. Ideology can be a very dangerous thing.

I also believe my takedown started with a very cynical and corrupt Liberal Party. They were desperate to stay in power. All the announcements Premier Wynne was making, all her promises of "free stuff" paid for by taxpayers, wasn't moving the needle on her popularity one bit. I think they launched the "Find Shit on Brown Campaign" early on.

After all, I was the perfect subject. I am a white, single male. I happen to like partners from the opposite sex, and I dated and I pursued women whom I found interesting and attractive. But here was my crime. At 39, I still wasn't married, and for the sanctimonious Liberals under Wynne, it meant that something must be really, profoundly wrong with me. I must be a closet predator. And they were going to find out. And if I weren't, they were going to find someone to say I was. As a 39-year-old-single, white male, who wouldn't believe it?

I believe they got to these girls using various levers that may have included bribery and lobbying from other political opponents, and they convinced them to come forward. I believe they helped orchestrate everything, and they shopped the story around until an incompetent news outlet found it all too tantalizing to consider its veracity. How else could it be that some Liberal political staffers were sending signals to stakeholders during January 2018 meetings that a story was going to break, that Brown would not survive. Coincidence? It is possible, but in my mind, unlikely.

I believe there was also a campaign going on within certain elements of the PC Party that could not accept that I was bringing the party to a more modern and moderate centre. I believe that my team, hearing rumours, began hedging their bets, then planning to jump ship and throw me overboard, so that they could start anew with other candidates. The idea is that they would assist me just as long as things were going well, but if the kitchen got too hot, they would gut me like a fish. That is not how your executive team should respond. I believe some of the more ambitious members of my party stood to gain and jumped on board. Their concern now was that I would go off and die somewhere and not make a comeback. Their wrath was still to be inflicted upon me.

However, the big winner of the Blame Category for my downfall is awarded to CTV. It hung me in the court of public opinion without giving me the proper chance to defend anything, and it did so with a very poorly researched story.

Rumours are rumours. Politics runs on them. Mouths flaps constantly, and gossip abounds. There are always those shopping around lies and controversies. But without the media to legitimize these rumours, these stories never really gain traction.

CTV legitimized these allegations regardless of whether or not they were legitimate. CTV gave the public the perception that it was delivering a fully researched exposé on a pattern of abusive and predatory behaviour. Instead, it crafted a distorted and false narrative that omitted key facts and didn't verify the accuracy of others. CTV rushed the story out the door without giving me any reasonable opportunity to provide a defence that was counter to the narrative: Patrick Brown is unfit for public office.

Had I been given the time, I would have been able to provide the evidence that I put together, some of which is now the content of sworn affidavits from witnesses.

CTV should have understood the seriousness of what it was about to print, and it ought to have left no stone unturned. The story should have been properly vetted. CTV should have known that its "investigation" fell short of the standards expected for a premier news network.

CTV ought to have known that the story could have ruined me, the PC Party and the political careers of a number of candidates that I had recruited by knocking them off the political map in ridings where I was playing well. By doing what it did, CTV subverted the democratic process and changed the political landscape. That is not the role of the media.

There was no urgency in broadcasting and publishing this shit. What could have possibly justified failing to fully investigate and verify the facts? A competitive edge on other news sources is likely.

There were those who strongly supported the integrity of all journalistic organizations and concluded that because of its status as a news organization, CTV was beyond reproach. Martin Regg Cohn, a columnist for the Toronto Star, was quick to defend CTV on TVO's The Agenda with Steve Paikin. In a panel discussion right after my resignation, Regg Cohn simply could not allow for the possibility that media investigations are anything but thorough. His reasoning was pretty obvious: CTV is a legitimate news organization. Legitimate news outlets conduct proper investigations; therefore, by definition, it must be believed. And we are asked to believe that investigations conducted by legitimate news organizations meet the highest standards, whether or not we are able to verify or assess this claim.

This is mythology, and it's exactly why I believe CTV was so negligent. CTV has an assumed reputation, whether or not it is deserved, and CTV used it. And because it has people like Martin Regg Cohn perpetuating this idea that media outlets, such as CTV, are thorough and never get it wrong.

Nonsense. Like in everything else, there is good and bad journalism. There is no outside accountability or transparency unless it is called to task, which is what I am doing with my lawsuit.

Not everyone shared Regg Cohn's position. Eventually, as the inconsistencies in the reporting began to surface, some journalists were critical of CTV. The Toronto Star's Rosie Di Manno referred to the story as a "sketchy narrative." Christie Blatchford slammed the standard of journalism and raised a number of possible ideas for more accountability. In her January 25, 2018, piece she wrote:

> Perhaps "investigative" journalists should have to take the same courses cops do, in how to interview people without leading them or suggesting the answers they want.

> Those are facetious suggestions. Here's one that isn't: Reputable news organizations should swear off anonymous allegations of sexual misconduct unless there is a substantial body of evidence and an overwhelming public interest imperative.

> Despite the mountain of horse manure from the likes of Wynne, Horwath et al Thursday about the courage of the two women, I can think of almost nothing that requires less fortitude than accusing someone else of wrongdoing when your own face, name, and identity are hidden.

Thank you, Blatchford. Journalistic sources are often undisclosed; I understand why. But we are expected to blindly trust that their stories have been researched and vetted properly, according to some special set of rules. What most people don't know is the degree to which rules are adopted, enforced or even documented somewhere within the organization. Different media go by different rules and different enforcement mechanisms without consistency. There's no college of journalists that can remove your licence or your company's licence if you break the rules. If it sounds a bit loosey-goosey, it's because it is. There is no independent arbitrator except the courts, if you have the money to take on the media.

But we are asked to believe that no one cuts corners in an environment where the company brass, while beating the drum for journalistic integrity, is also responsible for ensuring corporate solvency and prosperity in a very competitive marketplace. Let's face it: a good story is a good story. If you wait too long on a story with too many mouths flapping, some other outfit is likely to scoop you.

It's a bit of a conflict of interest, if you ask me.

***

There were reasons behind these awful allegations that had nothing to do with my own actions on the evenings in question. I now believe I had a pretty good idea of what happened to me and how. This gave me at least some closure.

If I still had any doubts that there was a movement to remove and discredit me, my final confirmation came in March 2018. I was forwarded an email sent to my former assistant, Logan Ross, that the township of Oro-Medonte had received a six-digit tax payment that was logged toward my home tax account. In it, the revenue clerk for the city wrote:

> Good morning Logan,
>
> We received a large payment from Mr. Brown's tax account. The payment is very abnormal and it is from a different person. Mr. Brown is on our Pre-Authorized Payment plan, so this payment

should not be applied …. I am not really sure how to deal with it. I would call but I do not have a contact phone number for you or Mr. Brown.

Thank you,
Vanessa Cooper, Revenue Clerk

The size of payment was somewhere in the order of $175,000. To me, this was the final proof that someone wanted to ensure that I was caught with this large sum of cash in my tax account and use that to cast further aspersions on me. It never got to that. I instructed the city to refuse the payment. Seriously, you can't make up this stuff.

Enough. Now I needed to figure out what I was going to do next to get my life back.

On April 23, 2018, my lawyers filed my $8-million lawsuit against CTV.

CHAPTER 7

FIGHTING BACK

Vic Fedeli took over as interim leader with Lisa MacLeod as his finance critic. But he wasn't happy. He wanted more.

He wanted to be the party leader who would take the PCs into the June 2018 election.

Once I had poured a considerable amount of energy into trying to figure out what had happened, my mind turned to what I was going to do next with my life. At this point, I was looking at everything and weighing my options together with my family and closest friends.

The letter in which I had resigned as party leader had been sent out without my agreement, approval or authorization. Hell, I didn't even see it. Paul Martin said it best when asked if he quit or got fired by Jean Chrétien. He said, "I got quit." That was a great way to describe what happened to me.

Now I considered the question of whether or not I should put forth a complaint to the executive of the party that, as far as I was concerned, I hadn't actually resigned. We had the votes on the executive to cancel the leadership and reject the letter; however, Jag Badwal was refusing to call the meeting, which complicated things. We could have forced him to do so.

In the end, I decided not to fight it because it would have resulted in a protracted and ugly court battle, and with an election coming up, it was too short a runway for a legal challenge. In retrospect, and despite all that, I should have gone down that path.

Meanwhile, my lawyers Howard Winkler and Julian Porter had been reviewing the facts and interviewing the witnesses. Both came to the view that my case against CTV was very strong. This gave me a renewed hope of justice, and on February 14, 2018, I posted this on Facebook:

> CTV News fabricated a malicious and false report about me from two anonymous accusers. After a long three weeks, CTV News has now admitted that it got it wrong.
>
> Initially, the reporter (and I use that term very loosely) claimed my first accuser was a high school student under legal drinking age. Running scared over its lousy reporting, CTV News now says my accuser was out of high school at the time and was of legal drinking age. Clearly concerned about the backlash it has been receiving as a result of its biased and false reporting, CTV News is trying to change its story and claims the incident happened one year later. The significance of this changed story is monumental.
>
> Not even having the decency to come clean and admit that they recklessly published a poorly researched report, CTV is burying this new fact, hiding it in the middle of an online story. In fact, CTV is doubling down on its terrible reporting, digging a deeper hole for itself, by featuring more of my accuser's lies.
>
> I can also tell you that CTV News did not disclose last night that their reporter, Glen McGregor, called an acquaintance of mine yesterday to ask him if he had driven my first accuser to my home – a claim that was made by her. He categorically told CTV that this was completely untrue.
>
> I thought surely, CTV News would report on my acquaintance's evidence. I was wrong. CTV chose not to report the truth because the facts contradict their phony, made up narrative.
>
> Here is my message to CTV News. You lied. You defamed me. I will not allow your brand of trashy journalism to hurt another person in this country.

And here is my message to my accusers – both of them. If you truly stand by your allegations, then I urge you to contact Barrie Police and have them lay charges. Barrie Police can be reached at 705-725-7025. These types of allegations should be dealt with in a proper and fair forum.

I will be telling my story tonight on Global News. Please watch. Finally, and most humbly and sincerely, thank you to the dozens of candidates and caucus members, thousands of Ontario PC Party members and tens of thousands of Ontarians who have supported me and my family through this very difficult time.

This is not over.

Soon after my "getting quit," Vic Fedeli took over as interim leader with Lisa MacLeod as his finance critic. But he wasn't happy. He wanted more. He wanted to be the party leader who would take the PCs into the June 2018 election. Rumour had it that MacLeod and Fedeli cut a deal. She would back him to take over as the permanent leader, and in return she would be finance critic. Likely, the deal included a senior post after the election, when and if the party won.

Now the games began in earnest. Who would ultimately lead the party into that next general election, which was only five months away? I began to hear reports that Velshi, now Fedeli's chief of staff, was upset at the possibility that I might consider making a comeback to provincial politics — perhaps run for PC Party leader to replace myself — which wasn't my interest right up until the morning of my announcement, as I will discuss later.

By now, Velshi was bragging to Conservative friends that he was the grand puppet master who was calling the shots. Velshi's return to work at that office meant that he had access to my personal records and the people who could unlock those records, which he would now use to orchestrate a campaign against me. I needed to be despised by the public and cast out, so I could never return.

Fedeli, Alykhan Velshi, Richard Ciano, Nick Kouvalis and the PC caucus were pushing hard to allow Fedeli to lead them on election day: June 7, 2018. They were also pushing to hold a leadership convention afterwards. According to the party's constitution, the ultimate decision-making on this request resided with the party's executive, not caucus.

Since Fedeli would likely be premier if the PCs won the election, he'd have a massive advantage in any leadership race after that. In fact, the race itself likely wouldn't matter. It would be a coronation. But the party executive wasn't inclined to allow this to happen.

Team Fedeli and the party executive headed by party president Rick Dykstra were headed for a massive showdown. Velshi turned on Dykstra and threatened that if he blocked Fedeli in any way, he'd be "shot in the head." They'd finish him politically.

The executive was under tremendous pressure not to have a general leadership contest before the election, but rather to install Fedeli. Dykstra knew the stakes were high going into that first executive meeting held on a Saturday.

Kaydee Richmond, Mike's wife, who was on the party's executive, began making her remarks. At that point she was rudely interrupted by Richard Ciano who began yelling over her. Kaydee shot back calmly but sternly "You will not interrupt me again." Ciano didn't open his mouth again for the rest of the meeting.

Some who attended believe that that one exchange between Ciano and Kaydee turned the tide of the meeting and gave the rest of the executive the confidence to stand up for what they thought was right – to allow the members to decide. Ciano's failed bully attempt may well have cost Fedeli the leadership and the premier's office.

Ultimately, the executive did not succumb to caucus pressure. Instead, it ruled to hold a general leadership contest prior to the general provincial election. Fedeli lost. The vote wasn't even close. It was 15 to eight in favour of proceeding with an immediate leadership contest. The eight on the executive who voted for Fedeli's position were his loyalists and included

Ciano and hold overs from the Ciano period in the executive, when he was the party president.

Fedeli's group had tried to seize the party undemocratically, but it didn't work. It was when Fedeli started bumping up against the party executive that he began talking in front of the media about the "rot in the party" that he had to root out. These words made headlines and likely made many caucus members feel uncomfortable knowing the words would come back to haunt the party during the impending election campaign.

There were those who really felt it would have been better to have a leader who was a known quantity lead the party into the election. In these unprecedented circumstances, I may have been inclined to agree with them, except for the fact that the person in question was Fedeli.

I believe that Fedeli was really becoming power hungry, and that this hunger was being fed by Kouvalis, the same person who scripted Kellie Leitch, the federal Conservative leadership candidate. Leitch was prone to extreme and inflammatory remarks. I saw Kouvalis's fingerprints all over Fedeli's demeanour and his "rot in the party" comments.

My experience with Fedeli was that he was extremely competent, but that he was also duplicitous and too ambitious for his own good. And the events that unfolded in the weeks that followed reinforced my concerns that in my view, Fedeli would do anything to be in power for the sake of being in power. That doesn't make for good leadership.

Kathleen Wynne is a good example of someone who, in her second term, governed to stay in power. She governed exclusively for those niche constituencies she thought could mobilize to support her during an election. That became a hallmark of her administration.

Once it was established that a leadership contest was needed before the June 7, 2018 election, the next question was: "Could Fedeli, now interim leader, run in that leadership race?" He hoped so, and there was really nothing preventing this, technically speaking; the constitution of the PC Party in Ontario allowed for this possibility. Fedeli could have run for leadership, even though he was the interim leader — a scenario that he wanted and said so openly.

Regardless of the rules, there's a tradition that interim leaders should not run for leadership because they have an unfair advantage. They have access to the resources of the office they hold and they have access to information that other candidates don't have. In fact, it is unprecedented for an interim leader who has been appointed to run for leadership of a party because it is inappropriate. And the fact that Fedeli didn't understand that is significant, in my view.

A number of people weighed in. I was told that Mike Harris, former premier of Ontario, believed that Fedeli had to pick: Did he want to be interim leader or did he want to run in a leadership contest?

On January 30, 2018, the sexual allegations against Fedeli brought forth by the staff member came forward via a press release provided to the media. It is my understanding that the communication sent from the staffer's lawyer was intended as a shot across the bow to Fedeli, signalling that if he ran, the staff member would move forward with the allegations. She was pissed at his attitude toward the allegations against me, and she had told me that. I think this is the main reason that Fedeli didn't run for leadership of the PC Party.

Fedeli was very disappointed. His henchman, Velshi, had been active in trying to finish off Dykstra as party president before the executive meeting that ultimately dashed Fedeli's master plan. While the timing didn't work, the end result did.

Suddenly, all these old stories about Dykstra started making media headlines. While Velshi was quoted in the media as "knowing nothing" about any of all this, he was bragging in the office about his campaign to destroy Dykstra using sexual allegations made during Dykstra's time in Ottawa as an MP. These stories were leaked on the days just prior to the executive meeting that did not go well for Team Fedeli.

Velshi had worked in the PMO. It was during his time there that inappropriate sexual conduct allegations against Dykstra had surfaced. The PMO had called both Dykstra and the girl in the story to talk about it. I don't know the details, except that it was resolved; it was settled. From what I understood, both parties had different perspectives about what had happened, but it was agreed to by both parties that the issue was over. I am not going to weigh in on who was right or wrong, or whether or not the story should have been resolved the way it was. The point is, it was settled with the agreement of the woman in question at the time, and nothing was made public.

But Velshi would have known about this. He may even have kept notes and emails from the PMO in 2013 and 2014, where he worked at the time. This certainly would have been in character, and besides, he had threatened as much. And when Dykstra became a barrier to Fedeli's plans, I was told by a co-worker of Velshi that he leaked the story to Steven Maher, who wrote the devastating Maclean's article. Dykstra was done and resigned. Velshi delivered on his threat.

By now, Velshi was a very busy chief of staff. Apart from running the office and leaking shit on Dykstra to the media, he was also conducting "black ops" on me. This was confirmed to me by a number of staffers.

Yes. That is correct. My former chief of staff, only months before a provincial election, was heading up a war room — with me as the target. Many told me that Velshi was extremely proud of his role as puppet master and bragged around the office and to others.

We found out about this operation soon after that awful Night of Knives. Ryan Amato had been one of my drivers and an assistant for me when I was leader. At my sister Fiona's request, he came to her office after my takedown. When he arrived, he found a reporter at her office as well. Fiona was hoping Amato would say something on the record about me being the subject of surveillance that had been going on since December, as we were trying to piece things together. Amato knew we were being followed because he was my driver. The party executive did as well.

Amato freaked. He pulled Fiona aside and told her clearly, "Fiona, don't you understand? There's an entire PC war room at Queen's Park now that has been tasked with taking out Patrick. Alykhan told me that they will not stop until he's criminally charged and arrested. Are you fucking out of your mind, Fiona? Stop this now. Patrick has to play dead."

Well now, that was encouraging — not that I was surprised. By now, everyone was fighting over who would lead the party I built. Anything that might prove that I was unjustly convicted in the court of public opinion could dash their own leadership plans or the plans of the candidate they were going to support. They wanted me dead politically. But as candidates entered the leadership race, they began to understand that the apparatus of the party was still very loyal to me.

It seemed Velshi was, orchestrating new media drops to discredit me using any personal information he had. I was told by my former staff that he had given direction to leak whatever they could to discredit me. He told them not to be concerned about what happened in the Legislature. That was apparently not relevant. Velshi tried to scare them by saying that if Patrick Brown came back, they would all be fired. Everyone's only job was to find dirt on Brown. He turned the communications office into a war room against me. The task at hand was to scour through every single email of mine, anything that could be found that could condemn me. While Velshi had fired many, he hadn't fired everyone, and these people told me that Velshi was "a man possessed."

He had an ace up his sleeve with Bugeja, who had served as my personal assistant. She had all the passwords to my private stuff.

It was around this time that James Dodds, a close friend of mine and an executive with the Toronto-Dominion (TD) Bank, told me that Velshi had asked him for a meeting. It was pretty clear that the purpose of the meeting was to deliver a threat to me through a messenger, who Velshi knew was close to me. Velshi said to Dodds that while he didn't mind a tweet I had posted essentially defending myself and stating that the truth would come out, if I tried anything else to defend myself or make any other move like entering the leadership race, there would be a negative story about my house mortgage. I was to play dead, to go away or there would be hell to pay. He made good on that promise.

A few days later, on February 8, 2017, Robert Benzie and Rob Ferguson of the Toronto Star published an article on the size of my mortgage, my pay and other tidbits of information that had been extracted from my own personal records without my knowledge or consent. This was only the beginning.

Now the leadership games began.

Fittingly, Caroline Mulroney announced her intent to run on Sunday, February 4, 2018, the night of the Super Bowl game. Walied had been invited to a campaign meeting happening at her house. He basically wanted to clear it with me first. Was it OK if he went? I told him he had better go, and to make sure they didn't make any stupid mistakes. In spite of all that had happened to me, I really felt that Caroline was the one who would promote the kind of party I tried to build — one that represented a more moderate Ontario, which is what I believe Ontario is.

It was then that I found out that they were hiring Boddington and Robertson. *Wow — how did that happen?* I told Caroline and her husband, Andrew Lapham, that these guys were going to blow the campaign for her. I didn't trust either and believed that he would screw her over. In retrospect, I believe that's what happened. Caroline's campaign spent four times the amount spent by everyone else, and she almost finished last. I believe they did not run a good campaign at all.

Once candidates got serious about running, I became a huge commodity if they could land my support. They all knew that I could unlock many voting blocks in key ridings; after all, I had signed up these people and I had grown the party. Having me onside could help swing the leadership vote in their favour. They were all nice to me (with the exception of Granic Allen).

During the early stages of the leadership contest, I spoke to Lapham almost daily. He was supportive of me and he would call me and ask me if I had seen Caroline's media statements. The statements were suddenly much nicer than the one that had been posted the day after the Night of Knives.

On CP24, for example, she said that I deserved to have my side of the story told.

Caroline was someone I was thinking of backing for leadership, having no interest in running myself at that point. I also tried to convince Neil Davis, the son of former Ontario Premier Bill Davis, to consider running. Ultimately, he decided against it.

I was also being romanced by Elliott, who made the most attractive offer to me. We met for lunch in the TD Tower in Toronto on the Wednesday before I announced to run for leadership that Friday. That was because I still wasn't considering running for party leader, even though some around me had gathered up the requisite papers so that if I changed my mind, I could make the filing deadline.

This meeting was to see what deal I might make with Elliott if I were to back her. Elliott was unbelievably nice. Her son, Galen, told me that in the event of a PC majority, his mother really only wanted to serve one term as premier. That could open up the possibility for me to be premier in four years if I ran, if I won and if the party were to be re-elected. He told me that he understood from Storseth that I really wanted to be deputy premier. Elliott was very straightforward. She told me that she could promise me deputy leader/deputy premier, but not minister of finance because she had already promised that to someone else. It was refreshing to hear her honesty and clarity. It reminded me of my conversation with McNaughton years before during the 2015 PC leadership race. That was the best anyone could have promised me.

I told her that one of my inspirations in politics was Modi because he made Gujarat the economic titan of all of India. I shared with her how Modi conducted his trade conferences. Then I asked her if she'd consider merging the ministries of economic development and international trade and making me minister of this new portfolio? As minister, I would work tirelessly to bring jobs and industry to Ontario.

Elliott loved the idea. After about 15 minutes, we turned to discussing the mechanics of her campaign. What could I do to help? I explained about mobilizing my forces.

We also agreed that we would hold a joint rally together on the weekend, at which time, Elliott would announce to the media that she would sign my nomination papers, so that I could run in the election and represent my riding of Barrie, which many candidates were debating whether or not they would allow me to do until I "cleared my name." So that was the deal.

Ford had also been calling everyone around me, asking me to join him at breakfast. He was saying that I could have any position I wanted if I threw my organization behind his candidacy. Ford, too, was prepared to make me an offer.

I finally told Lapham that Elliott wanted my support and that she was prepared to make me deputy premier if we won the election. I told him that they were willing to put it into a contract. I also told Lapham that, frankly, the Mulroney camp was the only one that hadn't made it clear to me where I stood in terms of any possible position in exchange for my help. I thought that was odd. After all, weren't Caroline Mulroney, her husband and Brian Mulroney the ones who should have been the most supportive among all the other leadership candidates? I didn't recruit Ford, I had a bad relationship with Granic Allen and I ran against Elliott on the last go, the 2015 leadership race. But Caroline was my pick, and I worked hard to recruit her to the team. Yet Team Mulroney was silent.

Lapham's response was simple: "The Mulroneys will always be here for you — for life. These others will not." Listening to these words made me smile. Clearly, years of being around Brian had worn off on him.

I had made my point. Lapham then suggested that we get together with Brian at his hotel suite when he came to Toronto. He also suggested that we leave Caroline out of this particular meeting.

The meeting took place at the InterContinental hotel on Front Street West in the presidential suite, where Brian was staying. It was late at night, around 10:30 or so.

I had Rob Godfrey with me, who was there for my support. Paul Godfrey, his father, also attended as a neutral intermediary, knowing both Brian and me. Paul had arranged for Phillips, another star candidate whom I had recruited to run as MPP, to support Caroline's bid for leadership.

The three of us, Paul, Rob and I, made our way up to the presidential suite. In the room to greet us were Brian and Lapham. We made small talk for a while.

I then said to Brian, "Obviously, I have a lot of goodwill for your daughter. After all, I'm the one who recruited her so aggressively to run. But," I continued, "I can't be involved if you have those traitors running her campaign. And frankly," I went on, "I am a little dismayed that you haven't made me any clear commitment."

First Brian said that they would "look into" the issue of the traitors. But he added that there weren't many good campaign managers out there. I told him that I could give him a great campaign manager, Storseth. But that didn't get any bites.

Brian then began his offer with these words: "Mulroneys don't need to put anything in writing. All I can tell you," he added "is that you're going to be on her front bench! Of course! How could you not? You're going to be on her front bench."

I asked, "OK great, but what does that mean?"

He answered, "We can't get into specifics, but you will be at the centre of her government."

So, I asked again, "OK, but what does 'the centre of her government' mean? I've been told by others that I would be deputy premier."

Again, Brian responded, "You're going to be at the centre of her government."

At that point, Lapham told me not to worry; it was all good. Brian then added that once I agreed to being at the centre of her government, they needed me to send my organization to the Mulroney camp right away. So I asked if I would be part of a joint event with Caroline. Mulroney Senior responded, "No." He was worried that other women would be coming forward.

Whoa! What? Brian was sitting there saying that I was so important to Caroline, to her bid, to her team that I'd be at the centre of her government. But at the same time, he actually believed that there could be other girls coming forward? Why would you agree to let a slimeball participate in a central role in your daughter's government?

Mulroney Senior replied, "Yes, I heard that from a conservative friend of mine."

I said, "Yeah? Well that's bullshit!"

Brian continued to press for a handshake deal with the following terms: I would be in the front bench in exchange for handing over my organization to his daughter's bid — tonight.

I told Brian, "I'm not going to shake hands on anything tonight. You're worried about other girls coming out? You go back to your conservative friend."

Mulroney cut me off, "Look, Patrick. I hear there could be another story coming out in the next 48 hours."

It was then that it dawned on me. If I agreed to a handshake deal, might that actually precipitate another concocted story against me? Such a story would certainly scuttle any obligation that Brian had to honour any promise he made me. At the same time, I would have already delivered all of my organization to his daughter's campaign. Sure, it seemed like a Machiavellian plot considered by a paranoid person. And three months earlier, such a plot would never have crossed my mind. But after the surreal events of the past few weeks, the fact that it was far-fetched made me believe it all the more.

So I said, "Look, Brian. We don't have to shake hands. Let's let these 48 hours go by, and if there's no story, then you can shake my hand with confidence on this."

"No, no," Brian said. "Let's shake hands tonight! We trust you. We don't have to wait the 48 hours."

And I said, "No. I don't want you to have any doubts."

Paul, who was there as the neutral party, chimed in, "Come on, we actually have a deal tonight, guys! Let's get the deal done!"

I said that I didn't want to have any deal where there was uncertainty. And then I asked Brian "The Question": "Listen, if some other girls were to come forward, would the deal be off?"

"Well, of course it would have to be off," Brian muttered.

"OK, then, let's not agree on anything tonight. If you think there are still some loose ends out there, then you go investigate. I'm telling you this is all bullshit, but you go ahead and investigate it."

They were desperate to get a deal with me that night. But I told them I wasn't doing any on-the-spot deal. I put his own words right back on him. I was doing this to protect him, Brian. So it was best that we wait. I was really pissed off, and likely he was as well.

Rob Godfrey and I left with the understanding that we would all talk again in 48 hours. There was no deal. I gave no handshake. I was already unnerved that they had Boddington and Robertson working for Caroline, two of the traitors-in-chief.

I told Rob that this was all bullshit. No formal commitment? A handshake deal that could evaporate? Just "trust him?" Yes, right. After everything I had been through, trust was certainly not high on my list of criteria for self-preservation. That night, Team Mulroney lost me.

During the same week, I also gave an exclusive sit-down interview to Carolyn Jarvis from Global News, which aired in two parts on February 14 and 15, 2018. This was a way for me to be able to tell my side of things once I was finally able to digest and investigate the allegations. The interview took place in Fiona's condo, in Toronto. I was extremely nervous. I knew my opponents were watching from inside and outside the party.

In this interview, I told the world that the accusations against me were lies, but now I was able to explain the inconsistencies that I had discovered. It felt good to have someone go through the allegations line by line and to have the time to actually address the claims one by one. Viewers were able to hear first-hand the shock and damage I had suffered. But they were also able to hear my anger, and I was plenty angry.

Jarvis started with my personal life. "Do you want to address the rumours about you? Do you know what they are? That you're a playboy ... that you like younger women."

I explained that I had dated women who were my age, younger than me and older, too. I also pointed out that I started my political life formally at the age of only 22. Usually, politicians are older, with grey hair and are married with kids. I grew up in politics, a career where I spent half my life on planes without much time to dedicate to someone else. I told Jarvis that I had loved and had my heart broken, like most people. There was nothing that I'd like more than to meet the love of my life, to settle down and have kids and a family. The responsibility for failed relationships was mine. I didn't dedicate the time because my focus was on politics. Finally, I told her that the one silver lining in this tragedy was that I would now finally have time to have a family.

While I spoke from the heart, I left the audience with the view that I was not seriously involved with anyone at that time. That was deliberate. I was concerned about opening up new scrutiny on me and GG after all that had happened. But as could be imagined, that really hurt GG. For her, that interview punctuated the problems in our relationship; the denial of her existence. Everyone had advised her to remain in the shadows because media attention would all be negative. And while she obviously wanted the normalcy of being officially recognized as my partner, she, too, was frightened of all the potential negative publicity.

The interview rolled on, and now the interviewer concentrated on the actual string of allegations against me. This opened with questions dealing with the specificity of information CTV shared with me (or not).

"Did you know the last name of the first accuser? Did you know the date of the allegations? The year?" Jarvis appeared surprised when I responded "No" to most of these questions. At times, it appeared that my answers left her without words. She'd go silent after my response before resuming the interview.

What almost left *me* silent was when Jarvis shared that my staff had apparently known about the story that was about to break days before I did. This caught me off guard. The best answer I could give was to say that maybe the staff didn't tell me because they were trying to shelter me. No sooner were the words out of my mouth than I thought to myself, *Yeah, fat chance.*

Jarvis also seemed surprised at the lack of time in which I had been given to respond by CTV. She asked me if more time would have made a difference.

Yes, of course it would have. I would have been able to put together some key discrepancies in these stories, as I was finally able to do. With these on the table, I believe the story would have played out very differently. It felt like a hit job, and that CTV didn't care about the truth.

Jarvis questioned me about what happened on the Night of Knives and asked me if I thought I had the support of my team. I believed at the time that I did. There was no talk about trying to convince me to resign. I was completely blindsided when I discovered that at 9:53 p.m., while I was standing up at the microphone to deliver the statement prepared by my core team, at a press conference dreamed up by my core team, they were tweeting out their resignations. And I explained to Jarvis that it was their resignations that caused caucus to demand my resignation. It was politically expedient at the time to throw me under the bus.

The big bombshell I dropped during the interview was when I said that the resignation went out without my approval. This point was not actually the central point I was trying to make. I was trying to explain that the evening just got worse and worse. Jarvis stopped me cold.

"I just want to make sure I am understanding what you are saying here. Are you saying that you didn't actually agree to the resignation?" she asked.

I responded that I had not even seen the resignation, nor had I authorized anyone to send it out. Jarvis seemed shocked and repeated her question differently. And I reiterated my answer.

"So you might *not* have agreed to resign?" she countered.

The short answer was that I didn't know what I would have done the next day. But I would not have resigned that night, for sure. I wanted time. That was something I didn't get. I would have expected to meet with caucus. I would have expected to see the statement of resignation and to have authorized its release, if that is ultimately what I decided to do. None of that happened. I was of the view then, as I am now, that I needed time to determine what was best to do next.

It took Jarvis a bit of time to move on from this declaration. After a few more questions, the interview was over.

It was likely that interview really spooked Velshi and my political opponents from within the party. It showed that I was starting to fight back. Might I challenge my unauthorized resignation? I understand that was a question they were worried about. The king was not dead. Could he try to retake the throne? All this must have terrified them, especially with all these candidates in the race.

Elliott's campaign began to hear rumours that I wanted to run for the leadership myself. Fred DeLorey, Elliott's campaign manager, began emailing Storseth, asking if the deal was "still on." I was clear with Storseth: I was *not* running for leadership. No way.

MP Gord Brown called me, asking me about rumours he had also heard. "Are you running for leader?" I told him the same thing: not a chance. Brown told me that he had been planning to commit to Mulroney, but that if there were any chance I was running, I needed to tell him. I told him to go ahead and commit to Mulroney because I wasn't running.

Why was I meeting with Elliott and Mulroney? Why was I turning down offers of help from good supporters? Why? Because I didn't really want to run.

There were a few pushing me to run. Some of these folks got the forms I needed to sign "just in case" I changed my mind. They were mobilizing to collect money and get signatures. But I wasn't having anything of it. I had been hurt enough.

On the Thursday before the deadline to enter the leadership race, we held a meeting Richmond's house. There were about 40 people there. Everyone was pleading for me to run. They said, "We have the money and the signatures." I told them that I wasn't doing it.

That Thursday night, I reached out to a few people I believed in who weren't there. I got great advice from some. One in particular wrote me a text in which she argued that I was young and had my whole life ahead of me. Perhaps it would be better to back an existing candidate, who could provide me with the assurances of a cabinet post. She went on to say that she didn't know many of the candidates personally. She had never met Mulroney, but she did know Elliott. Her view was that she was a very straight-up candidate, and that perhaps I should seek a deal with her or someone whom I believed in. She felt it was a wrong move for me to run for leadership, as it would be too early.

Also on Thursday night, Watsa, the Canadian billionaire and chief executive of Fairfax Financial Holdings, gave me exactly the opposite advice in a long conversation we had.

He said, "Patrick, this is your destiny. This is your party. You go for this."

I have so much respect for Watsa, but I still responded less than enthusiastically. "I don't know, Prem." Still, he got me thinking, and at that point I was about 60 per cent against and 40 per cent for running for leadership of the PC Party.

There were others who did not have my interests at heart and just wanted me out of the picture. Ken Zeise, vice-chair of the Provincial Nominations Committee (PNC), did not want me to run. He was unofficially supporting Mulroney. He had called me earlier and told me that if I filed my papers, I would be kicked out of caucus on Friday morning. Friday was the deadline to file.

I told Zeise clearly that I wasn't running for leadership, and he could tell that to Fedeli. I added that they didn't have to make any threats. Zeise explained that Fedeli didn't believe me and fully intended to kick me out of caucus. The reason for Fedeli's suspicion was that my supporters had asked for the leadership forms. As I mentioned, they did this so they could ensure that if I had an interest, we would have the requisite signatures and money.

On February 14 and 15, 2018, I took and passed a lie-detector test that was conducted in two stages by John Galianos, one of Canada's top polygraph experts with over 40 years of expertise.

I was asked to respond to a set of questions involving each allegation that had been made against me twice.

Galianos's seven-page report included the following conclusions:

> In each case, Brown not only answered truthfully, but exceeded the standards use to determine truth by the FBI and RCMP. Upon evaluating the lengthy pre-test interviews and the polygraphic charts, I am of the opinion that Mr. Patrick Brown is being truthful while answering the relevant questions asked of him during the tests.

"There was no deception," Galianos told the Toronto Sun in an article published on February 16, 2018.

On Friday morning, February 16, 2018, I was still against running for leadership. It was that morning that Fedeli made the announcement that I would be kicked out of caucus. Those who were against me had an interpretation of the party rules that if I were kicked out of caucus, I couldn't run for leadership of the party because I was not a member in good standing. A member who is not in good standing in the party cannot run to lead it. They presented this position to the president of the party, Badwal, and to the Leadership Election Organization Committee (LEOC).

No one called me to tell me this. I found out that I had been kicked out of caucus through a live news report. That announcement put me over the edge. Being kicked out of caucus was definitely the straw that broke the camel's back.

My supporters erupted. "Patrick, you're foolish to think these guys are going to treat you well."

I was angry and now I felt I had no choice but to run. At 12 noon on Friday, I met my supporters at my sister Fiona's law firm. They reminded me that this was my last chance. The deadline to enter the race was that day, at 5 p.m.

I had a meeting with Dodds and my sister Fiona in a side room. Dodds had reminded me of something else — the threat that Velshi made: that if I ran, he'd finish me off with a number of charges and stories against me.

I held a conference call with Storseth and Dodds. Dodds maintained his position: "Don't do it. Don't run. There's too much risk."

Then there were the 40 supporters who had gathered at the law firm of Aird & Berlis LLP. They were all pleading with me to run.

Was it worth it — all the hell that I would go through in the next few weeks? With 40 people in the boardroom waiting, I sat alone in another room. I was torn, really torn, and I needed time to think. I just sat there by myself. The vision of Fedeli's sanctimonious face puking out those words, "I am removing him from caucus" kept playing in my head. *Why was I being turfed now? Why not before?* I believe that Fedeli, Velshi and Kouvalis, the Toxic Three, had masterminded this phony narrative about "rot in the party," so that they could play this card if I tried to get my life back.

By now it was around 3:30 p.m., and the 5 p.m. deadline was fast approaching. "Fuck it," I said. "Let's do it!"

Everyone jumped up and cheered. They had already arranged that MPP Toby Barrett would walk into party headquarters with me. Barrett was en route from his riding. Barrett, Nagalingam, both of my sisters, Fiona and Stephanie, and I led the pack. Other supporters followed. We walked down to party headquarters to register me to run for leader of the PC Party.

Before I went to party headquarters, I personally called Brian Mulroney. I told him that I felt I had to do this. His response was, "You have to do what you have to do." It was a short conversation, but I always admired him, and I felt I needed to give him the respect of a phone call.

Dodds told DeLorey what was happening. Basically, he was told I had no choice after being kicked out of caucus. But Dodds also told DeLorey that we should not assume that the conversation was over because while I felt compelled to run, Dodds didn't believe I would remain in the race. He had asked me if it was OK to keep the lines of communication open with Elliott. I gave him permission to do so.

It was about 4 p.m. when we arrived to sign the documents at party headquarters in downtown Toronto.

Fiona had organized some supporters to be on standby for a rally in front of the PNC at party headquarters. They stood there and chanted outside the building while the party committee interviewed me upstairs.

The media had been alerted. There was pandemonium at party headquarters. I couldn't even move. We all walked in. There were chairs that had been set up, which the media continued to knock over.

That was when I found out that Fedeli and Velshi had already filed a paper saying that I could not run as a candidate because I had been kicked out of caucus.

A supporter was there and started arguing the technicalities of the issue. He said that the party must let me register, and that disallowing my registration was illegal under the party's constitution. Fiona was taping everything.

I went to Steve Gilchrist, the deputy director of the party, and my sister asked if everything was in order and in accordance to party rules. He confirmed everything was. And my sister said, "So if Fedeli tries to intervene, we have confirmation that everything is in accordance?" His response was: "Please don't do that!"

We filed the papers. Two days later, on February 18, 2018, Hillier tweeted out his full statement on why he felt I was "unfit" to be a member of the PC caucus, the leader of the PC Party or the premier of Ontario.

The attacks just kept coming. Velshi was delivering on his promise to leverage my personal information to crush me in the media and anywhere else.

The morning of February 20, 2018, I woke up to a front-page Toronto Star article that made my blood boil. It was the photo that I noticed first. The Star has used the image of a smiling GG with a barbecued rib in her hand with me sitting beside her. The photo had been taken in summer 2015 at an event called Ribfest (three years earlier, before we were seeing each other) with her good friend Adam Ibraham.

In the photo printed by the Star, however, you couldn't see Ibraham because someone had conveniently cropped him out of the picture completely. So the photo leaves the reader with the impression that this was a picture of us, a couple, out on a date, which wasn't remotely the case.

I read the article in its entirety and with disgust because the Star got some key facts wrong — facts that were put in to prop up the narrative of a guy who hits on his staff and flies them around the world on party dollars. The fact that none of this was true, especially in this case, didn't matter. It had Velshi's fingerprints all over it. It was co-authored by Benzie, who, as I recall during my time in office, was the person to whom Velshi regularly leaked stories. I suppose that the other reporter on the story, Kristin Rushowy, was in charge of pursuing GG, and Benzie got the dope, most of which was incorrect, from Velshi.

As I wrote previously, after the night of January 24, GG asked for and received three weeks off from SickKids Foundation. During that time, she returned to her workplace on a few occasions.

It was during these short visits to her office that GG received a call that was routed through the main reception. It was from Rushowy. At the time, we believed that reporter was interested in a comment on the allegations against me from the girlfriend I was rumoured to have.

GG had never been called by a reporter before and was totally taken off guard. She explained that she was at work and wasn't interested in answering anything on the subject. After that, the calls persisted. GG kept seeing the number come up on her call display at work.

Once out of the office, Rushowy continued to harass GG by email, text and cellphone. What had started with the Star grew to include reporters from a variety of news outlets. It became ridiculous.

The hospital foundation had to send out foundation-wide communication to all staff, saying that if anyone received any media requests about the Toronto Star story or GG, to forward those to the foundation's PR department. Another staffer bumped into a reporter wandering around the halls of the foundation. When she questioned him, he asked about GG. She shooed him out of the building. It was crazy.

GG called me and complained. She felt that the Toronto Star reporter was a real low life for the tactics she was using. At the same time, however, GG didn't want anyone to think, given all that had happened to me, that she didn't have anything good to say about me.

It was our belief at the time that the reporter was working on a bigger story, not just about GG, and likely just wanted a comment to include in the article. So we came up with a comment that Genevieve could offer: "Patrick is the kindest, most genuine man I have ever met, and I don't believe the allegations."

We were naïve. As far as this reporter was concerned, GG was the story. Her comment became the hook for an entire front-page Toronto Star exposé that I refer to as "Ribgate."

They say power loves a vacuum. So does rumour. When the facts aren't being provided, people fill them in, or they turn to people who claim they can help to fill them in. In this case, that person, we believe, was my former chief of staff, Velshi.

The finished story was appalling, and many of details provided in it were completely incorrect and damaging to us. The Star reported that GG had been my intern in Ottawa, which was false. She had never been my intern in Ottawa, nor at Queen's Park. In fact, we met at the time I was running for leader of the Ontario PC Party, and we were both seeing other people.

The article wrote that that GG had gone to India and Lebanon as an intern — she was not. The way it was written, it left the reader with the impression that GG was a staffer, and I was flying her around the world on the party's dime. On none of these trips was she a staffer, nor was her ticket paid for by my office or the party or a third party. In fact, GG had purchased her own ticket to India and went with her sister. I purchased her ticket from India to Lebanon when I was going over to visit a refugee camp. It was my birthday gift to her — we would visit the refugee camp together.

GG was devastated by the article. It was particularly hurtful because travelling together was really the only sense of normalcy in the relationship, and now even that was being misrepresented. She couldn't understand how one comment she provided to this reporter yielded such a tabloid-like story packed with inaccuracies. And why would the Toronto Star put such a piece of garbage on the front page? I told GG that if her biggest pet peeve was being hidden, now she wasn't a secret anymore. It was clearly not much of a consolation. GG had never had her privacy invaded. She felt violated and misrepresented. But what bugged me most is that our story was not told on our terms.

On February 20, 2018, Hillier followed up with his initial claim that I was unfit to be a member of the party, its leader or premier. He had now submitted a litany of complaints to Ontario's Office of the Integrity Commissioner, which was provided to the press. In it, he accused me of a series of ethical breaches. These were based on numbers located in my personal information to which my former assistant, Bugeja, had access. Velshi now had unfettered access to Bugeja.

The many allegations against me could be whittled down to a few basic buckets:

1. I failed to disclose gifts of travel to the integrity commissioner (in his charges, Hillier accused me of having third parties pay for my and GG's travel);
2. I failed to disclose a source of income (rental on my home) to the integrity commissioner;
3. I received money (mortgage on my home) from Jaswinder (Jass) Johal, which I failed to disclose; and
4. I influenced the outcome of a nomination race for Johal.

In the hopes of bolstering these claims, Hillier's submission to the integrity commissioner included a photo of a landscape, which GG had taken on one trip and posted to social media. I'm not certain what that was supposed to prove, other than she was with me on a trip.

GG had deleted that photo from her social media in spring 2017. So how did Hillier (or whoever put the piece together) get that image to use? He didn't. Velshi did. And for this we had proof.

In spring 2017, Velshi had asked my permission to talk to GG about what she was posting to her social media account. He told her he was going to go through a "clean-up" exercise to ensure that she deleted anything posted to her social media that he felt could disclose the relationship between us or be used by the Liberals to discredit me.

He took screenshots with his phone of what he considered to be the questionable photos, and he sent the screenshots to GG, so she could delete the items in question. These screenshots included a picture of the landscape during one of our trips. But it also included the image of the battery icon, and the time that was displayed on Velshi's screen. GG promptly deleted all the photos that were also now screenshots taken by Velshi. One of these photos was included in Hillier's complaint to the integrity commissioner. It also showed the icon of the battery level and the time on Velshi's phone. Obviously, Velshi had kept all his screenshots of her social media posts and was using them as evidence against us.

Seeing that screenshot from Velshi's phone was further evidence that he was a louse. The fact is that all my trips were paid for by the party, and there were receipts proving this. None of my travel was a gift from anyone. And when GG came with me, she either paid her own way or I paid her way out of my pocket.

In his ruling, released two months later, the integrity commissioner agreed with me: there was no evidence that I accepted or failed to disclose gifts of travel, period.

With regard to the other charges related to my house and mortgage, I will explain the issue and then provide the rulings. I had promised party officials that I would move into the riding of Simcoe North after I won my by-election in 2015. I sold my Barrie home and started house-hunting in Simcoe North. Homes there were not cheap.

After a long search, I found one with a sticker price of about $2.8 million. Instead, I offered $2.3 million, certain that the sellers wouldn't accept my offer. They did. The agent said that this was really a steal; the house was worth a lot more than I had paid.

To make the higher down payment, I sold my BMW, which I didn't need because as leader of the party, I had a driver. Then I considered selling my share in the Barrie restaurant, Hooligans, which I owned with some friends. I really didn't want to sell the business because it was something I did with my buddies, and it was personal for me. We invested a great deal of sweat and toil, and my buddies didn't want to have a partner they really didn't know.

It was my hope we could turn the place into a huge sports hang-out, and it would increase in value. In retrospect, it was a big headache and a money pit. Business was so dependent on how well the local sports teams were doing.

Then I heard that one of my friends, Johal, was also a personal mortgage broker. At the time, Johal was not running for any nomination for the PC Party, nor had he expressed any interest in running. Johal offered either to buy my share in the restaurant or give me a loan in the form of a second mortgage on the house. I preferred to take out a loan with Johal, and officially registered the title of that second mortgage. But I didn't report it to the Office of the Integrity Commissioner. Mistake.

The house deal was completed in July 2016.

My game plan was to wait for the house to increase in value and then remortgage it, discharging the loan with Johal. In the meantime, I made the payments with the help of my parents. I also invested in renovations to enable me to rent rooms from time to time, which I did. The cost of the renovations was significant and more than offset the rental income, which wasn't much, so I didn't declare the rent. Mistake.

The integrity commissioner found that I should have disclosed the loan from Johal since it was significant in size, and voters should know my personal financial liabilities. That was considered an important omission. He also found that I should have declared the rental income; although, this was not considered to be as significant an issue.

In November 2016, Johal, who had loaned me the money, decided to run for the nomination of the PC Party in the riding of Brampton North. He was nominated by acclamation. As I discussed in Chapter 4, few candidates were vying for the job in that riding, and one was disqualified for immigration fraud. Johal signed up a record 6,600 memberships in this riding. It was huge by any standard. In one riding, he signed up more than 60 per cent of the total number of province-wide party memberships under Hudak's leadership. After he delivered these memberships to party headquarters, the other two candidates dropped out of the race. Johal was the acclaimed candidate.

Johal was not acclaimed because he gave me a second mortgage, nor because I pulled strings to help him, because I didn't. Anyone who walked into party headquarters with 6,600 memberships sold in one riding with no competitors would have been acclaimed, unless he or she had been a known axe murderer.

The integrity commissioner could find no evidence that I influenced the outcome of the nomination process that resulted in Johal being acclaimed as the candidate in Brampton North.

TD Bank eventually completed a full valuation of the home after about a year, and it showed a healthy increase in the value. I could now remortgage the property and rid myself of the Johal loan. I was working on doing so. The transaction was finally due to happen in January 2018, the month I was deposed as leader of the PC Party.

So that's what happened.

I will say that I was shocked that Hillier and the party accused me of unethical behaviour when they were rifling through all my personal information, including all my personal finances, without my consent and then leaking it to the media and making allegations based on my personal records. All of that is unethical, in my view, and I would love to know what the integrity commissioner would have said about that.

The day after Hillier's complaint to the integrity commissioner (which they promoted heavily to the media) was February 21, 2018. I was scheduled to appear before the PNC to get its final approval to ratify my candidacy. It was clear to me that this bottom-of-the-ninth-inning submission was part of the coordinated strategy to have me disqualified from the race, under new party rules.

The PNC had been tasked to ratify each leadership candidate on the basis of his or her commitment to the party and to public life, as well as the candidate's financial, ethical and social media history. None of this is a bad thing. What I had a problem with, however, was that this process had never existed before. The new process had been invented expressly for this specific leadership race and because of my potential candidacy; the rules were changed to allow the PNC to be able to toss me out. In every leadership race in the past, a candidate needed to have a certain number of signatures, and if you could put the money together, you could enter the race. The timing of Hillier's public complaint to the integrity commissioner was deliberate.

I also believe that there was an attempt by some on the PNC to apply the "rules" differently to me than to other candidates. Think about it. Granic Allen managed to be ratified by the same group, even though she had made a number of highly offensive and public statements to the media, which included comparing abortion to the Holocaust and burkas to Spiderman masks and bank-robber garb. She had been recorded on video in 2014 spewing homophobia and hatred.

How is it possible that the PNC was unaware of that? After all, Granic Allen was a highly controversial candidate, who seemed to make it a point of being offensive. The new PNC process, in its application, was a joke.

Granic Allen's outbursts were later used by the new leader, Ford, to terminate her nomination as a riding candidate in the general election. Many believe, including me, that these pieces of evidence had always been in the party's hands and were leaked to the media in a well-orchestrated effort to get rid of Granic Allen. She was a problem for the party in a general election. They let her run for leadership to placate the religious right, knowing that she didn't have a hope in hell of winning.

And so, on that Wednesday, I presented myself before the PNC to see what bullshit they could throw at me now.

PNC members were supposed to be neutral judges, according to the rules. No one could be associated with supporting or being against a specific candidate. Zeise was not a supporter of mine. It was widely known that he supported Caroline Mulroney. Zeise began arguing that I couldn't be a candidate because, as he said, he had my personal financials and emails that contained information that would indicate that I should be disqualified from being a candidate out of the gate.

This made other members of the committee uncomfortable. They didn't want to see these personal documents, as they felt this was inappropriate. They felt these documents had been taken without my consent.

Mike Richmond launched a counter attack on Zeise. He pointed out that in the rules of the PNC, each member had to be neutral. "Ken," he asked, "is that the case? Are you neutral or are you associated with a specific candidate?"

Zeise responded that he was neutral.

Richmond fired back, "Ken, we have a recording that says otherwise."

We actually did have a tape recording, and it clearly showed that Zeise was not neutral at all. Richmond then called Zeise into the hall and asked if he should play the recording in front of the entire PNC. He didn't want to make him look foolish, but he would if he had to. Richmond advised Zeise to go back to the committee and recuse himself from the decision. Unbelievable. And Zeise was among those who stood in judgment of me.

Zeise went back into the room and recused himself. Eventually, the committee reached a consensus that I should be allowed to run.

By now, I had jumped over every hurdle, and five days into my leadership run, I was finally able to concentrate on my campaign. My campaign staff included Dodds, in charge of fundraising; Storseth, my campaign manager; and Nuttall, my campaign chair. Heading up communications for me was Alise Mills. Nagalingam was my chief organizer.

I knew that my candidacy would completely gut Caroline's because I had sent people over to her, and with me in the race, they'd leave and come to me. She had about 20 committed candidates, and within about 48 hours it was down to six or seven. I had gone from zero candidate support to 35 endorsements from candidates whom I had recruited to run for the PC Party.

The person who headed Caroline's Sikh campaign left. The head of her Muslim campaign left. The guy running her fundraising left; mind you, fundraising was an area in which Caroline excelled, so his leaving didn't hurt her too much. She raised and spent four times more than any other candidate. But people who had endorsed her were leaving her. Her campaign went into a spiral the moment I entered the race.

Since I hadn't been a candidate at the time when the provincial broadcaster TVO had held an all-candidates' debate, I was offered up an interview on The Agenda with Steve Paikin. Upon entering the studio, I was greeted by the TVO brass. They had greeted all the other candidates the week earlier, and I suppose they figured they owed me the same respect.

TOP
Announcing one of my star candidates, Caroline Mulroney.

BOTTOM
Thanksgiving weekend with the Mulroneys.

TOP
The PC Party was now targeting full out Liberal strongholds.

BOTTOM
International Plowing Match with MPP Toby Barrett.

TOP
Project 234 event in Toronto with Tom Currie; MPP Peter Bethlenfalvy; Dean Baxendale, our host; and Bill Sceviour. This was one of four fundraisers held that day, which helped to erase a $7.2-million deficit.

BOTTOM
With Prem Watsa, founder, chair and CEO of Fairfax Financial Holdings.

XII

TOP
Nephew Colton campaigning
for Patrick.

BOTTOM
Fighting against government
autism cuts.

TOP LEFT
Shan Gill, my dedicated event co-ordinator, organizer and driver.

TOP RIGHT
Alykhan Velshi former Chief of Staff.

BOTTOM
With my sisters, Stephanie and Fiona, and my brother- in-law Charles Carver at the Pride Parade, Toronto, 2015.

TOP
Unveiling the Peoples Guarantee at the party convention. A platform and party that would have delivered over 100 PC candidates to Queen's Park.

BOTTOM
Campaigning for the lost leadership.

TOP
Campaigning for all Ontarians.

BOTTOM
With former premier Bill
Davis, campaigning in
Brampton Mayor's race.

TOP
With Genevieve at our
bridal shower.

BOTTOM
A photograph from our
wedding day.

The interview went well, and for the first time I was not feeling encumbered. I could be myself. I was pleased with the interview, but I didn't feel the same way about my campaign. It was in a bit of disarray. That was confirmed to me by an unfortunate event that certainly didn't help matters.

People around me were booking me for interviews, and I was completely out of the loop. I didn't know that I had been booked on the Jerry Agar Show on the radio station Newstalk 1010. Meanwhile, I was at TVO for my interview when someone informed me that at the same time, I was supposed to be on with Jerry Agar.

What? I was disappointed by this disorganization, which became fodder for social media: Patrick Brown disses Jerry Agar. I am a great organizer, and my campaigns have been focused and strategic. This was not that. On the other hand, this was no normal campaign. Everything was a hill to climb laden with a thousand grenades. Still, on the ground and at functions, the communities loved me out there. We were monitoring polling, and I was told that that my numbers were going up each day.

Despite my change of heart to run in the leadership race, Elliott was not nasty to me. We still were communicating. Ford was also staying out of the fray and messaging that he wasn't interested in commenting on me, but rather was focused on defeating Wynne. Caroline Mulroney, on the other hand, went negative on me. I think it is because she felt that I had betrayed her by entering the race, or perhaps she was being coached by her new (my former) campaign manager.

I don't think it is worth describing Granic Allen's views about me. They were part of a very public display throughout the leadership race, including during candidate debates. She made me part of her campaign and spent equal time promoting her extremist ideas, as well as her views on me. She was toxic.

That week was tough. But there were also some victories. As I mentioned, 35 candidates committed to support me. To put that in context, Ford had three candidates supporting him. Mulroney and Elliott had about 20 each. We had a rally in Mississauga, which was attended by 20 supportive candidates the Sunday after I filed my papers. It didn't make up for the fact that I was running for a job that I felt was mine and had been stolen from me. I lacked the enthusiasm and the positive energy that was such a big part of who I was and why I had been successful in politics. I love public service and I love people. But now there was something missing in me. Everything that happened had taken a huge toll.

On Thursday, only one day after I was cleared by the PNC, I held a private meeting at the law offices of Norton Rose Fulbright. I decided not to include Nagalingam because he was so committed to my running.

When I had told Rob Godfrey about the second mortgage on my home that was being used against me, his response was, "Who cares about a second mortgage?" He may have been right; after all, the title of the second mortgage was registered and the payments were being made. I realized, however, that he, too, was such a supporter that I could not include him in this meeting, either. For this reason, the meeting was held with only three people present: Walied Soliman, James Dodds and Brian Storseth. We discussed it all in earnest. I had a decision to make. I had emailed Dodds to restart negotiations with Elliott. Was the deal with her still on? Dodds explained at the meeting that the deal was still on, minus the promise of deputy premier. That annoyed me, but that was the price I had to pay for jumping back in the race.

I also knew that Velshi didn't just want dirt on me, but also on friends and family. He was ordering staff to find dirt on my sisters, Richmond and GG. When the target was me it was one thing, but now I was seeing the toll it was taking on my friends and family. That was quite another matter completely. My mom was bedridden with anxiety. She spent hours watching Diana Davison's YouTube videos. Davison heads up a Canadian not-for-profit organization called The Lighthouse Project, which offers free assistance to people who have been falsely accused.

I had to ask myself, *Was this all worth it?*

That weekend, I was doing events in southwestern Ontario. It felt great to be away from the toxicity of the party elite. We had a big rally in Windsor on the Saturday, and the candidates were there to endorse me. We went to

London, where we had meetings with the Muslim communities. These events were going well. I was rolling out endorsements, and communities were firmly behind me. People were encouraging. These activities would serve us well in the race, but I knew that more importantly, they would help in my negotiations with Elliott.

I knew this was it. I knew I had to get back to the table with her. I was done.

By the end of Sunday, I had an agreement with Elliott that I believed I could accept. I would still be the minister of economic development and international trade. And if I performed well in the campaign, then deputy premier could be put back on the table. Storseth had a signed agreement that he locked away in a safety deposit box at his home in Ottawa. He had a lawyer notarize it. DeLorey signed it on behalf of the Elliott campaign. Elliott was counting on me to help bring in the cultural communities to support her. I prepared the letter that I would drop out of the race on Sunday night. That letter was released Monday morning, February 26, 2018, just 10 days after I had entered the race. They say in politics a week is a lifetime. In my case, that turned out, quite literally, to be true.

In my statement, I cited three main reasons for my decision. First, my desire to focus on my case against CTV News; unpleasant as it was, I needed to give it some oxygen. Second, I would free up the PCs to focus on defeating the Liberals; it was clear my opponents would not permit me to join the race in any productive way. Third, and perhaps the one that I felt the strongest about, I needed to protect my family and friends. I concluded with the following words:

> While I am discontinuing the pursuit of my goal to lead this great and proud party into government as our next premier, I remain steadfast in my love for Ontario and Canada.

> It was a crazy week, and now I was at peace to be out of the race. I had entered largely because of my anger surrounding Fedeli throwing me out of caucus. Had he not done so, I would not have run. Note to self: never make a decision based on anger.

But Elliott's campaign made a fatal mistake. They felt that I was tainted goods, and they didn't want me out there stumping for her. I had to be hidden. They told me to go away — take a trip somewhere.

What could I have done for Elliott, had they let me? I could have won her Scarborough, Brampton and Mississauga. I had tons of support and communities that loved me. I could have convinced them to vote for her, had her team allowed me out of the stable. After all, I had signed up many of these people as members, and they trusted me. But I had been vanquished, and with that, so, too, were Elliott's chances. In the end, it was not a question of votes; it was a question of distribution.

Her team was telling her that she was polling at 65 per cent and 68 per cent. They told me to go away — go on vacation. They didn't need me. They were overconfident. She lost badly in those races, and in the end the leadership vote was razor-thin. With those communities, she'd have won. I could have delivered them for her.

Instead, Genevieve and I took our trip to Florida. We also visited Jekyll Island, Georgia. That is where we got engaged. And that is when I began my new life.

CHAPTER 8

REFLECTIONS AND LESSONS LEARNED

I've admitted to the mistakes I've made and I would argue that I paid dearly for them as well as for the politically motivated allegations which I did not do.

Two questions that I frequently get asked are: "Did I follow the leadership convention?" and "Did I watch the provincial election?"

Yes, and yes.

The day of the leadership, March 10, 2018, I was with GG driving back from Georgia, and I followed the entire race live-streamed on TVO. It actually turned out to be a marathon, with results that were so close that candidates demanded recounts and called in lawyers. It was a shitshow. Finally, at around 7:30 p.m., everyone was kicked out of the convention hall, because apparently, the venue had a wedding function in the same space. I wouldn't want to be getting married in that hall — the karmic energy must have been awful. Members of different camps were deflated and bewildered, still not knowing who won the leadership in a race that was "too close to call."

When the leader was eventually announced, I was in disbelief that Elliott lost the race, even though she won the popular vote and also the majority of the ridings. However, the contest was based on a point system that considered the margin of victory in each riding.

The results were extremely close, and there were rumblings that certain voters were counted in the wrong ridings. In the end, Elliott's team conceded defeat. But that didn't happen for a day or so.

After all the drama the party had already been through, the messy convention was the icing on the cake. The media highlighted a poorly handled, disorganized event that was punctuated by a lack of updates. The media were left trying to fill hours and hours of coverage with content as they waited for someone to explain what was going on.

There was some irony to the eventual result. All the people who had knifed me in the back and tried to kill me off as a candidate had done so in order to seize power for themselves and their preferred candidates. Those candidates did not include Ford. In fact, back in fall 2016, many of my PC Party adversaries, including Robertson and Ciano, almost lost their minds at the thought of Ford running to be the PC candidate for the riding of Scarborough-Rouge River. At the time, they thought he was all wrong for our brand. The majority of caucus did not back Ford for the leadership race. Now they'd all end up with him as leader of the party. I mean no disrespect, but he was not the candidate they hoped for then or now.

All my enemies thought they were so clever, and in the end, this would have been the last result they would have expected or desired. Personally, I never thought Ford could beat Elliott, but he did, albeit by a hairline amount. Still, close only counts in a game of horseshoes.

I had been approved to run for the nomination in my own riding by the PNC. Two days later, on the Monday after the leadership convention, I received a call from a top adviser and supporter of Ford. This call was to discuss the type of role I might play if the party won the general election in June. More specifically, could I reconcile my positions with the new leader, so that I wouldn't be a distraction? Would I change my positions on climate change, carbon taxes, Islamophobia and sex education?

My response was that I shouldn't have to change my views on these issues. The federal party was able to accommodate a broader tent. I gave the example of Michael Chong, who has been the MP of Wellington-Halton Hills since 2004. He was among the 13 Conservatives who opposed reopening the same sex marriage debate. Yet, Chong had been welcomed in the Conservative Party under Harper and also held cabinet posts. This is the way you build a broad-based tent and win elections — not by ostracizing and pushing aside opposing views. Let's face it: next time, there will not be a Wynne to run against.

The response from the other side was that my stated position just "wouldn't work." It was then that I knew that my response dictated my exit from provincial politics. Now it was only about the format of my exit. At this point, everyone was still friendly and amicable. I was told that I could announce my exit from provincial politics on my own and that I would be provided with a week in which to do so.

I booked a meeting with the riding association executive, so that I could first announce my exit to them. The riding association had told me that the candidate who could replace me was quite close to me. It was Nuttall, who was promised a cabinet position and was willing to make the move from federal to provincial politics. It actually made sense for him because his family was young, and the travel to Toronto would be a much easier issue than his commute to Ottawa. I was OK with all of this.

Then in a total surprise move, one day before my riding association meeting, the party leaked out to the media that I was being disqualified as a candidate by the PNC. I couldn't believe it! My friends on the PNC told me that this was a direct order from Ford and his close associate and adviser Dean French. I didn't know French and had never even met him. I have no idea what he held against me at all. I had always worked well with Ford, and frankly, I had built a good party that had maximized the chance of winning in the general election. I handed Ford a turnkey operation. To this day, I really don't get it.

In my opinion, it was tasteless and unnecessary. A few weeks later, they pulled the offer to Nuttall and appointed someone from a different riding to run in Barrie–Springwater–Oro-Medonte.

With the party's leadership decided, the next battle was the general provincial election on June 7, 2018. A little-known fact is that during the election, I had been approached by the Trillium Party to see if I would take it over. Actually, the Trillium Party approached Storseth and pitched him to pitch me the idea of leading that party.

Of course, given my views, I would have been exactly the wrong person to do that. They had built up candidates everywhere and they were going to get trounced. In the polling data, they had discovered that if I were leading the party, it would become more relevant on the Ontario political scene. They'd still finish in fourth place, mind you, but rather than being at one per cent, they'd be at seven per cent or eight per cent. This would enable the Trillium Party to participate in debates and be part of the conversation. I figured that if I agreed to lead the Trillium Party and if I worked my ass off, I might get them to 15 per cent. But I also knew that it could kill the PC Party's chance for a victory. Had Ford and the PCs lost 15 points to the Trillium Party, it would mean losing the election. Much as I am angry at the backstabbers who threw me overboard, there are many good people in the party, and I wanted them to win.

During the election campaign, many in the left-leaning media did their level best to discredit Ford. They ran clips of him praising Donald Trump after he was elected president of the United States. There were articles that were recycled from five years earlier — old stories and headlines of Ford as a high-school student involved in selling hash. Ford managed to keep his cool.

Finally, election day arrived. Many people thought it would be good for my own sanity to get away — leave the country. My view was no. I'm a political nerd and I couldn't *not* watch the election that I had been gearing up to win. I knew every riding upside down and I knew what the numbers should be. Many of these people running were *my* candidates — candidates I had recruited. I wanted to know every single detail of the election as it unfolded.

And so, on the night of June 7, 2018, I went over to Mike and Kaydee Richmond's house and watched with GG, my sisters and their partners and Nagalingam. Everyone was surprised. How could I want to watch election night unfold? But I did, right until 1 a.m. Of course, it was painful and sad because I kept thinking, *This should have been me.* And despite every knock I was handed, I had built a tremendous organization with lots of money in the coffers, which I was proud of. That night, I was getting all kinds of messages from candidates saying things like, "I'm here because of you" and, "Thank you, Patrick." People were saying, "This is your victory as much as it is Doug's." Of course, those messages ring a little hollow when you're not there.

That night, as I watched the riding returns, I realized that I was really stupid to have allowed my resignation to stand. I've since struggled to come to terms with this reality.

Ford was a polarizing candidate. People either loved him or hated him, and for those who hated him, that hatred was palpable. But none of it mattered in the end. The people of Ontario wanted change desperately. And they, frankly, didn't give a shit. On June 7, 2018, Doug Ford was elected to be Ontario's 26th premier.

I often wonder whether or not those around Ford realize that most people didn't vote for him or the PC Party; they voted against Wynne. Her party went from a 55-seat majority government just before the election, to only seven seats, one shy of the number required to have "official party status" in the Legislature. The Liberals, for the first time in Ontario history, no longer had official party status. We could have run anyone, and it would not have mattered. The people of Ontario were done with the Liberals and had no interest in more of the same left-wing government from the NDP, even without the corruption.

After I left politics, I met up with Charles Sousa, minister of finance in the Wynne government. Sousa had lost his seat. We got together for a drink: he had a drink, and I had my Diet Coke. I told him that I always viewed him as Liberal with a blue tie. I told him that I liked him, but always felt he had to carry Wynne's baggage. And he told me that the Liberals were always scared of me. It wasn't just that I stole their territory on issues, but what petrified them the most was that no one could believe my work ethic. They just couldn't believe how many events and ridings I was visiting. They didn't understand that that has always been in my DNA from the time I was a young politician.

After my takedown, I got calls from a number of people wanting to do something with me or to offer me employment — a prestigious university asked me if I would consider teaching, and major law and financial firms on Bay Street reached out to offer me lucrative jobs. I was also offered fascinating employment opportunities in India and Florida that would have allowed me to make more than I dreamed of. It was then that I began to realize that this was not the end of the road for me.

REFLECTIONS AND LESSONS LEARNED

I really don't know if any of those who tried to destroy me have wasted a moment thinking about what they did to me or what they might have done differently. I don't know if these people feel any remorse or whether or not they have learned anything. I know I have. All that I have been through over the course of the last eight months has shaped me, matured me and, in some sense, transformed me into a wiser person and a stronger politician.

The biggest lesson I learned is that you can only move a political party as fast as its members are willing to be moved. Some of the moves I made were done much too quickly. I was trying to change the nature of the conservative movement overnight. You cannot take a party that includes people who hate unions, who are homophobic or who are climate-change deniers and move them to a new centrist party overnight.

I had been clear on my belief that climate change is man-made, and we have to do our part. Just acknowledging that really grated a faction within the conservative movement. After I announced at my first policy convention that polluters must pay, I attended a number of meetings with landowner groups, and they were aghast at the idea of a carbon price. People were sending me research papers denying climate change. I believe that climate change is an extremely difficult concept to accept for a certain faction within the conservative movement.

Robertson, my former chief strategist, insisted that I make a splash at the first policy convention by announcing my belief in a carbon tax. I believe now that it was advice I should not have taken. Oh sure, it garnered a great deal of media attention and was highly successful as a communications tactic; however, as a means to start a serious conversation, it backfired terribly. It caused the party internal agony and division.

There were those who agreed and supported me. As I mentioned, Brian Mulroney called me after the leadership convention in 2015, reminding me that he had been the greenest prime minister in Canadian history, and that if you had cared about the environment in 1988, you were more likely to have voted Conservative than Liberal.

And there are also conservatives who are substantially more right wing than Brian Mulroney, and they support economic measures to combat climate change. Preston Manning, leader of the now-defunct Reform Party, reached out to me in a meeting at Queen's Park and told me that he felt I was going in the right direction. Manning has been trying for some time to bring the conservative movement in on the issue of climate change. He has been trying to convince members that being a conservative as well as an environmentalist is *not* a contradiction. Manning often says that "conserve" is part of what it means to be a conservative. I strongly support Manning's push on green issues.

Unfortunately, there are still those, such as Kenney, who are rabidly against a carbon tax, and at this time, it is still a divisive issue in the conservative movement.

With all that said, do I believe that I could have brought the members along? Yes. I believe that, had we done consultation sessions as I did with caucus, it would have been more productive. We should have had the ferocious debate, and after that we should have let the party decide, rather than dictating the policy on carbon pricing. We didn't do that because we were worried to call for a vote among party members, thinking that we would lose it. I now believe that, had we done so, we'd have won it because the party was now 20 times the size it was when I became leader. There were now more modern and moderate voices in the party that would have offset the naysayers and climate dinosaurs. I believe now that any resolution on a highly divisive and contentious issue should have been preceded by a thorough debate before being put before the membership for a vote.

During the creation of the platform the People's Guarantee, there were some riding associations that wanted a direct, clear motion and that asked whether or not members were favourable to a carbon tax. These requests were submitted to the environmental Policy Advisory Committee (PAC), which is in charge of creating policy options to be put into resolutions and voted on by the members.

The PAC also had the power to determine which resolutions made it to the floor for voting, so that it could weed out absurd or fringe ideas that we as a party would never run on. In this case, however, a proposed carbon tax, regardless of how controversial it may have been, was not a fringe issue and should have been proposed clearly.

Instead, we suffocated all clearly worded carbon tax motions. In the end, the resolution that was put before the members was deliberately ambiguous. These were all mistakes I made.

Kaydee was one of the policy convention co-chairs who provided me with the right advice. She believed that we had the numbers to win the vote. Velshi and others didn't want to risk losing the vote. I should have taken Kaydee's advice.

Interestingly, Ford said publicly during a televised debate that he believed in climate change and that he also believed that it is man-made. But he didn't go further to say that he would put a price on carbon, and instead, promised not to. I pulled off the bandage.

The errors I made were tactical in nature. But on the substance of the matter, I believe strongly that we need to come to terms with the idea that climate change is real, that it is man-made and it is threatening our existence. The planet Earth will survive. The question is, "Will we?"

When it comes to my own team, I would have paid more heed to Davis's advice. I would not have been so dependent on a team of paid mercenaries selected by others. I would have listened to my gut, which would have eliminated some who had been hand-picked by Velshi.

Would I have handled that awful night of January 24 differently? Absolutely. First, I would not have allowed my staff to coax me into an urgent press conference, when I had not had enough time to analyze the allegations against me. I'd have put out a simple statement, which would have pointed out that six months before the election, there were allegations dating back years. This was a fictitious smear being presented to the public, and it was politically motivated.

I would have held a conference call with senior staff and told them that I was not going to resign, and if there were any dissenters, they were free to go. If some on my staff resigned, I would have replaced them. Instead, with my resignation, my former staff now had access to all my personal records, which they used to try to cobble together a case against me to the integrity commissioner.

And I'd have taken the same approach with caucus. On a caucus call, I would have explained that these allegations were orchestrated, and that I intended to have them investigated. In the meantime, if there were any members who were not comfortable, I would accept their resignations. There were many people who would have been anxious to take their place, and I could have appointed candidates if someone left. This is exactly what Harper did with the Democratic Alliance Caucus when it rebelled. He told them it had a certain number of days to return to the fold; otherwise, he would appoint a candidate in that riding. I should have said, "Lisa, you want to resign? Randy? Great. Go for it."

We should have gone into a full operation the next day to analyze the allegations. We should have had the party's lawyers and other party resources going after CTV.

REGRETS

Regrets? I've had a few. The one that really stands out is the treatment of MPP MacLaren by my office.

He made some joke about the Liberal MP, which was viewed as derogatory and sexist. Everyone was asking me why I didn't fire him over this. MacLaren argued that his fellow MPP, Hillier, had sent someone out to record him MacLaren had made some comments to a Liberal MP at the Annual Carp Agricultural Fair, while I was leader. At this fair, politicians had to stand up and do comedy. He was convinced that Hillier was out to get him. Velshi told me that MPPs like Hillier and MacLeod were losing their minds over the fact that MacLaren was participating in events in their ridings with the landowners' association. MacLaren believed that Hillier and MacLeod didn't like the fact that he was my eastern Ontario lieutenant representative. MacLaren asked me to stick by him. We found a compromise solution, which was to send him to sensitivity training. I also removed him from the role of opposition critic for natural resources.

Later on, Velshi had heard that MacLaren was flirting with the Trillium Party and that he was going to defect. Velshi's advice to me was to fire him first. Then Velshi suggested that he would use and leak "the worst stories" about MacLaren to the media. This consisted of some anti-francophone remarks from four years earlier. Velshi leaked these to an Ottawa radio station. In these remarks he made to his own constituents, MacLaren was essentially challenging the need for all communities to have francophone employees and services. These politically incorrect mutterings certainly hurt MacLaren, who became a target. But it is also true that in certain communities without French populations, it is an accepted position among the voters. And MacLaren was essentially sticking up for the views of his constituents. All politicians do that at some time or other. But not all politicians have taped meetings leaked to the media by a member of their own team.

The point is that these very old statements were leaked and used as the justification to kick MacLaren out of caucus. And I approved that. And I regret that. It certainly weakened me to have one of my eastern Ontario organizers dismantled. I believe now that MacLaren was likely set up and quite possibly by MacLeod and Hillier.

It was true that MacLaren was meeting with the Trillium Party. But that was only after a great deal of water had passed under the bridge. I believe that MacLaren had finally had enough of being ostracized and set up by his own colleagues. My taking away his role as natural resources critic, a role he was very proud and excited to have, would have been a significant blow. We drove MacLaren to the Trillium Party and then we crushed him for going.

I have also come to realize that I should have been less fixated on stories that are one-day news. It is amazing how much time is spent in political offices on stories that are really "inside baseball." No one out in the real world actually cares. The media get hooked on something, and everyone in the political bubble dedicates hours of time and research to try to spin, dispel and position around a story that no one in the real world cares about.

In the immediacy of the moment, you're convinced that your whole career or your party's fate depends on it. The reality is, it doesn't. And to destroy a person's career because of these one-day blips is simply wrong.

When I think back, it is quite possible that MacLaren was reacting the same way I reacted when Fedeli threw me under the bus and removed me from caucus. He, like me, was likely jaded, and at that point, all bets are off. I do acknowledge my role in these events.

I have never spoken to MacLaren again, even though I would like to reach out and see how he's doing. I am sure we'd have much to share in terms of experience. In any case, I regret how I dealt with him.

I have other regrets at a personal level. In retrospect, I wished that I had acknowledged my relationship with GG openly early on. I should not have allowed myself to be convinced by an overly risk-adverse team that my relationship with GG was a political liability. I find it somewhat hypocritical that in an age where we are encouraged to accept individual sexual preferences, I was made to feel that being a heterosexual male in love with someone 16 years my junior would be viewed as wrong.

We should have disclosed our relationship on our own terms. Over the last six months, since GG and I have been engaged, I can honestly say that no one cares about our age difference.

GG was always skeptical that I would ever be prepared to settle down. Having been the product of older parents, she had always hoped to marry young in life and start a family. The truth is that most men her own age are not ready for this sort of commitment. So it was always in her mind to find an older man, who would be open to marriage.

In March, I went to visit her father to ask permission to marry GG. Dr. Angelo Gualtieri is a real renaissance man — a student of history, a lover of books. I told him that I was convinced that we would be good together. He said that he and his wife, Silvia, had been hoping for us to marry. Silvia was instrumental in helping us work through the difficult years, when the stress of our clandestine relationship took its toll. She helped us sort things out. Both Silvia and Angelo felt that we were meant for each other. Angelo gave us his permission. The permission part of the conversation took all of maybe 10 minutes. For the next 45 minutes, Angelo and I discussed Napoleon Bonaparte and other historical figures. I am a lucky man to have married into a family that is so rich with culture, tradition and exceptional intellectual curiosity.

On September 30, 2018, at 2:30 p.m., GG and I were married in Kleinburg, Ont., at The Doctor's House, a lovely, little, white wood-framed chapel. It was moving to see good friends and family there to support what had been a rather difficult journey. I was especially touched to see Bill and Kathleen Davis, as well as Neil and Ruth Davis, who came out to wish us well.

When GG walked through the doors accompanied by her father, I melted. All I could think to whisper to her when she joined me at the altar was, "You look so beautiful." And she did.

The reception was a grand affair, which I had absolutely no part in organizing.

A few months earlier, I told GG that a friend got an elephant for his son's wedding to take the bride and groom into the hall. "Hey! What a great idea! Let's rent an elephant to take *us* into the hall!"

That was the moment in which GG determined that regardless of my other contributions, I would no longer be involved in the planning of the event. She shut me out of any input early on, which was probably a really good thing. While I had done a tremendous job organizing Charest's visit to my high school back in the day, this event was a certainly a cut above. GG has much more taste than I do and a tremendous eye for detail. For example, all the colours matched with the invitations — cream and soft pink. I mean, who thinks of that, right?

When it was finally our turn to address our guests, GG and I made our way to the microphone together. My wedding speech required little preparation. It practically wrote itself. I told GG that marriage is for the long haul, and I was always touched by my grandfather Joe Tascona taking his walker and going to see my grandma Edna every day, when she was too ill to leave her nursing home. I told GG in front of all our guests that I look forward to growing old together and doing what my grandpa Joe did. Without missing a beat, GG smiled and said, "Yes. But in our case, it will likely be me taking my walker and visiting you." The room erupted with laughter.

I shared with everyone one specific quality in the many qualities that GG possesses that I find so attractive — her spontaneity. I recounted one incident that took place when I was leader of the PC Party. We were taking a floatplane on a sweltering hot day. I was due to participate in an event in Lansdowne, Ont. En route, I said, "GG? What do you say if we were to have the plane land just north of the event, and we could go for a swim in the lake?"

GG answered, "Patrick, I have my good dress on! I can't get it wet."

I said, "Sure you can. It's light, it's hot and it'll dry by the time we get to the event. Come on!"

GG smiled. "Sure! Let's do it!"

After our swim, which cooled us down, we loaded ourselves back into the floatplane and took off. By the time our event started, GG's dress was dry. GG rolls with the punches. She has a sense of adventure and never takes herself so seriously that she gives up on an opportunity to experience something new or out of the ordinary. I love that about her.

After the wedding, we went back to our new home in Brampton. Life with GG is going to be great, and I can't wait to start a family of our own.

ON THE MEDIA

With regard to the media, I believe that the traditional media are waning in influence. News is, for better or worse, being accessed through different sources, and more people are able to put their views forward with little control or expense. Traditional newspapers are being challenged by outside voices that now can use social media platforms. You can't live in fear of what voices may or may not say. You have to live your life honourably and be true to yourself.

My staff had warned me that the media are not to be trusted. Don't talk to them, don't engage with them. This was the old Harper mentality. I don't agree. My initial reaction was to build relationships, to go to lunch with reporters. Since all of my misfortunes, I have spoken to many members of the media, and it's far better to have good relationships. I really don't think that a hostile relationship serves the politician well. I feel it is a failed component of the Harper era. I believe my office bought into that far too much. We allowed our opponents to talk to the media and we didn't advance our own perspective.

The dominant perspective of the Toronto Star is left wing, and the Toronto Sun holds a right- wing view of the world. But in the end, it balances out in the wash. I do believe you are better off engaging with reporters than shutting them out or making them your opponents. Obviously, I knew which members of the media would write positive articles. For example, Christina Blizzard, when she was in the press gallery, was a guaranteed good article. When I was first there, Richard Brennan, a long-time reporter with a number of papers over the years, including the Toronto Star, was still a member of the press gallery. Brennan was relentless, earning the nickname "the Badger." He had been a member of the press gallery since 1979 and had held every premier since Davis to account. You had to respect the man. I had read that he apparently never called premiers anything but their first names and would often be heard shouting out, "Just answer the question!" I only caught the tail end of his work at Queen's Park and really regret that. He retired in 2015, soon after I became leader. Keith Leslie of the Canadian Press was another giant in the press gallery. But at the end of December 2016, he, too, retired.

Regg Cohn of the Toronto Star loved Wynne and the Liberals. I would call him out on this in my scrums. To be fair, Regg Cohn's job is not to be a journalist and report objectively. He's a columnist, which is someone who is paid to have an opinion that is in keeping with the newspaper's political slant.

I remember pulling Regg Cohn aside and saying, "Martin, you hate everything about the conservatives. Well, you finally have a conservative who is trying to emulate Bill Davis. A Progressive Conservative. Rather than criticize me, you should actually praise the fact that now you finally have a debate that is less polarized or you might get stuck with someone like Trump here!"

Once in a while, Regg Cohn would give me credit, for example, on my stance on being opposed to carding. And he did write an article praising me on my strong words against Islamophobia. He praised me on climate change, but then attacked me on the positions I took when I worked under Harper. I suppose you can't win them all. Once in a while, I would get an accolade from him, but he typically showed more adulation for the Liberals than any other media on the ground at Queen's Park. I was disappointed in his assumptions that CTV must have conducted a thorough investigation before tarring me with these allegations. I think that was naïve on so many levels.

I found, however, that Benzie and Ferguson were good, solid reporters at the Star though writing for the Star they were harder on me than on my Liberal or NDP opponents during that time.

ON LEGISLATIVE ACCOMPLISHMENTS AND REGRETS

From a legislative perspective, there were items I was proud to have helped pass and others that were a great source of frustration. People wondered whether or not I should have voted for that fundraising bill that included getting rid of corporate donations. Personally, I believed it was good for democracy. I don't think it's right that elected officials spend half their time fundraising. I estimate that half my schedule was taken up with fundraising. Nothing else took up more time in my day when I became leader. After the new rules were put into effect in 2017, that all changed. I praised the government publicly, even though I believe the policy was long overdue.

However, there were ideas that were never passed, even though all three parties agreed. One of these was on the issue of pensions for MPPs.

Harris, in a move to demonstrate that politicians would also be required to curtail spending, eliminated the provincial pension for MPPs.

A number of MPPs including Dave Orazietti, a Liberal MPP from Sault Ste. Marie, and Gilles Bisson, the NDP MPP from Timmins were pushing very hard for a provincial pension for elected members of the Legislature. From our bench, the initiative was pushed hard by Jim Wilson, MPP for the riding of Simcoe-Grey, and backed by all caucus. Wilson is considered to be the caucus "dean," having been first elected in 1990. Julia Munro, MPP for York-Simcoe, was the PC representative on the pension committee that was struck to examine the matter.

Dave Levac, Speaker of the House and Liberal MPP, finally convened a meeting of the three party leaders: me, Wynne and Horwath. All three of us agreed that a provincial pension should be restored. After all, federal MPPs have pensions as they should. I have heard stories of MPPs who lose their job after years of service and a successful career, and they simply cannot find a job. Many MPPs, who lose elections, find themselves destitute after years of public service.

I told my counterparts that if we wanted to get good people into politics, the lack of a pension was a definite barrier. I felt strongly that it is disingenuous to be accepting of pensions in the greater public sector, but not to consider those who work to represent Ontarians and whose jobs are far more precarious.

I addressed Wynne: "I'll tell you. Normally, a political party in opposition, especially a Conservative party, would make political hay over the creation of a provincial pension. Instead, I won't make a single criticism of the government if you introduce this. We could even bring it in as joint legislation, with all three leaders co-sponsoring the bill."

Wynne observed that every member would have to sign on, and I assured her that I was fine with that. And if they didn't sign on to it after 30 days, they would no longer be eligible for it. We all agreed. Levac pulled me aside and thanked me for my leadership and for not being political on this. I responded to him that it was the right thing to do.

It looked like it was going to happen. Then Wynne came back and told us that she was afraid that she would wear it more than anyone else because she was the government. She didn't want to own it, so she didn't want to do it.

After a month of negotiations, Wynne pulled the chute on it. We were so close. Levac had managed the issue, and I thought we three leaders had a deal. But it didn't happen because Wynne got cold feet. This is the same person who fought for union rights and for the rights of every other greater public sector constituent except for MPPs. It was clear to me that Wynne was afraid to risk any political capital on this, even though I had agreed to co-sponsor such a bill. I never understood that. With my co-sponsorship, the media could not use this against Wynne in an election.

ON POLITICAL OPPONENTS

Most people see politicians slagging colleagues from opposing benches. I, however, got along well with a number of Liberal and NDP MPPs.

I also often ran into Dipika Damerla, the Liberal MPP, at Indo-Canadian events and got along quite well with her. I was very impressed with John Fraser, the Liberal MPP for Ottawa South (now the interim leader of the Liberals), and his passion for hospice care. Given my own involvement with hospice care in Barrie, I was very sympathetic to his push in that area.

Bob Chiarelli, another Liberal MPP, was, in my view, a very reasonable gentleman, and I got on very well with Levac, who was very good to me. Levac told me that he felt I was different from the ideologues of the PC Party, that I was reasonable and he enjoyed watching me. He really thought I would get to the finish line. I had a good relationship with him and always found him to be very fair in his role in the Speaker's chair. Levac was good friends with Phil McColeman, the Conservative MP for Brantford, who is also a friend of mine.

And I had some friends on the NDP bench, too. I got on well with Percy Hatfield, the NDP MPP from Windsor. We had both attended law school there, and I'd often tell him that he'd make a good conservative. Hatfield believed that I would one day be premier, and the prospect didn't frighten him. In fact, he felt that it would be very good for Windsor; he knew I loved Windsor and would visit it once a month. I was also a fan of Jennifer French, the NDP member for Oshawa; she was very diligent and well-prepared. We both interacted closely with correctional officers. I recall attended a police conference at which French spoke as the critic for public safety. She stood up and started her speech: "I know you are probably all friends of Patrick Brown and likely play hockey with him, but I'm here to tell you that the NDP support your issues, too."

I had a great relationship with Cheri DiNovo, former MPP for Parkdale-High Park, who is a United Church minister. When she announced that she was running for the federal leadership of the NDP, I put out a tweet, saying that she was not to be underestimated. DiNovo made a real mark in the Legislature; whether it was her post-traumatic stress disorder (PTSD) bill or same sex benefits, she went all out. She would message me anytime I made a big move, like taking a stance on climate change or Islamophobia or marching in the Pride Parade, and she'd tell me that I was doing the right things. What was really great was that after everything happened to me, it was DiNovo who messaged me. She said, "You were too good for your own party." That really meant a lot to me coming from her. She is a real class act.

Not everyone in the NDP benches were people I got along with, though. The MPP for Niagara Falls, Wayne Gates, was always combative. He was angry because I dared to go into his riding for an event, and he actually confronted me: "What! So you think you're a tough guy going into my riding?"

I thought to myself, *What the hell do you think an opposition leader's gonna do? You travel the province!* Just on account of his reaction, I committed to visiting his riding more often.

And there were those with whom I sparred in the Legislature, but I didn't dislike them. I sparred a lot with Deb Matthews, the deputy premier, but I believed she was a really effective communicator.

I thought that Eric Hoskins, former minister of health and MPP for the Toronto riding of St. Paul's, believed himself to be better than everyone else. He is arrogant and pedantic. And frankly, I thought Hoskins was a huge gift to the PC party. So many health-care constituencies hated him in that he was actually allowing me to reshape health care as a PC issue. Health care as an issue had always been a weakness for the PC Party, but it was Hoskins who revitalized our voice in that sector. I could wedge him on issues: "Why aren't you giving PTSD leave to the nurses? Why are you treating the physicians so poorly? Why are you building big bureaucracies and not providing patients with more care?" I could go on. The litany of complaints was enormous.

Hoskins's office leaked to the media the total billing of a few physicians, which reflected the entire amount that the physicians billed and also covered their overheads and staff expenses. I had a great deal of fun with this. I compared it to the amount of money his office required to pay him, his staff and his operating expenses. "Minister Hoskins, the highest-paid physician in the province is actually *you*, if you count overhead."

I believe that originally the Liberals thought Hoskins was a great asset. He was articulate and smart, and had been involved in travelling the world to war-torn countries and practising medicine. He also received the prestigious Order of Canada. But he was arrogant and calculating. He was all about the politics and did little to improve the health-care system. Many believed his worst trait was his remarkable ambition.

I remember him being worried when they had the cabinet shuffle that he'd be shuffled out of the health minister role. The rumours at Queen's Park were rampant. Hoskins was going to be shuffled from the position after the complete botching of the physician negotiations. I didn't want that to happen. Hoskins was a gift to the PC Party.

So what did I do? I knew that Wynne was stubborn. I also knew that Wynne did *not* want me to have a victory. The cabinet shuffle was happening in a

263

week, so I said to caucus, "Every day until then, we need to ask for Hoskins to be fired. If we're asking for him to be fired, she won't fire him."

We would go to the Legislature, and I would stand up and say, "Premier, you are about to have a cabinet shuffle. Well, this minister has let down nurses, misled physicians. Please, do us one favour and fire him!" Then Yurek, health critic, would stand up and give a similar plea, and PC MPPs followed suit. I figured that was the way we could guarantee that Hoskins remained health minister. There was no way in hell that Wynne would accept the optics that she had allowed the Leader of Her Majesty's Loyal Opposition to dictate her cabinet choices. So while many were saying, "Patrick, what are you doing? That's so silly to be demanding the minister be fired," I was actually doing it to keep him there.

Physicians felt that Hoskins betrayed them and more so because he was a physician, even though they felt he didn't practise much. I think when you are betrayed by one of your own you, it's worse. I remember one incident in which Hoskins was supposed to show up for a vote on Opposition Day. We had put together a motion to reverse the cuts to physicians. His office put out a statement saying that he would not be able to show up because he had stakeholders' meetings. Then a photo surfaced of him at a Blue Jays game during the vote. That was among the most-discussed incidents on the Ontario Medical Association Facebook page.

Personally, I don't think his treatment of the doctors was up to him at all. I believe it was the premier's office that dictated those parameters, and he was just the messenger. Truthfully, I believe that Hoskins's power was very limited. It has been confirmed to me by former ministers that it was typical in Wynne's cabinet that your power was quite limited. Wynne's office was extremely controlling, I was told.

In my view, Liz Sandals, MPP for Guelph-Wellington and minister of education, was awful. She really believed she was better than everyone else. Hoskins did not come close to the level of arrogance of Sandals. She really couldn't control her elitism. I recall what happened when she was asked by the media what people who ride the GO train should think of the massive salary hikes that were being proposed for senior public sector executives.

As reported by the papers, she replied, "When you really stop and think of it, most people sitting on the GO train probably don't have high-level ... qualifications, or the business qualifications, to run a multibillion-dollar corporation. The talent is exceptional to be in those exceptional positions." Wow.

When she was education minister, Sandals argued that the Liberal government didn't need itemized receipts for the $2.5 million it was giving to teacher unions to cover the cost of their contract talks with the government. After all, she knew the cost of hotel rooms, meeting rooms and pizzas. She didn't feel it was necessary for her office to ask for receipts.

Of course, to many, the idea that taxpayers were footing bills to cover negotiating expenses and pizzas for a union lobbying to get more tax dollars was completely sickening. One journalist referred to her as "Marie Antoinette," reminiscent of the alleged response given by the queen of France when asked what should be done with the starving people who had no bread. "Let them eat cake." The tone deafness was stifling.

ON KATHLEEN WYNNE'S LOSS

I refer to the loss of the Liberal Party on June 7, 2018, as Wynne's loss for a very simple reason. As far as I'm concerned, it was, and in the process she blew up an entire party. I don't buy into the idea that they were in power for too long. That may well be true, but other premiers had managed to keep it going. Besides, people didn't just vote the Liberals out. They threw them out with fervour.

When I think about Wynne, I think of a real ideologue on the left who was too wrapped up in the equity agenda to govern well. Wynne took a centrist party and drove it all left. It worked in the 2014 election when she won a majority because she dismantled the NDP, and the election became a choice between the hard right or the hard left.

In the 2018 election, they tried the same thing. But this time, it was their own party that collapsed.

The Liberals were preparing for a campaign against me. They had spent $4 million or $5 million producing attack ads against me in fall 2017. They also had Working Families, a group made up of unions, going hard after me. Wynne tried to compare me to American President Donald Trump. There were TV commercial saying, "Stephen Harper, Donald Trump, Patrick Brown."

Then I was out of office, and the campaign for which they paid $5 million evaporated. With Ford's victory, the Liberals really wanted to compare *him* to Trump. It would have been easier in some ways, but they had already compared me to Trump. So they lost credibility. As one Queen's Park reporter told me, it was like crying wolf once too often. First, it was me who was Trump, and now Ford, too? They wasted money and bullets. They blew their attack ads on someone they never had to run against. That certainly didn't help their strategy.

But people were genuinely tired of the constant hands in their pockets, funding sprees on taxpayers' backs, ideological policies aimed at bolstering unions, the Liberals' disdain of the private sector and small business.

One week before the election, Wynne came out with the statement that she knew she would not be premier, something that was self-evident to most people. I still don't know what she was really trying to accomplish by making that statement. She claimed it was to rally people to vote Liberal, without the worry that she would be premier. But that showed me just how out of touch she was. People in an election need hope. It showed me that, once again, Wynne lived in a bubble of theories and ideologies and grand movements, yet she forgot about the everyday issues facing people. These everyday issues seemed unimportant to her, that she always had bigger issues to solve. That was her problem — she became a crusader. If people or businesses got crushed by her bigger picture policies, so be it. Let them eat cake.

I think that when issuing the statement that she would not be premier, Wynne should have gone full circle and immediately stepped down and appointed an interim leader. Even had she promised to step down as Liberal Party leader after the election (which she did not), that would not have helped because, by this point, people didn't trust her. She could have and should have appointed someone to take her place right then and there. That would have been real to people, and I believe that the Liberals would have fared much better.

Naturally, passing the torch would have been much more beneficial to the Liberal party had it happened long before the election. The point to me is that most people realized she wasn't going to be premier. But what pissed them off was that she wasn't ready to step aside or give anything up. If she said "I will step down now," it would have been better.

I also think the people she put around her failed miserably. She had a campaign team of people who were considered brilliant, including Tim Murphy and David Herle. I don't think they showed brilliance at all. I believe that they didn't speak truth to her. What made this clear to me was her appearance in the Whitby-Oshawa by-election to campaign, when everyone knew the Liberals weren't even contenders there. They lost that by 30 points. In my mind, it meant her strategists weren't sharing accurate polling. I really don't think she had people around her who told her how bad it really was.

Had I been in her place and truly wanted to "save the furniture" of the Liberal Party, I would have announced that, after reflection, I was going to call a leadership race. And I would have done that in March 2018, at the latest. Once there is a leadership race, the election could have been put off until fall 2018. They might have selected a new leader outside of the caucus, maybe someone federal who wasn't tainted. I also believe that had they done that, it could have been a very competitive election.

ADVICE

Not that he asked, but my main piece of advice for Ford is that the team around him should look for inspiration in Davis, not Trump, because ultimately, Ontario is moderate on matters of social values. They are not hard left or right. Ontarians may want fiscal restraint and responsibility because we haven't had much of that over that past 15 years, but on social values, most people don't want the sanctimonious, left-wing, social justice warriors, nor do they want the intolerant right.

I remember when Ford had referred to Trump as the greatest thing. I called him and told him that he couldn't be saying that if he wanted to run for me. We were not going to be the party heading into an election pounding our chests about how great Trump is.

I know Ford respects Harris, who is a very smart man and very seasoned. I think Harris will give him good coaching. Harris is definitely not a social conservative. I had private chats with Harris during my time as leader, and he privately coached and supported me on attending the Pride Parade and on climate change and carbon pricing. So many people say that Harris would never have supported a carbon tax. Well, he did.

I would say to Ford that the social conservatives are dinosaurs who are becoming less and less relevant every single day. Ten years ago, they may have been a real force, but I believe that their influence is waning with every year that passes. They are people yelling at the sky. They have influence in a political party because they are organized. But they are few in number and they are out of sync with a modern Ontario. And I don't think that they represent conservatism of any stripe. Conservatism is about getting government out of your business. So how does that work for social conservatives? We won't tell you what to do, but we're going to tell you what to do in your bedroom or whom to love? It's so disingenuously hypocritical. Social conservatism is an oxymoron.

Ford said the right thing when he criticized Trump for his totally inappropriate words against Trudeau or his stance on NAFTA. That's the correct approach. When it comes to the interests of Canada, a premier must always stand with the country and be non-partisan.

I look forward to seeing what Ford and the PC Party will do for Ontario. Ontario was left by the previous government with a mess of debt and deficit, and cleaning it up will take time. It won't be easy, but it's the right thing to do for our kids. It's my hope that his administration will end the division in the party and reach out to people who, like me, represent different voices in the Big Blue Tent. Our party needs to be modern and reflective of Ontario if we ever hope to have a dynasty.

AFTERTHOUGHTS

Throughout this book, I have bared my soul, for better or for worse. I've admitted to the mistakes I've made and I would argue that I paid dearly for them, as well as for the politically motivated and false allegations against me. But despite it all, I know now, more than ever, that I love public service. It's always been my calling. I love people, I care about their issues and my impulse is to try to help. Politics is a means to that end.

What I have lived through has forced me to learn, to mature and to grow. I hope my story can shine a light on what needs to change in politics, to bring it back to a more honourable time.
Politics is not about the game. It's about service. It's not about payback. It's about accomplishment.

We politicians leave far too much power in the hands of our hired strategists, who, rather than guide us, script us. We are often the chess pieces, while these unelected officials control the board. They are often too focused on tactics and too dismissive of principles. Frequently, they are too busy settling scores, rather than trying to fix problems.

The *game* of politics shouldn't trump the pursuit of public service.

My name is Patrick Brown, and I am committed to continuing in that pursuit.

ACKNOWLEGEMENTS

There are so many who have contributed to my pursuit of public service and who have supported me in my darkest hours. These are the people to whom I owe much gratitude for successes and my resolve to overcome the obstacles I have endured.

First, I want to thank all of those who inspired me to run for office and who have volunteered to help me make a difference. There are too many to mention but they know who they are and I am grateful for the support, loyalty and hours they have dedicated to my campaigns.

Thanks to my closest friends who have sustained me during the rough times and celebrated my victories; Kevin Bubel, Robert Faissal, Stew Garner, Gurdev Gill, Rob Godfrey, Justin Heran, Steve Martin, Mike Mccann, Babu Nagalingam. Con Di Nino, Alex Nuttall, Garry Perkins, Laj Prasher, Naresh Raghubeer, Mike and Kaydee Richmond, Walied Soliman, Bob Stanley, Brian Storseth, Daniel Tascona, Sri Vallipuranathar, Joe Villeneuve, and Frances Waldinger.

I owe much to my late grandparents Joe, Edna and Walter, as well as to my grandmother "nanny" Teresa who at 104 remains my biggest fan. They have all been tremendous inspirations to me throughout my life. I owe a special thank you to my family – my sisters Fiona and Steph and my brother-in-law Chuck Carver, my mother Judy, my father Edmond, my in-laws, Angelo and Silvia Gualtieri and, of course, my wonderful wife and partner in life, Genevieve who always stands by my side. My family are beyond incredible. Words don't describe how lucky I am.

Finally, a sincere thanks to all those who don't know me well but who have put their trust in me to represent them in public office to build a better future. You are an inspiration and the reason for my commitment to public service.

Thank you.

APPENDIX

Figure 1 - the collection of evidence

Most appendixes provide a list of documents to support the research and claims made in the book. Before I agreed to publish this book, I spent a week with this binder pouring over the documents and most interestingly the telephone records between PC Party employees, Liberal operatives and lobbyists prior to and just after the 24th of January. A full record of the e-mails, surveillance pictures, taped conversations, internal and external communications, newspaper articles and much more are documented and contained in the binder.

With over 1,000 pages in this volume, it was a vast trove of information and evidence that has supported Patrick's assertions, opinions and many of the conclusions that you read in the book.

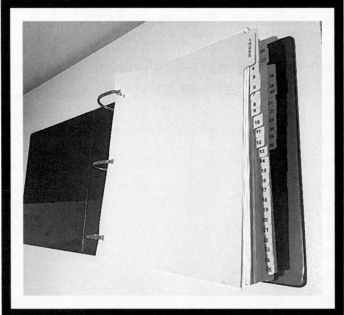

Figure 2/3 - close to 40 tabs and over 1,000 pages of evidence

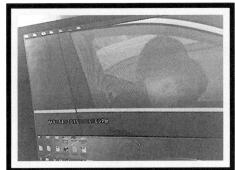 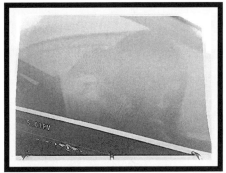

Figure 4-7- date and time stamped surveillance footage

From: Thomas DeGroot
Sent: February 4, 2018 12:20 AM
To: Badwell, Jag (External) <jagbadwal@gmail.com>
Cc: Marc Marzotto <marc.marzotto@ontariopc.com>
Subject: Memberships
Importance: High

Hi Jag and Marc

As requested, I have looked into the memberships. In Patrick Brown's email dated Jan 13th to the Membership he stated that if he became Leader of the Ontario PC Party he would grow our Party's membership to over 100,000. He indicated that this was an ambitious goal as we were a party with only 12,000 members when the race stated. When this email was sent out he stated that he had grown our party to over 200,000 members. This has come under scrutiny recently with OLO and Caucus who has insisted that the membership couldn't be more then 76,000 and then on Feb 3rd they said it was over 130,000.

After, reviewing our memberships I can confirm to you that during Patrick Brown's tenure the Progressive Conservative Party of Ontario's membership has grown to over 200,000, to be exact it has grown to 234,066 members.

1

Figure 8 the email that confirmed that the party membership had grown to well over 230,000 members

INDEX

and inconsistencies in sexual misconduct allegations, 36, 187, 188, 192
law office, 38
PB's retreat after sexual misconduct allegations, 172
Toronto apartment, 7, 142
Toronto Star story on, 219
homophobia, 80, 107, 117, 239, 250
Hong Kong, 181
Hooligans (restaurant), 91, 236
Horwath, Andrea, 147, 158, 208, 260, 261
    See also New Democratic Party (NDP) of Ontario
Hoskins, Eric, 263–64
Hudak, Tim
    in 2009 PC leadership race, 70, 73, 74
    in 2014 provincial election, 67, 68–69, 92
    and A. Boddington, 91
    approach to policy, 80
    deputy leader under, 87
    and fundraising for political parties, 103
    job cuts announced by, 68–69, 163
    northern Ontario seats as write-off under leadership of, 115
    and number of candidate nominations, 119
    and number of PC memberships, 118, 237
    riding of, 116
    selects speech pathology as charity of choice, 23
Hyder, Goldy, 13, 15, 142, 145

Ibraham, Adam, 232
iChannel, 35
India, 54, 58, 62, 122, 234, 249
    See also Gujarat (India)
Indian community, 54–62, 69, 75–76, 92, 96, 127
Indo-Canada Chamber of Commerce, 55
Innes, Jennifer, 185
Innisdale Secondary School, 9, 187
interim leaders and leadership races, 216
internally displaced persons (IDP) camps, 48, 50, 51
International Association of Firefighters, 63
investigations into PB's past, 201–2, 205, 218, 235–38, 242, 253

influence on PB's political leanings, 27
and PB's bid for 2018 PC leadership, 231
PB's childhood letter to, 25
on quitting drinking, 24
youth support for, 31
Mulroney, Caroline
in 2018 PC leadership race, 219–20, 221–24, 227–28, 229, 239, 240, 241
ad inviting young PCs to "deflower," 175
on carbon pricing, 100
nominated as PC candidate, 130–31
on PB and GG's relationship, 95
response to sexual misconduct allegations, 166–67, 169–70, 219–20
Mulroney, Mila, 95
Munro, Julia, 130, 260
Murphy, Tim, 267
Muslim community
and 2018 PC leadership race, 240, 243
and by-elections, 94, 114
Islamophobia against, 239, 246, 259, 262
misgivings about sex education, 112
and Ottawa West—Nepean nomination, 127
Muttart, Patrick, 91
Mykytyshyn, John, 70, 71–72, 124, 125, 131

NAFTA, 268
Nagalingam, Babu, 49–50, 70, 75, 114, 231, 240, 242, 248
Nash, Rick, 47
National Council of Canadian Tamils, 52
National Post, 168, 195
Navigator (consulting firm), 185–86
New Democratic Party (NDP) of Canada, 22, 25, 26, 55
New Democratic Party (NDP) of Ontario
by-elections, 94, 111, 112, 114, 115, 117
debts, 102
electoral defeats, 249, 265
and fundraising, 105
media coverage of, 259